PEACE AT ANY PRICE

Crises in World Politics

TARAK BARKAWI
JAMES MAYALL
BRENDAN SIMMS
editors

GÉRARD PRUNIER
Darfur—the Ambiguous Genocide

MARK ETHERINGTON
Revolt on the Tigris

FAISAL DEVJI
Landscapes of the Jihad

AHMED HASHIM
Insurgency and Counter-Insurgency in Iraq

ERIC HERRING & GLEN RANGWALA
Iraq in Fragments—the Occupation and Its Legacy

IAIN KING • WHIT MASON

Peace at Any Price

How the World Failed Kosovo

Cornell University Press

Ithaca, New York

Originally published in the United Kingdom by
C. Hurst & Co. (Publishers) Ltd, London

First published 2006 by Cornell University Press

ISBN 978 0 8014 4539 2

Printed in the United States of America

Librarians: Library of Congress Cataloging-in-Publication Data are available.

Cornell University Press strives to use environmentally responsible suppliers
and materials to the fullest extent possible in the publishing of its books. Such
materials include vegetable-based, low-VOC inks and acid-free papers that are
recycled, totally chlorine-free, or partly composed of nonwood fibers. For
further information, visit our website at www.cornellpress.cornell.edu

Cloth printing 10 9 8 7 6 5 4 3 2 1

CONTENTS

PREFACE AND ACKNOWLEDGEMENTS

The announcement that millions in the Balkans had been anticipating for years with either volatile hope or sullen dread came on 7 October 2005 in the form of a short, matter-of-fact letter from Kofi Annan to the President of the UN Security Council. The Secretary-General accepted the assessment of his special envoy, Norwegian ambassador Kai Eide, that 'while standards implementation in Kosovo has been uneven, the time has come to move to the next phase of the political process'. After administering Kosovo for six years and four months, the UN accepted that its usefulness had come to an end. Annan announced that he would 'initiate preparations for the possible appointment' of a special envoy to preside over the process that would finally resolve Kosovo's status. 'Resolving status' is the official parlance; in reality, a process of shuttle diplomacy will make Kosovo a new, sovereign country, while building in safeguards for minorities, leaving some international officials in key positions and trying to leverage a bit more progress before calling it quits.

Eide's assessment of conditions in Kosovo was mostly negative: 'The current economic situation remains bleak'; 'respect for rule of law is inadequately entrenched and the mechanisms to enforce it are not sufficiently developed'; 'with regard to the foundation for a multi-ethnic society, the situation is grim'. Uncharacteristically, all parties in Pristina agreed his criticism was fair.

Albanian leaders could afford to be magnanimous because their goal was finally in sight. Independence was coming, not because Kosovo was ready but because the status quo was unsustainable. Kosovo had ceased to evolve under international stewardship. As Eide put it: 'Kosovo can either move forwards or slide backwards. Having moved from stagnation to expectation, stagnation cannot again be allowed to take hold.'

Eide's verdict came more than six years after the end of the Kosovo war. Kosovo remained in a peculiar legal limbo, a non-country ruled by everyone and no one. During this ambiguous period the territory had seen riots and murders, impressive achievements and savage disappointments, pioneering innovations and catastrophic systemic failings. The most generously supported and ambitious nation-building exercise in recent history (if not ever) is now a humbling reminder of humanity's limitations. Kosovo has exposed the weaknesses of all the most powerful global international institutions, including the United Nations, NATO and the European Union.

Despite its shortcomings, Kosovo looks like a great success compared to the debacle in Iraq. It was also a substantially more straightforward proposition. Kosovo is much smaller, the terrain is easier to dominate, and the population is not generally disposed to use violence against its occupiers. There is no danger of roadside bombs here, no 'Fallujah triangle'. There is greater international consensus on how Kosovo should be tackled, a high level of legitimacy, and relatively generous levels of troops. Kosovo aspires to join Western institutions like NATO and the EU, giving the international community much more leverage to transform the territory.

These advantages make Kosovo a better measure than Iraq of the international community's current capacity to rebuild failed or dysfunctional states. No one is likely to repeat the series of mistakes that led to the current Iraq imbroglio any time soon. But the international community will be called on to intervene in societies ravaged by ethnic and other conflicts. It is imperative that we learn as much as possible from the institutional weaknesses and mistakes that contributed to the international community's underperformance in Kosovo, and its failure, despite enormous effort, to transform the society into one in which all its people can live in security and dignity. We hope that this book may be of use to the UN's new Peacebuilding Commission and the post-conflict reconstruction units now operating in national capitals.

Peace at any Price casts a critical eye over one of the most ambitious ventures by the so-called international community — an act of Good Samaritanship that reached across national borders and did much to define the humanitarian dimension of globalisation. The authors have attempted to convey a sense of the drama played out by a few thousand international officials, soldiers and local leaders, who were never perfect but generally well-motivated, well-meaning and reasonably competent.

This book is *not* a history of Kosovo as a whole, nor an ethnographic study of its peoples. Nor is it a comprehensive history of the international community's engagement with the Kosovo problem before the creation of the UN administration. Rather its subject is the international community's attempt to meet a series of challenges at a particular juncture in Kosovo's history, to halt atrocities and to help lay the foundation for a more peaceful society.

Both Iain King and Whit Mason served in the UN Interim Administration in Kosovo, the body that was charged with administering the territory, as well as in other capacities.[1] While drawing liberally from our personal experiences, we have been promiscuous in our use of other sources: interviews, years of conversations with both local people and foreigners, internal documents, academic studies, and media reportage.

The first main section of the book is a chronology, beginning with the histories of Kosovo's two biggest nationalities and of international intervention, including the steps leading to the NATO air war in 1999. Subsequent chapters chronicle four distinct phases of the international presence which began when the war ended: 'Emergency', 'Consolidation', 'Confrontation and Stagnation', and 'The Reckoning'. No periodisation could be perfect, but we believe that ours roughly captures the changing relationship between the mission and its local counterparts, from both the internationals' and most locals' perspectives. Each chapter covers the five fields in which the crucial decisions were made: security and the rule of law; interethnic issues; political development; hearts and minds; and the economy. In these chapters we have tried to eschew the benefits of hindsight in favour of conveying how the landscape appeared to decision-makers on the ground at crucial moments in Kosovo's development.

The second section aims to explain 'why the world failed to transform Kosovo'. We assess the international community's performance in Kosovo, and conclude that — despite notable successes in certain areas — the international presence must be judged a severe disappointment. Then we identify six causes for this failure and offer several 'lessons learned', with a realistic look at the institutional and ideological constraints to applying these lessons in current and future nation-building exercises.

Kosovo was the most intensive intervention ever, receiving more international money, staff and effort per local person than any mission before or since.[2] While this makes it a fair measure of the best that the world can currently manage, it also means that many of the lessons to be gleaned from it will only be relevant to other high-investment missions. *Peace at Any Price* concludes by arguing that future nation-building efforts will have either to scale back their ambitions dramatically or, preferably, to rethink both their institutional infrastructure and strategic approach. Remedying the deep-rooted problems of post-conflict societies requires more robust instruments and longer time horizons than were available in Kosovo.

This book attempts to fill a surprising void in literature both on Kosovo and on nation-building. There have been many fine works in English on the collapse of Yugoslavia, on Kosovo's history leading up to the NATO air war, and on the legal, ethical and political issues surrounding

the 1999 military intervention. There have also been a large number of
articles on various aspects of Kosovo since the intervention, and some
excellent policy papers — particularly by the International Crisis Group
and the European Stability Initiative — analysing individual problems
and recommending tactical adjustments. A large portion of the extensive
literature on peacekeeping produced in the past few years makes reference to Kosovo. And yet, so far as its authors are aware, this is the first
book explaining the international protectorate in Kosovo as a whole. By
being more comprehensive than other studies, *Peace at Any Price* can avoid
missing the forest for the trees; by focusing on a single enterprise, we also
hope to avoid missing the trees for the forest.

Anyone looking for signs of bias towards either the Albanians or the
Serbs — or, for that matter, the 'internationals' — will be wasting their
time. The only bias of which the authors are conscious is a general antipathy towards nationalism. This stance obviously puts us at odds with many
Albanians and Serbs. While there are certainly individuals who have at
moments played sinister or heroic roles, members of all the groups involved — including the so-called 'internationals' — have displayed the
full range of virtues and vices of which people are capable when living
under the pressure of opaque and potentially threatening change.

In using place names, we have generally given both the Serbian and
Albanian names in the first reference and thereafter used the name
most appropriate to the context. The Patriarchate of the Serbian Orthodox Church, for instance, is in Pec (the Serbian name) not Peje (the
Albanian name for the same place). Similarly, the town that has been a
centre of Albanian nationalist activity is Gjakove (Albanian), not Djako-
vica (Serbian). 'Kosovar' is only used in quotations by others; 'Kosovo
Albanian' and 'Kosovo Serb' are only used when we need to distinguish
them from people in Tirana and Belgade; and 'Kosovans' means people
of more than one ethnicity living in Kosovo. This means that most of
the time we're just talking about Albanians and Serbs. When referring

to the territory, we use the politically neutral international standard 'Kosovo' unless quoting someone who says 'Kosova'.

One reader of an earlier draft decried it as a manual for 'how to manage barbarians'. This could not be further from the authors' perspective. While this book will inevitably be read, especially in the US, within the context of the culture wars that dominate university campuses and debate in the media, it was conceived in a world of harder-edged struggles. Its aim is not to score ideological points but to help those who are working to heal societies that have been ripped apart by violent conflict. When UNMIK and KFOR failed to assert their authority with sufficient decisiveness, they let down the great majority of people in all communities who want to live in a peaceful and prospering society. International pusillanimity did not honour local mores — it benefited a small minority of self-styled militants and outright criminals who live by extortion. Hence, descriptions of terrible behaviour by some local people are not meant to denigrate Kosovans in general, or to justify prejudiced conceptions of primitive savages yet to be tamed by 'Western civilisation'. Crimes against humanity were committed in Kosovo, as they have been all over the world and throughout history — that is beyond doubt. The tragedy is that the attitudes and structures of power which permitted these crimes still persist.

Our view that the mission had a moral responsibility to protect civilians in Kosovo is hardly radical: Articles 13 and 27 of the Fourth Geneva Convention and Article 46 of The Hague Regulations charge occupying powers 'with adopting measures to protect the inhabitants of the occupied territory from violence from third parties'. Certain values, such as the need to uphold the law and respect people regardless of their ethnicity, we regard as universal, not uniquely 'Western', and we assert them with conviction.

Our call for consistent enforcement of the law is also echoed by countless people in Kosovo. Blerim Krasniqi, a 28-year-old Kosovo Albanian who has worked as a journalist and for the UN administration, for example, argues that UNMIK has done Albanians a huge disservice by promulgating rules without enforcing them. The Albanian custom of 'laying down the dust' by hosing down the sidewalk in front of shops, even during a drought, would end immediately, Krasniqi argues, if the police were simply to write a few tickets. That is precisely what happened when police began enforcing speed limits after a brief traffic free-for-all in 1999.

ACKNOWLEDGEMENTS

Kosovo under international administration was a whirlpool of activity. Although circumstances for local people were often difficult and some-times brutal, life for internationals in the territory was often thrilling and fulfilling — a dichotomy we have tried to convey in our writing. If the authors have succeeded even modestly in achieving the book's immodest ambitions, it will be because of the help of dozens of people, many of them former colleagues, comrades and friends. It goes without saying that no one but the authors is responsible for any shortcomings that remain.

Iain would like to thank Ben Rich for putting his name forward; Roy Dickinson, whose April Fool's Day email first drew him to Kosovo; Joly Dixon for keeping faith with him; and Andy Bearpark for support even when he didn't deserve it. Particular thanks to Tatjana Radenko-vic, Besnik Vasolli, and Enisa Rashlanin, without whom he would have achieved nothing while working in Kosovo for the EU and UN; and Terence Bellingham for helping him out of a potentially fatal Mitrovica car crash.

Whit would like to thank Peter Bird Martin, the long-serving Ex-ecutive Director of the Institute of Current World Affairs, for allowing him to first follow his nose to Kosovo against his own better judgement; Serif Turgut for showing him the ropes in Pristina and Prizren; Bob Churcher for giving him his first job in Kosovo; and Simon Haselock for giving him a fascinating role and being a good friend and stimulating boss. For friendship and good conversation that helped shape his views he would like to thank: Fisnik Abrashi, Antonella, Ajri Begu and Flora Brovina, Stacia Deshishku, Michaela Friberg-Storey, Bukurije Gjonbalaj, Dukagjin Gorani, Baton Haxhiu, Father Sava Janjic, Genc Kelmendi, Blerim Krasniqi, Damijan de Krnjevic-Miskovic, Shkelzen and Alisa Maliqi, Migjen Kelmendi, Tina Kraja, Filip Pavlovic, Nebi Qena, Adam Storey, Henrik Villadsen and all his colleagues in DPI.

Both authors would like to thank Michael Dwyer, Maria Petalidou, Dr Brendan Simms, Blanca Antonini, Jeff Bieley, Catherine Clarke, Tim Cooper, Andrew Cumming, Guy Edmonds, Dana Eyre, Sarah Fradgley, Massimo Gambi, Jeremy Gilling for his meticulous editing, Victor Gomes and the EU Pillar regional offices, Monique de Groot, Michael Hartmann, Reno Harnish and many others who have worked at various times in the US Office in Pristina, Bjorn Hauksson, Karin von Hippel, Oliver Ivanovic, Minna Järvenpää, Kara Johnston-Molina, Izabella Karlowitz, Christer Karphammer, Kumrie Kelmendi, Sandra Khadouri, Michael King, Verena and Gerald Knaus, Agnieszka Klonow-iecka-Milart, David Kruiff, Nikolaus Lambsdorff, Jeremy Lidstone, Andrew Lloyd, Susan Manuel, Tania Mechlenborg, Stella Messenger, Jolyon Naegele, Bill Nash, John Naughton and the Fellowship scheme at Wolfson College Cambridge, Leonora Nezeri, Hilary Pennington, Bajram Rexhepi, Carne Ross, Esther Rutter, Jonathan Shaw, Siobian Smith, Michael Steiner for having vision and passion worth articulating, Dana Stinson, Rebecca Sutton, Lars Tummers, Tony Welch, Victoria Whitford, Phil Williams, Nick Wilson, Andreas Wittkowsky, and the many other people who enriched our understanding through conversation over the years or who contributed directly but chose to remain anonymous. Both authors would particularly like to express their gratitude to all the people from Kosovo who patiently indulged the interests of yet another two foreigners, and gave them an understanding of their society — and an attachment to it — that never would have been possible without their friendship and conversation over the years.

Iain dedicates this book to his wife Tori, without whose love, understanding and comradeship he couldn't have made it, and to their first child, due to be born the week this book is published. Whit acknowledges the invaluable emotional support of Fergus, Mert, Micro and Winifred, and devotes his work on the book to his brilliant and lovely *hayat yoldashım*, Amanda Wilson, for keeping her smirking sense of humour through countless misadventures.

London 2006   I. KING • W. MASON

ACRONYMS AND ABBREVIATIONS

AAK	Alliance for the Future of Kosovo (a Kosovo political party)
ABL	Administrative Boundary Line
AKSh	Kosovo National Army, a paramilitary group
ANA	Albanian National Army, a paramilitary group
BBC	British Broadcasting Corporation
BPK	Banking and Payments Authority of Kosovo
CFA	Central Fiscal Authority
CIMIC	Civil Military Cooperation
CivPol	(International) Civilian Police
COE	Council of Europe
COMKFOR	Commander of Kosovo (International Security) Force
DFID	Department for International Development (UK)
DJA	(UNMIK) Department of Judicial Affairs
DM	Deutschmark
DPA	(UN New York) Department of Political Affairs
DPI	(UNMIK) Department of Public Information
DPKO	(United Nations) Department of Peace-Keeping Operations
DSRSG	Deputy Special Representative of the (UN) Secretary-General
EAR	European Agency for Reconstruction
EC	European Commission
ESI	European Stability Initiative (a think tank)
EU	European Union
FRY	Federal Republic of Yugoslavia

FYROM	Former Yugoslav Republic of Macedonia
GDP	Gross Domestic Product
GSZ	Ground Safety Zone (between Kosovo and Serbia proper)
IAC	Interim Administrative Council
ICG	International Crisis Group (a think tank)
ICTY	International Criminal Tribunal for the former Yugoslavia
IDP	Internally Displaced People
IMC	Independent Media Commissioner (a Kosovan)
IMF	International Monetary Fund
IOM	International Office for Migration
IWPR	Institute for War and Peace Reporting
JIAS	Joint Interim Administrative Structure
KEK	Kosovo Electricity Company
KFOR	Kosovo (International Security Force)
KLA	Kosovo Liberation Army
KPC	Kosovo Protection Corps
KPS	Kosovo Police Service (comprising Kosovans)
KTA	Kosovo Trust Agency (UNMIK's privatisation agency)
KVM	Kosovo Verification Mission
LDK	League for a Democratic Kosovo (a Kosovo political party)
MUP	(Serbian) Military Uniformed Police
NATO	North Atlantic Treaty Organisation
NGO	Non-Governmental Organisation
OPA	(UNMIK) Office of Political Affairs
OPM	Office of the Prime Minister (of Kosovo)
OSCE	Organization for Security and Cooperation in Europe
PDK	Democratic Party of Kosovo (a Kosovo political party)
PIO	Principal International Officer (international official assigned to the PISG)
PISG	Provisional Institutions of Self-Government (the Kosovan institutions)
RTK	Radio and Television of Kosovo
SOE	Socially-Owned Enterprise
SRSG	Special Representative of the (United

	Nations) Secretary General
TMC	(International) Temporary Media Commissioner
UCPMB	Liberation Army of Presevo, Bujanovac and Medvedja
UCK	Ushtria Clirimtare E Kosoves (English: KLA)
UK	United Kingdom
UNDP	United Nations Development Programme
UNEP	United Nations Environment Programme
UNESCO	United Nations Educational, Scientific and Cultural Organisation
UNHCR	United Nations High Commissioner for Refugees
UNMIK	United Nations (Interim) Administration Mission in Kosovo
UNSC	United Nations Security Council
UNSCR	United Nations Security Council Resolution
US	United States
USAID	United States Agency for International Development
USD	United States Dollars
USIP	United States Institute for Peace
VJ	Yugoslav Armed Forces
WFP	World Food Programme
WHO	World Health Organisation

INTRODUCTION

Around the middle of every day of the week, a unique collection of people queue up at Terminal C of Vienna airport. A more diverse group of commuters the world has never seen. On a given day it may include a contingent of policemen from Fiji or the Philippines, Scandinavian engineers, administrators from Peru and Ethiopia, riot control experts from Pakistan, German soldiers, American lawyers, Australian specialists in such niche industries as mine clearance and border security, and well-heeled fifty-something civil servants and diplomats from the four corners of the world. Alongside this cosmopolitan crowd are Kosovo Albanians, the young often sporting outlandish fashions, middle-aged men wearing dark suits and even darker expressions, and elderly men and women in skullcaps and kerchiefs nervously waiting to board a plane for only the second time in their lives. This is the daily Austrian Airlines flight to Pristina.

A little over ninety minutes after take-off, the pilot announces the beginning of the descent toward the capital of Europe's most famous non-country. Below lies a landscape of unkempt fields and villages hiding in narrow valleys separated by forested hills and mountains. To the west, snow-capped, saw-tooth peaks mark Kosovo's natural borders with Montenegro and Albania, and block out the gentle climate of the Mediterranean beyond. To the east, a lower line of hills traces the softer boundary with Serbia proper. Pristina's most visible landmarks from the air are grumbling smokestacks that belong to an aged power plant kept alive by European largesse. In the smokestacks' shadow stretches

1

the notorious Field of Blackbirds where in 1389 the Serbs suffered (at least according to their collective historical imagination) a fateful defeat that ushered in centuries of Ottoman domination. It was here, six hundred years after the battle, that Serbian strongman Slobodan Milosevic metamorphosed from politician to demagogue by exploiting the Serbs' sense of injustice.

Looking down at this overwhelmingly rural country, it is hard to believe that on the cusp of the millennium it had been the obsessive focus of the greatest military alliance the world had ever known. For the first and only time in its 50-year history, NATO had gone to war, its goal to stop massive human rights abuses. Between 24 March and 10 June 1999, NATO warplanes flew 38,400 sorties and dropped or fired 26,614 bombs and rockets on Kosovo and Serbia.[1]

To many observers at the time, the Serbian government's oppression of Kosovo's Albanian majority appeared to follow the same pattern as previous wars in Croatia and especially in Bosnia. Indeed, many journalists and international aid workers who had witnessed the war in Bosnia, in which some 200,000 people were killed and two million displaced from their homes, vowed not to allow a similar tragedy to befall Kosovo. The scale of violence in Kosovo had not been comparable, but they knew from Srebrenica that vast destruction could be wrought by sudden spasms of violence.

But in several respects the situation in Kosovo was unique. The violence was on a different scale: an estimated 10,000 Albanians were killed between the outbreak of serious hostilities in 1997 and the arrival of the NATO-led Kosovo Force or KFOR in June 1999.[2] Yet the rift between Serbs and Albanians in Kosovo was deeper than that between any of the other nationalities in Yugoslavia. Bosnians, Serbs and Croats all spoke the same Slavic language. Albanians spoke a unique language that was incomprehensible to virtually all non-Albanians. Most Albanians had never wanted to be part of Yugoslavia or its antecedent, the Kingdom of the Serbs, Croats and Slovenes, and Albanians never enjoyed equal status in either state. The clashes that culminated in the guerrilla war of the late 1990s began with riots in 1981, when the rest of Yugoslavia was quiet. For decades, inter-ethnic marriage rates in Kosovo had been among the lowest in Yugoslavia: Kosovo's rate of intermarriage in 1982, 5 per cent, was less than half that of Serbia or Bosnia.[3] The recent years of conflict are only the latest turn in a cycle of brutal tit-for-tat violence that began in the nineteenth century and ran right through the twentieth.

NATO's immediate military objective had been to compel Serbia's authoritarian leader, Slobodan Milosevic, to withdraw his soldiers and police from Kosovo. Milosevic refused and instead his forces stepped up their repression of ethnic Albanians. Kosovo was convulsed by terror, and a stream of almost a million refugees poured into neighbouring countries. After 78 days of bombing, NATO achieved its goal of driving Serbian soldiers and police out of Kosovo.

Having gone to war for moral reasons, the West sought to impose a moral peace. Its ultimate goal was not just to end a wave of human rights abuses, much less to turn the tables in the Albanians' favour, but to pave the way for constructing in this poor, mountainous and largely clan-based land a new entity based on 'Western' values. The international community believed it had the power to transform Kosovo — for the first time in its long, strife-ridden history — into a society based on the rule of law being applied equally to all citizens irrespective of their station or ethnicity.

What few spectators fully grasped at the time was that NATO and the UN were wading into a long-running civil war between two nationalities each of whom asserted its right to dominate a single piece of territory to the detriment of the other.[4] Certainly there were liberal Albanians and Serbs who envisaged a regime for Kosovo that could accommodate the rights of all its people and peoples without discrimination. But they were a minority. Most people on both sides took it for granted — sometimes resignedly, sometimes enthusiastically — that whichever nationality dominated Kosovo would run it for its own benefit, and that other nationalities would be second-class citizens. The great majority of Kosovo Albanians who took up the struggle against Serbian oppression had no quarrel with this model — they just wanted to be on top. Recognising this fact does not mean that one has to conclude that the West was wrong to intervene; NATO's bombing undeniably saved hundreds of thousands of people from being evicted from their homes or killed. But failing to understand the nature of the larger conflict of which this wave of oppression was part had grave consequences for the planning and execution of the intervention and the subsequent protectorate.

With Serbian soldiers and police evicted from the territory by the Military Technical Agreement between NATO and Belgrade and the passage of UN Security Council Resolution 1244, Kosovo, which was a centre of the Serbian medieval kingdom and regarded by Serbs as the crucible of their nation, thus became a UN protectorate. The UN Security Council created the UN Interim Administration Mission in Kosovo — UNMIK — and gave it a mandate of undetermined duration and theoretically almost unlimited powers. UNMIK was mandated to administer the territory, build democratic institutions that would allow the people of Kosovo largely to govern themselves, and create the conditions that would lead to the resolution of its final political status. The essence of this mission was distilled into a single promise that UNMIK officials repeated thousands of times: to transform Kosovo into a society in which all its members could live in security and dignity.

The task of maintaining a secure environment would fall to a NATO-led multinational military force called KFOR. Because Russia and China — both veto-wielding permanent members of the UN Security Council — opposed rewarding separatists, Kosovo's political status was left unresolved. Prejudging Kosovo's final political status was the one thing UNMIK was forbidden to do. Whether Kosovo would gain its independence — the dream of its Albanian inhabitants and the nightmare of its Serb minority — would be determined once institutions of self-government had been constructed and the international community judged conditions 'ripe'.

Five years after NATO's bombing began, the international community was looking for the exit. It had already changed Kosovo dramatically, but now seemed content to sit back. KFOR, the military component, was drawing down its personnel. UNMIK, the civilian administration, had passed responsibility to administer most things in Kosovo over to a locally elected government that it rarely dared to criticise and which had lost much of its moral authority. Since neither part of the international mission in Kosovo could do much to change the status quo, they both had to hope Kosovo would stay reasonably calm. Hope is a fragile bulwark at the best of times; the spring of 2004 was not the best of times.

Explosion

On 17 March 2004, thousands of Kosovo Albanians rampaged across the territory. Some set about murdering Serbs; others picked out Serb houses and set them alight — more than 700 Serb homes were damaged or destroyed along with thirty-six Serbian Orthodox churches or cultural sites, some of them centuries old. Over 4,000 Serbs and members of other minority groups perceived as being close to the Serbs were forced to flee. Several Albanians were killed in clashes with KFOR and UNMIK police. In all, nineteen people died[5] and more than 1,000 were injured, several of them KFOR peacekeepers or members of the newly created local police force.[6]

Kosovo's media, above all its foreign-funded public broadcaster, played a leading role in whipping up enthusiasm for this pogrom. Most of Kosovo's new political elite, appointed with UN approval and subject to removal by UNMIK's chief, the Special Representative of the Secretary-General, offered tacit support or, at best, half-hearted condemnation. As the riots progressed, Albanian mobs turned their collective fury on their international overlords, throwing rocks at UN buildings, burning UN flags and destroying more than 100 of the administration's ubiquitous white Toyota 4Runner 4x4s.[7]

After five years as an international protectorate, with peacekeepers from 37 countries, thousands of experienced civilian engineers, police, jurists, economists and administrators, and billions of dollars in reconstruction aid, hopes that the world would turn Kosovo into a society in which all its members could live in security and dignity had gone up in smoke in a mere 48 hours.

This book explains how the most ambitious and best-supported peacekeeping operation in the UN's history failed to save Kosovo, on the face of it a relatively easy case among candidates for nation-building. Unless and until it takes on board the lessons from Kosovo, the international community will remain ill-equipped to implant the seeds of tolerance and stability in other war-torn societies.

Many of the lessons that would-be nation-builders need to learn lie amid the ashes of March. Not only was that two-day spree of looting, arson and murder a watershed for Kosovo; it exemplified UNMIK's failure to control the levers of 'soft power' — education and the media — and KFOR's and the police's failure to marshal the 'hard power' necessary to maintain physical security. Without commanding these heights of security and social change, UNMIK's domination of the middle ground of administrative authority counted for very little when violent national chauvinists decided to test its resolve. All of those experts passing through Vienna Airport had become powerless to stop a local mob.

Background

The omens before the March pogrom did not all augur ill. Political officers in the UN mission who had been monitoring indicators of inter-ethnic tolerance were seeing progress. Returns of displaced Serbs had increased along with support for them by the Albanian-majority government. Talks between Belgrade and Pristina about a variety of 'practical issues of mutual interest' had recently begun, with working groups on energy and missing persons meeting in Pristina. Minority representation in the Kosovo Police Service had improved, while in the civil service it was holding steady.[8]

But there were also signs that tensions were reaching breaking point. The success of nationalist parties in presidential elections in Serbia proper set the stage for political grandstanding in Kosovo. The Kosovo Assembly, the territory's elected parliament, had marginalised the significant number of minority members elected under UNMIK-imposed quotas, rejecting their nominee to the presidency and dismissing their concerns about several pieces of new legislation. The official opening of the Assembly's refurbished hall was marred by Kosovo Serbs' understandable complaints about murals depicting scenes that reflected only the Albanians' view of history — effectively erasing that of the other ethnic groups who have inhabited Kosovo for centuries. Relations between the Kosovo government and UNMIK were also strained.[9]

Alongside this political backsliding, Kosovo had been overshadowed by threats of violence by groups whose political allegiances were not always clear. A party of Serbs visiting their former homes in southern Kosovo on a 'go and see' tour, which was arranged by UNMIK to encourage them to return and escorted by Austrian KFOR troops, was stoned. The visit was cancelled and no attackers were ever apprehended.[10] An intelligence agency had discovered a plan for a Kosovo-wide uprising in November 2003; the plotters had shelved the plan when the original pretext evaporated but were looking for a new catalyst to put it into effect.[11] There had been sightings of paramilitary guerrillas in black uniforms and balaclavas — suspected members of the shadowy AKSh (Kosovo National Army) — near Caglavica and Gjakova during the summer. On 21 February 2004, an improvised bomb planted in an official vehicle injured three people, including one of the government's ten ministers. The arrest of senior KLA veterans on war crimes charges had angered many Albanians, who saw the charges as intended to discredit the war of liberation as a whole.[12] On 12 March a grenade exploded near the home of President Ibrahim Rugova, damaging the building but causing no injuries. A homemade explosive device containing five kilos of TNT was planted near UNMIK headquarters just ahead of a visit by Jean-Marie Guehenno, the UN's Undersecretary-General for Peacekeeping Operations.[13] Every year early March has been marked by nationalist demonstrations by Kosovo Albanians to mark the beginning of the NATO air campaign against Serbian forces. This year the occasion was used to protest against the arrest by UNMIK authorities and by the war crimes tribunal in The Hague of veterans of the separatist Kosovo Liberation Army (KLA) on war crimes charges. Demonstrations on 16 March attracted 18,000 former fighters and their supporters, but remained peaceful.[14]

In retrospect, these events may have indicated that long-standing grievances on all sides were ready to erupt into violence. The tipping point occurred when unidentified gunmen, almost certainly Albanian extremists, shot a young Serb, Jovica Ivic, in a premeditated attack near Caglavica, an all-Serb village near Pristina. A few hundred local Serbs reacted by blocking the main highway connecting Pristina with Macedonia to the south. This roadblock understandably infuriated many Albanians, as the road was their main connection to the outside world and its blockage by a small group of angry Serbs seemed to have become a fairly regular occurrence. Serbs from Gracanica blocked another important highway running from Pristina to Gnjilane and some Albanians' cars were stoned as they drove past the demonstrators. Venomous articles in the Kosovo press about the roadblock said it proved that the 'Serbs can get away with anything'.[15] Tensions were thus already heightened on the day that three Albanian boys drowned in the Ibar river. And, after an unusually long winter, 17 March 2004 happened to be the third sunny spring day in a row.

The trigger

On the evening 16 March three Kosovo Albanian boys, ages 9, 11 and
12, went missing and were presumed drowned in the Ibar river that
divides the rest of Kosovo from the Serb-dominated north. What happened to them is not absolutely certain, but it is clear that what few
facts were known were distorted.

Thirteen year old Fitim Veseli told reporters that he and five friends
had been walking along the Ibar when two Serbs in a distant house, who
had a dog, began yelling at them. The kids took fright and four of them
jumped into the river. Of those four, only Fitim survived. No reporter
ever talked with the two kids who stayed on the river bank and made it
home unmolested.[16]

When the public broadcaster, RTK, first aired news of the drownings, the anchor in the studio immediately identified the children as
victims of 'an attack by a group of Serbs'. The reporter on the scene
amplified that the children 'had fallen in [the river] after being chased by
a group of Serbs'. The correspondent's report lasted two minutes and
sixteen seconds. It was followed by a 12-second statement by an UN
police spokeswoman saying that there was no evidence that the incident
had been ethnically motivated. This brief soundbite was followed by
an interview with Fitim, the sole witness. He said: 'Some cousins and
friends of mine and I were walking close to the river when some Serbs
with a dog swore at us from a house.' He never claimed that the children
had been chased by anyone.[17]

Agitators immediately swung into action. In an interview immediately after Fitim Veselli's, Halit Berani, a member of the Council for
the Defence of Human Rights and Freedoms, proclaimed that 'a group
of Serb bandits had attacked these children, the Serb bandits also had a
dog, and, swearing at their Albanian mother, they forced the Albanian
children to run away'[18]. On the basis of such reports, even many intelli-
gently sceptical Kosovo Albanians remain convinced that Veselli claimed

that the kids had been chased by a group of Serbs with a dog and that jumping in the river offered the only possibility of escape. Key national- ist instigators in Pristina and elsewhere became aware of the drownings before they were reported through the media.[19]

The Ibar was running high on the day of the drownings. The Inter- national Public Prosecutor who led the investigations into the incident, Peter Tinsley, concluded that 'something other than free will caused the children to enter the river, whether it was accident or a threat of a nature greater than the river itself'. However, his investigation found no evidence of any criminal act.[20] Serbs in the area wonder why six Albanian kids would be strolling through a Serb area, and speculate that they may have been on a dare.[21] The barking of a dog, of which most Kosovo Albanian children are taught to be terrified, may indeed have startled them into making a fatal leap into the swollen river. People living in the area who were questioned later told security service opera- tives that the children were most likely chased by a pack of wild dogs unconnected to any Serbs. If this is true, intimidation would deter the Veselli family from ever correcting the version that proved so expedient to the nationalist fanatics.

'Almost all citizens are heading toward the village of Cabre to learn more about the fate of the three children missing in the Ibar river,' intoned an RTK reporter who was 'on the scene'. At that point only a handful of people were actually moving toward the Ibar, but the report- er's exaggeration became self-fulfilling.[22]

Overnight and into the following morning, Kosovo Albanians di- gested the distorted news. 'People had a black look on their faces as they walked into the streets that morning,' said one local.[23] 'Some peo- ple were really outraged; others just wanted to fight.' School directors in many towns ordered their students to take part in demonstrations against 'this monstrous crime'. Nothing more vividly demonstrates UNMIK's failure to prevent the schools from perpetuating ethnic enmities than school directors reacting to nationalist broadcasts on the public TV channel by ordering their own pupils to rally to the nationalist cause.[24]

On 17 March an organised demonstration by more than 500 Albanian students and teachers was stopped by police on the south side of the main bridge across the Ibar in the centre of the ethnically divided town of Mitrovica. While the students were demonstrating peacefully, a second crowd 1,000-strong moved through them, overpowered the riot police and headed north, throwing stones at the Serbs on the north side of the river. Some Serbs threw stones at the approaching Albanians, and a few police managed to place themselves between the two mobs to prevent a direct confrontation.[25]

Their main route blocked, a group of Albanians used a footbridge to cross to the Serb-majority area north of the river. Shots were fired and Molotov cocktails were thrown between the two crowds before police managed to push the Albanians back across the river. The two mobs continued to exchange fire and there were deaths on both sides.[26] According to one senior UN official: 'French KFOR [who were responsible for security in Mitrovica] were wholly inadequate in Mitrovica and made no attempt to prevent anyone from crossing the bridge. On the contrary, they stood aside.'[27]

Two Albanian snipers shot and killed two civilians in Mitrovica across the riverbank. The Serbs believe that the weapons were moved by ambulance to the park area behind the Mitrovica municipality building. One of the dead was the father of Dragan Spasovic, a leader of the 'Bridge Watchers', a paramilitary group dedicated to defending the Serb part of Mitrovica. The other person murdered was a young pregnant mother of two who was well respected in the local community. The mother was buried locally but apparently KFOR did not allow a large crowd to attend the burial.[28] (This is in sharp contrast with the 2,000 Albanians attending the funeral of one of the Albanian children.) Some Albanians in Mitrovica blamed KFOR for the deaths, as the bullets found in the bodies of the Albanian casualties were of a type used not by Serbs but by KFOR.[29]

Enraged by the situation they saw unfolding on the television, several hundred young Albanians assembled and began moving towards the Serbs' roadblock in Caglavica, which by then had swollen to 1,000 people. In Pristina, KFOR's Multinational Brigade Centre initially underestimated the threat and decided to allow the UN's police, CivPol, to take the lead in managing the gathering crisis. The police formed a line across the main highway leading from Pristina towards the Serb enclaves; the crowd of protestors simply walked around them. KFOR received intelligence that the crowd intended to sack Gracanica, including the church complex that was one of the most important Orthodox sites in Kosovo. If Gracanica fell, KFOR anticipated that the Serbian Army would roll into Kosovo. Having repatriated its heavy weapons, KFOR could not have withstood such an assault. Because the ground between Caglavica and Gracanica would have been impossible to hold, KFOR decided to make its stand against the mob before Caglavica. Heavy fighting between the Albanian rioters and security forces continued late into the night. Several houses and cars were set on fire. Despite suffering several gunshot wounds, KFOR soldiers under a Norwegian commander prevented both villages from being torched — but at the cost of pulling in troops from the surrounding area.

Thus exposed, Serb areas of Lipljan, Obilic and Kosovo Polje were all sacked.[30] Crowds in different areas displayed different levels of organisation. 'I saw local networks being activated and they were connected to networks in other areas,' said a KFOR source. Around Lipljan the network told local Albanians to mark their houses with red paint; unmarked houses, belonging to Serbs, were ransacked. The networks varied in quality. The one in Lipljan was tightly disciplined and led by a former KLA commander well connected to the PDK. Agitators in Obiliq/c were just 'the dregs'[31].

Late that evening, a crowd of Albanians attacked with rocks and automatic weapons a block of flats that was the only place in Pristina where Serbs
still lived. The besieged residents phoned for help and locked themselves
away in an emergency room specially prepared for such an attack. They
listened nervously as the apartments they had just vacated were ransacked.
One UN staff member, George Huber, who also lived in the building and
tried unsuccessfully to hide, was surrounded by men in his apartment and
stripped. He was only spared when they discovered he was American. He
was allowed to leave untouched, holding his passport over his head as he
walked through the seething crowd. This discipline convinced Huber that
the attacks on minorities had been carefully planned and coordinated. After
six hours, an eleven-man KFOR rescue team finally arrived and managed
to escort the Serbs to safety.[32]

Another mob massed near the gate of the UNMIK HQ compound,
threatening to overrun it. Rioters also rampaged through Kosovo Polje
— a village near Pristina inhabited by both Serbs and Albanians that is
named after the nearby site of the legend-shrouded fourteenth-century
battle at which the Ottomans first defeated Serbs. In Kosovo Polje,
Serb houses, medical facilities, the police station and a school were all
torched in quick succession. One Serb was murdered.[33]

Violence spread west to Peje/Pec, and south to Prizren and Gji-
lan/Gnjilane, where crowds attacked UN buildings and police stations.
The regional headquarters buildings in the latter regions were badly
damaged and staff had to be evacuated. In Prizren an immense crowd
was led around by militants carrying burning torches.[34] As mobs across
Kosovo attacked Serb houses and churches, many Serbs sought shelter
in KFOR bases and police stations. It seemed that Serbs who had tried
to integrate with the Albanians were targeted most: those who had followed the urgings of the international community were now being let
down by it.

Violent demonstrations resumed the following day. Now, however,
KFOR was fully alert and reinforcements were being brought in from

nearby Bosnia. Many hoped the internationals would be able to regain control, but it wasn't so easy. German KFOR in Prizren packed their bags and negotiated with the mob to be allowed to evacuate the Church of the Holy Archangels, a centuries-old site that the Germans were supposedly guarding. Once inside their protected barracks they even refused to venture out to rescue German policemen in distress, let alone deal with the crowd. Their reason was 'national caveats' — they took their orders from Berlin rather than from the local KFOR commander.[35] Incredibly, the non-commissioned officer who led this ignominious retreat was given a medal. American, Swedish and Finnish KFOR all had mixed records. Too often, KFOR troops protected themselves rather than confronting the mobs or helping their victims.

UNMIK had complained to NATO that KFOR was being reduced too fast, with numbers being whittled down according to a schedule worked out at NATO headquarters in Belgium without regard for circumstances on the ground. Some in the UN also noted that the Swedes and Finns were an inadequate substitute for the robust British troops who had formerly had responsibility for security in and around Pristina.[36] Apart from the Norwegians who made a stand at Caglavica, the only other national contingent that distinguished itself during these trying days were the Italians who stood their ground at the Serbs' magnificent fourteenth-century monastery, Visoki Decani. Although outnumbered, they held back the crowd, wounding several Albanians who were trying to lob Molotov cocktails over the monastery wall. The Italians likewise prevented the crowd from getting close to the Serb Pec Patriarchate.[37]

In the village of Belo Polje near Peje/Pec, six American police officers and fifteen Albanian KPS (Kosovo Police Service) officers faced down a crowd of thousands of rioters to save 35 Serbs from being burned to death inside a church. After repeatedly warning one man who was waving a stick above his head to stop advancing, an American policewoman shot him in the chest, killing him.[38]

Gun-toting young men prowled the streets of Pristina in crowds, stoning UN vehicles and threatening the foreign administrators. Signals from UNMIK were confused, partly because of the hasty departure of senior officials. Aware that it was inadequately protected, UN security distributed radios to its staff and ordered them first to stay, and then to leave, Mission HQ. But many, particularly those living in besieged Serb villages near Pristina, had no way of getting home.[39]

Two days after clashes began, a combined military-police operation led by KFOR succeeded in securing Mitrovica. Staff of both the Regional HQ of UNMIK and the Mitrovica police station, however, took the precaution of evacuating their buildings in the Albanian-inhabited south of the city and relocating to the Serb-dominated north. With Mitrovica calmed, violence finally subsided throughout the rest of Kosovo.

In the following days, order was superficially restored across Kosovo. Police apprehended over 260 people suspected of crimes related to the riots, including many believed to be ringleaders. UNMIK called on 100 extra police investigators, six prosecutors and three judges to assist with the investigations.[40] The KFOR reinforcements finally arrived, most of them at least three days after they were needed.[41]

In all, at least 33 riots had erupted throughout the Albanian-majority parts of Kosovo. Although most protestors were genuinely incensed by what they thought had happened to the drowned children, they reacted by attacking individuals who they knew had had nothing to do with the incident on the bank of the Ibar. A malevolent minority targeted every Serb house they could reach. In the words of one Balkans expert, 'This was attempted ethnic cleansing, all across Kosovo, all at the same time'.[42] Publicly, though, UNMIK was anxious to avoid giving the impression that it had been temporarily beaten by an organised enemy. The Police Commissioner and his long-serving spokesman were forced out of the mission, reportedly because they had publicly expressed their view that the riots had been planned and coordinated. Those Albanians who were ready to use violence to achieve their aims couldn't believe that they could get away with it so easily.[43]

Many Serbs believed the Albanians were acting on a long term plan — that the drowning created the pretext, but that really the systematic destruction of the enclaves in three days had been worked out well in advance. Many felt let down by UNMIK and KFOR, who, they say, failed to offer them the protection that they had expected in such a situation. What is certain is that the riots caught both the Serbs and the international community off guard.

Underlying problems

UNMIK and NATO had been exposed as powerless when it mattered most. Somehow all their authority seemed to have turned to smoke, and lives were lost as a result.

UNMIK had not always been so impotent: in the early days it had a seemingly clear purpose backed up by overwhelming moral, legal and military authority. What it lacked from the beginning was the people and structures through which to assert this authority. But as staffing levels rose, the mission's authority diminished. One insider admitted that by the time the riots erupted, the one tool left in the international community's armoury was to appeal to the Prime Minister to tell the rioters to stop. 'He could either say "no", or "I can't control them either",' explained the official.[44] In the end, the Prime Minister did all he could, but it still wasn't enough to prevent catastrophic damage to Kosovo's social fabric.

Reactions among both Serbs and Albanians understandably reflected deep frustrations with life in what many critics referred to as 'UNMIKistan'.

Some Serbs characterised the violence as merely a continuation of a long terrorist campaign that began before 1999 with attacks against police, soldiers and Serb state officials, with the targets now including not just Kosovo Serbs but representatives of the international community as well. They say that although international officials claim that only 'a few extremists' instigated the riots, in reality the overwhelming majority of Kosovo Albanians support both their goals and their methods. Many Serbs also criticised Nebojsa Covic, the Deputy Premier of Serbia and Montenegro responsible for Kosovo, for failing to visit the families of the Serbian dead when he came to Mitrovica to assess the situation.[45]

Albanians, on the other hand, had become increasingly frustrated. Hopeful expectations about Kosovo's future, so widespread after the 1999 war, seemed to have shrivelled away. The economy remained the poorest in Europe outside the former Soviet Union: one in six Albanians were living in poverty, and half had no proper work.[46] The privatisation process that was supposed to free up resources and attract foreign investment had repeatedly sputtered for reasons that were opaque even to many within the privatisation agency itself. But material privation and lack of opportunity can only explain some of the Albanians' frustrations: Kosovo has always been poor, but these riots were new, and they were instigated by many of the best educated in society.[47]

Many Albanians were livid about the lack of progress towards independence, which most are convinced is the prerequisite to serious progress in any sphere. Many Kosovo Albanians felt that every time a Kosovo Serb was killed, instead of arresting the perpetrators, UNMIK held their leaders to account. Since the international community's critical response put the Albanians' longed-for independence in jeopardy, incidents of violence gave rise to conspiracy theories that Serbian intelligence services were actually behind attacks on Kosovo Serbs.

Foreign observers felt that the tepid international response had shown Albanian militants that they could get away with murder. 'I've heard previously pro-Kosovo people remark that the Kosovo Albanians appear to walk around town with a bit more of a swagger now,' said one long-time international official in Pristina. 'They've done their worst and know they won't be punished for it.'[48]

'It was interesting to watch the change in most of the junior officers at the US Office,' said a diplomat working there. 'They all came to Pristina bright-eyed and ready to help the poor downtrodden Albanians. Now they gripe more than anyone, frustrated because they feel the Kosovo Albanians aren't even trying to make a democratic state for themselves.'[49]

The campaign of physical assaults and arson shook international policy towards Kosovo deeply. Despite five years of promises that Kosovo would never be partitioned, the UN, prodded by France and with the US ambivalent, immediately began considering plans to divide Kosovo along ethnic lines, just as nationalists had been calling for from the beginning. 'We're worried that they'll do it again and again, and we probably won't be able to stop them,' grumbled one EU official. 'After the violence, people tried to find an explanation. Some said we hadn't given the Albanians enough power — so now we're giving them more. Others said we had some of the wrong people in place — so some people the Albanians didn't like have been sacked. It's just appeasement now. We can't really do anything else.'[50]

Kosovo's Prime Minister, Bajram Rexhepi, one of the few local politicians who actively opposed the violence — even going to the barricades to try to disperse the angry mobs, with limited success — engaged in a field tour around Kosovo. The government launched a reconstruction programme, allocating 4.2 million euros for repairing damaged churches.[51] But both failed to reassure the Serbs. One Kosovo Albanian awaiting heart surgery was told the operation had to be postponed because Kosovo budget funds were being redirected from health care towards the reconstruction of Serb houses destroyed by rioters (an explanation which betrays a misunderstanding of the budget system).[52] Hence, even the reconstruction programme, which international officials had hoped would help conciliate the Serbs, has come to be seen as yet another provocation.

The US reaction to the violence was uncertain. US Under Secretary of State Mark Grossman visited Kosovo in the weeks following the riots and offered political leaders sympathy rather than admonishment. Only later did the State Department stiffen its tone.[53] If the US refrained from reproaching the Kosovo leadership, many others did not. EU External Relations Commissioner Chris Patten warned that Kosovo could become a 'gangster pariah state' unless it reined in the extremists.

UNMIK called on Prime Minister Rexhepi to take action to dismiss ministers and mayors who condoned violence. It would have been very difficult, possibly fatal, if the PM had done so. UNMIK's chief, the Special Representative of the Secretary-General (SRSG), had the power to dismiss the officials himself but never used it — the international community always feared it wouldn't be able to cope with the backlash.[54]

Meanwhile, the victims of the March violence continued to suffer long after the riots had ended. Police often refused to stop their damaged homes from being looted. 'A month after the riots,' said one international official who works with minority communities, 'I visited a group of 80-year-old women with broken arms and legs and bruises still visible from the beatings they'd taken at the hands of the crowd. In another village, someone managed to steal the entire roof off a recently reconstructed property without the police noticing. While the politicians repeated their diplomatic words, in the towns and villages displaced Serbs are being given every signal that their return is not welcomed.'[55]

President Rugova was asked by a young woman if he felt it was safe for Serbs to come to Pristina, the putative capital of the would-be Kosovo state. He said there was no reason for them to come, and that it was dangerous for them to be there. Serbs, he said, 'have everything they need in Gracanica' (a Serb enclave three miles from the city). During the violence, Rugova had pointedly refused to condemn the violence against Serbs.[56]

'Personally, I sat and watched more then a year's hard work go down the drain,' said one senior international official dealing with displaced people. 'We're almost back to square one with refugee return and I think any hope of a sustainable multi-ethnic Kosovo is laughable. Most people will admit that the March riots were a combination of factors including bad timing and it would take a lot of coincidences for them to be replicated. But the bottom line is that all the underlying factors that caused the violence are still there and very little has been done to address them.'[57]

What's at stake?

The murderous riots of March 2004 are a pitiful episode in the recent history of Kosovo. Nevertheless, some people may still be inclined to shrug their shoulders and ask why it matters. Anyone who is being invited to read this book, still move to condone the expenditure of some of their taxes or the dispatch of their soldiers, has a right to ask why they should care about the outcome of the world's presence in post-war Kosovo.

This book argues that there are three reasons: one local, one European and one global.

First, over two million people live in Kosovo; the quality of their lives, and those of future generations there, depends on what UNMIK and the current constellation of forces in Kosovo are able to leave behind.

Second, Kosovo threatens to become a black hole in the middle of Europe. Slovenia has already joined the European Union, and Bulgaria and Romania are slated to follow in 2007. Croatia is also en route to Europe, though less sure-footedly. Albania and the rest of the former Yugoslavia — Bosnia and Hercegovina, the cumbersomely named Former Yugoslav Republic of Macedonia (FYROM, hereafter referred to as Macedonia), and the union of Serbia and Montenegro, which still formally includes Kosovo — threaten to become a mire of poverty, unrest and criminality in the heart of Europe. In other words, failure in Kosovo will feed problems throughout the continent.

Third, the outcome in Kosovo will set precedents that will reverberate around the region and the world. By many measures the UN Interim Administration in Kosovo is the most ambitious peace operation in UN history: on a per capita basis, the world has invested 25 times as much money and 50 times as many troops as in Afghanistan. Kosovo puts the experience in Iraq in sharp focus. If Kosovo is deemed a success, it will bolster the UN's claim to be the most credible and effective nation-builder in the world; if it's seen as a failure, it will embolden those who argue that nation-building should be done either by powerful individual states or not at all.

The outcome will also send a powerful signal to would-be separatists. If Kosovo gains its independence without having embraced ethnic diversity or the rule of law, it will be a thundering confirmation of the axiom that might makes right. Ethnic cleansing, righteously challenged during the Kosovo war, will have eventually won, albeit in a subtler, more insidious form. If, on the other hand, international stewardship transforms Kosovo into a society in which all its members can live in security and dignity, then that too will notify separatists everywhere that international recognition of their aspirations requires them to live up to a certain standard of civilised behaviour.

Early promise, massive investment, serious effort

In Kosovo, the international community went from being all-powerful to being ignored, impotent and under attack. Three misconceived explanations have been offered to account for this fall from grace. One is that we shouldn't have intervened in the first place. The second is that all the shortcomings of the protectorate can be chalked up to the incompetence or cupidity of international officials. The third is that the problems do not exist. None of these views withstand serious scrutiny.

NATO's intervention in Kosovo undoubtedly saved many lives. Mass ethnic cleansing was prevented. The intervention made Europe a much safer place and Kosovo a much better place for the majority than it would have been otherwise. NATO's action may have also given pause to other murderous tyrants elsewhere. Given this history, it is facile to look at the problems in Kosovo today and say that the West shouldn't have intervened in the first place.

A wearisome number of observers, especially inexperienced journalists parachuted into Kosovo, have blamed all UNMIK's failings on its employees. If this were true, there would be little reason to scour the record of this international administration for lessons. The only change necessary to make future international administrations more successful than this one would be to start with better people.

In a mission made up of thousands of people from every corner of the globe, there were inevitably several examples of gross malfeasance and more commonplace ones of laziness, arrogance and ignorance. There were, no doubt, a few individuals who deserve to be held responsible for particular failures in Kosovo. But these explain only a small part of the puzzle; they do not explain why the world's mammoth investment has failed to transform Kosovo into a multi-ethnic, law-abiding society with a sufficient sense of public spirit to function effectively as a democracy. For all its flaws, the UN's neo-imperial administration in Kosovo has not been worse and in many ways has been better than most governments around the world. The failure of international efforts to transform Kosovo is tragic precisely because it occurred despite massive investment and serious efforts by thousands of imperfect but well-meaning, committed and generally competent people.

The third view is that no serious problems exist. Although some institutions and their employees have a clear interest in pretending Kosovo is problem-free, the events of March 2004 (and many other examples) belie this. This is not to deny that the international community has improved Kosovo immensely; perhaps it has done all that could be done. The fact remains that the world seems to have tried its best and has failed to achieve a creditable degree of ethnic integration, to embed the rule of law, or to regenerate the economy. An explanation is sorely needed.

Forecast: ethnic division, endemic crime, non-inclusive politics,
a dysfunctional economy

UNMIK began with an intentionally vague mandate to administer Kosovo from day to day, to build democratic institutions and to prepare the ground for resolving its political status. Interpreted in the context of a massive effort to bring a sustainable peace to a conflict-ridden corner of Europe, the mandate evolved into a set of eight broad goals, known as 'the Standards', that the international community embraced as representing the essential elements of a stable and decent society. It is against these standards that Kosovo's development under UNMIK must be judged a severe disappointment.

When UNMIK finally leaves Kosovo, probably towards the end of 2006, it will leave behind a place where the main minority group, the Serbs, still live in isolation — some of it self-imposed — from their Albanian neighbours. Though ordinary crime has been reduced to a level comparable to some EU countries, an Al Capone-like combination of violence and corruption continues to colour public life. Opposition and government political parties, dominated by the personalities of their respective leaders, hardly speak either with one another or with their constituents. The economy is practically moribund. Links to neighbouring countries remain tenuous.

This is not to say that Kosovo is doomed to remain poor and isolated forever. The passage of time without open conflict over the next decade or two, combined with continuing ministrations by the European Union, may well raise living standards dramatically. Perhaps investors will find the place more attractive after its independence is recognised, as it soon will be. Removing the distraction of political status may also put pressure on Kosovo's political class to turn their attention to its myriad practical problems. If this comes to pass, then in the grand sweep of history it will not have been a bad result. But it is not the dramatic transformation that the mission had promised during most of its tenure. On the contrary, few parts of the UN-led mission will be able to claim dramatic success.

What went wrong?

The failure of the international administration to transform Kosovo into a multi-ethnic society subject to the rule of law resulted from a misunderstanding and misappropriation of power. UNMIK neglected soft power by putting local politicians in charge of education, and attempting to regulate the media with cumbersome after-the-fact investigations and ineffectual penalties. The risk-aversion of much of KFOR and the police meant that the international community also failed to wield hard power effectively. Even economic power was given away. Instead, UNMIK dominated the thin middle ground of *de jure* authority and bureaucratic power. This paper power proved largely irrelevant to achieving the twin goals of leaving behind an entity that was multi-ethnic and subject to the rule of law. UNMIK failed to transform Kosovo as it hoped because it misunderstood the nature of Kosovo's ethnic conflicts and other weaknesses, and the kind of power needed to remedy them. How this came to pass is the story of this book.

KOSOVO AND HUMANITARIAN
INTERVENTION UP TO 1999

Both Albanians and Serbs use history as a weapon in contemporary political struggles, but they use it differently. For Serbs, the heart of the argument is Kosovo's historic status as the seat of their short-lived medieval kingdom and its mythical status as the site of a unique covenant between the Serbs' ancestors, their descendents and God. The Albanian counterclaim is much more down-to-earth: they claim to have been there first, long before the Slav invasions of the Balkan Peninsula in the sixth century, in the form of Illyrians. Albanians also correctly claim to be far more numerous in Kosovo than the Serbs or any other nationality in recent times.

Both Albanians and Serbs have reasons to see themselves as the victims of injustice, maltreatment and worse. Since 1999, these abuses have been framed in the language of the intervention: as issues of 'human rights'. But these abuses are embedded in a tradition of bullying that predates such notions. To understand — not justify — current antipathies, one has to look at the deep sense of historical injustice shared by both peoples. These rival perceptions of the past, distilled by ideologues and stirred by demagogues, fed on one another to create the intoxicating and explosive nationalism that ravaged Kosovo in the 1990s. Indeed, many people who lived through the collapse of Yugoslavia argue that Milosevic could not have come to power without the foil of Albanian nationalism in Kosovo, and Kosovo Albanians certainly could never have

25

secured a mammoth international intervention without a villain on the scale of Milosevic.

Illyrians and Slavs. There is some evidence that Illyrians speaking a proto-Albanian language lived outside the towns and estates in the Roman province of Dardania.[1] The Serbs descended into the Balkans along with the Croats, in the fifth and sixth centuries when the Roman Empire retreated, and were concentrated in Rascia, northwest of Kosovo. The territory and identity of both groups seem to be have been quite fluid in this period. Waves of Visigoths, Huns, Ostrogoths and Vlachs also washed over Kosovo.

The Byzantine Empire 'reconquered' Kosovo in 1014-18 but ruled for less than two centuries before the emergence of the new medieval Serb kingdom of the Nemanjids. King Nemanja conquered the eastern flank of Kosovo before abdicating the throne in 1196 to become a monk on Mount Athos; his son Stefan then took over the rest of today's Kosovo, and was crowned King of Serbia by a papal legate in 1217.

Nemanjid rule inspired a flurry of monastery-building, which benefited from the flight of Orthodox painters from recently sacked Constantinople. The seat of the Serbian Orthodox archbishopric moved to Pec (Peje) at the end of the thirteenth century. The Patriarchate buildings in Pec, and the great monasteries in Decani, and Gracanica and the Holy Archangels monastery in Prizren were built in the fourteenth century, made Kosovo a centre of the Serbian Orthodox Church.

A few more generations of Nemanjids continued to expand their territory, blinding and strangling one another in vicious power struggles along the way. Stefan Dusan, crowned in 1331, brought the medieval Serbian state to its short-lived apogee. His empire stretched from the Danube to the Gulf of Corinth, with its capital in Skopje. There, in 1346, the Serbian Archbishop was elevated to the rank of Patriarch and the Serbian Orthodox Church became entirely independent. At Easter the new Serbian Patriarch crowned Dusan 'Emperor of the Serbs and the Greeks'. But within just twenty years, the Serb king would be forced to pay tribute to a new power — the rapidly expanding Ottoman Empire.

The Ottomans. Over the next century the still young Ottoman Empire subjugated the whole Balkan peninsula. Their progress was marked by clear victories, such as the decisive rout of Hungarian-led forces at the battle of the Maritsa River in 1371, interspersed with military setbacks, often prompted by dynastic feuds within the Ottoman court.

One battle in this energetic westward expansion — militarily not the most significant — was destined to assume a mythical status centuries later: the Battle of the Field of Blackbirds. The battle was fought on 28 June 1389 near modern-day Pristina. What little else historians can tell us about this battle is that a local lord, Lazar Hrebeljanovic, elected to fight rather than become a vassal of the Ottomans. In the weeks before the battle, Lazar formed a coalition — which included Albanians — before confronting the Ottoman army. Lazar, Sultan Murad and the Ottoman heir were all killed before or during the encounter; historians agree the battle was a draw. But Serbian epics tell a far grander and, from the Serbs' point of view, more tragic tale. Lazar's decision to fight the Ottomans rather than submit to vassalage is eulogised as a choice between a 'worldly kingdom' of power and comfort without honour and a 'heavenly kingdom' of everlasting righteousness at the cost of death. Lazar is described as a martyr, fabled to have cried 'it is better to die in battle than to live in shame'.[2]

Both Albanians and Serbs now view their centuries under Ottoman rule as enslavement. Both were explicitly listed among the seven Christian peoples Ottoman sources claimed to have defeated in Kosovo. Instead of imprinting a new culture on their captured lands, the Ottomans reinforced differences between communities, classifying people by religion and ruling through each confession's religious officials. As long as they accepted the nominal supremacy of Islam, all members of the monotheistic faiths were considered protected people. This organisational scheme divided Albanians into Orthodox and Catholic groups, which probably retarded the development of a national Albanian consciousness.

Of all the Balkan peoples under Ottoman rule, Albanians converted to Islam in greatest numbers, which gave them the same status as Turks in the Ottomans' official registries and all the advantages of first-class subjects. Men would often convert while their wives continued to practice Catholicism, and many who had officially converted to Islam continued to practise Christianity clandestinely.[3] Albanians supplied many of the empire's top officials, including renowned grand viziers, notably the Koprulus. The Albanians' most famous hero, Skanderbeg, was an Albanian noble who entered the sultan's service and became a general before returning to his native Kruja to lead a thirty-year rebellion against the empire.

Most Albanians who stayed in their mountainous homes preserved a traditional culture little touched by the empire. They were a warlike, patriarchal people ruled by traditional quasi-legal codes. The most important of these, known as the Kanun of Lek, remained in force in many mountainous communities until the 1930s and still occasionally casts a shadow over social relations. The Kanun regulated all aspects of life, including the blood feud or *hakmarrje*. The Kanun decreed that if a man was seriously insulted, he was allowed to kill the malefactor, but that the nearest male relative of the man killed would then be entitled to exact a revenge killing against the original avenger's family. Family feuds running through generations resulted in countless killings of young men and many others spending years in hiding or holed up in homes built like fortresses. The Kanun also institutionalised the oath or *besa* which remains an important concept in contemporary Kosovo. (Today it is the name of a Pristina insurance company).

Whereas religion never played a central role in Albanian identity, Serb consciousness was inextricably bound up with the Orthodox Church. Although forced conversions to Islam were rare, Christian subjects of the Ottoman Empire suffered serious disadvantages. They had to pay higher taxes than Muslims — often including surrendering their oldest son to be converted to Islam and enrolled in the sultan's service; could not carry arms, which was the avenue toward winning large estates; were at an extreme disadvantage in legal disputes with Muslims; and were subjected to various indignities such as having to dismount while passing a Muslim.

Despite these differences, Serbs and Albanians often collaborated against their Ottoman overlords. It was only as the empire declined in the nineteenth century, and as Ottoman officials became more brutal and capricious, that nationalism in its modern form began to stir. In 1804 a peasant trader named Karadjordje — 'Black George' — led a rebellion that quickly evolved into a full-blown struggle for independence. The Ottomans defeated the rebellious Serbs in 1813 and inflicted vicious reprisals, which linked this event in Serbs' collective memory to the defeat in Kosovo over four centuries earlier. A second Serb uprising led by Miloš Obrenovic secured limited autonomy in 1815 and complete autonomy in 1833. Serb autonomy, reinforced by developments in language and education, crystallised in a new national identity. Albanian national consciousness emerged a few decades later, slowed partly by the lack of a single alphabet — Albanians in the south used Greek letters, those in the northwest wrote in the Latin alphabet, and the Albanians' Muslim majority favoured an Arabic script. As with Slavic nationalisms before it, the movement to standardise the language and promote education was essential in creating a shared identity.

Both Serb and Albanian nationalism took a more overtly political turn in 1877. Russia — later joined by Serbia and Montenegro — attacked and routed Ottoman forces in the Balkans. The Ottomans retaliated with Albanian auxiliaries against Serb forces and civilians. Some 30,000 Serbs were forced from contemporary Kosovo, while a comparable number of Albanians were forced from southern Serbia, as John Lampe observes.[4] 'It was the mass expulsion of Albanians and other Muslims from the areas conquered by Serbia and Montenegro in 1877-78 that persuaded the Albanians in Kosovo that Serbia — and the Serbs of Kosovo who were claimed as an unredeemed part of the Serbian population — represented a threat to their existence.'[5]

It was at this time that 300 Albanians met in the southern Kosovo town of Prizren and formed a movement known as the Prizren League. The League called on the diplomats then meeting in what became known as the Congress of Berlin to prevent further Albanian-inhabited territories from being ceded to the expanding Christian states of Serbia and Greece, and for the Ottoman government, the Porte, to unify the four Albanian-inhabited provinces of Janina (now in Greece), Monastir (Macedonia), Shkoder (Albania) and Kosovo. The League demanded a national assembly to govern the vilayet (Ottoman province); that all its officials should speak Albanian; that teaching should be in Albanian; and that some tax revenues should be retained for local use. In a letter to Britain's delegate to the Berlin Congress, Lord Beaconsfield, the League declared: 'Just as we are not and do not want to be regarded as Turks, so we shall oppose with all our might anyone who would like to turn us into Slavs or Austrians or Greeks. We want to be Albanians.'[6]

Animosity between Serbs and Albanians grew, as events and outside powers exaggerated differences and made peaceful coexistence increasingly difficult. The Great Powers and the Ottoman Empire all regarded Albanians, in particular, as a volatile element that threatened to upset the region's delicate balance of power. In 1901 Albanians went on a rampage around Pristina, killing many Serbs. The Empire struck back with mass arrests of nationalist agitators, and by criminalising the use of the Albanian language.[7] In 1910, the Ottomans brought in Kurdish irregulars to suppress a revolt against rigorous tax collection and political centralisation. Albanian leaders were flogged in public. The Kurds burned villages and drove 150,000 people from their homes, two thirds of them Serbs.[8]

In 1912 an alliance of Serbia, Bulgaria and Greece agreed to attack the Ottoman portion of Macedonia and divide it among themselves.

The Serbs mobilised 350,000 men, routed the Ottomans, and occupied Kosovo as well as most of contemporary Macedonia. For the Albanians of Kosovo, already a majority of the population, this meant being 'transported from the disorder and ethnic rivalry of the last Ottoman years into an arbitrary regime administered by the Serbian army'.[9] Reporting for *Pravda* in 1912, Leon Trotsky quoted this account from a Serbian army officer: 'The horrors actually began as soon as we crossed into Kosova: entire Albanian villages had been turned into pillars of fire; dwellings, possessions accumulated by fathers and grandfathers were going up in flames; the picture was repeated the whole way to Skopje. There the Serbs broke into Turkish and Albanian houses and performed the same task in every case: plundering and killing. For two days before my arrival in Skopje, the inhabitants had woken up to the sight of heaps of Albanian corpses with severed heads. Among the mass of soldiers you see Serb peasants who have come from every part of Serbia on the pretext of looking for their sons or brothers. They cross the plain of Kosova and start plundering, from the area around Vranje[10] the population has crossed over en masse into the Albanian villages to pick up whatever may catch the eye. Peasant women carry away even the doors and windows of Albanian houses.'[11] The Serbs justified their war crimes against civilians by accusing Albanians of having expelled 150,000 Serbs from Kosovo since 1870.[12]

The World Wars. As the First World War began and Serb forces buckled under the assault of the Central Powers, Belgrade propagandists instinctively reached back to the battle of the Field of Blackbirds. The battle had given rise to an ideal of martyrdom which inspired several Serb leaders to quixotic or even masochistic follies. 'In the disaster of retreat [during World War I] before the armies of the Central Powers, [King] Petar was seen as "the new Lazar", the prince of the Kosovo defeat and a saintly martyr for liberty. "The old man," said his elder son, Prince Djordje, "got it into his head to die and become a saint, like

Lazar at Kosovo. He put on the soldier's cap, took up a rifle, and joined the men in the trenches.'"[13]

During the First World War, Serbia had generated a great deal of admiration in Great Britain and France. Indeed, echoes of this affection coloured both countries' actions in the wars of Yugoslav succession 70 years later. At the Paris Peace Conference in 1920, it predisposed them to listen sympathetically to the Serbian argument that it needed Kosovo to help recover from the enormous trauma it had suffered during the war. The new Kingdom of Serbs, Croats and Slovenes was duly awarded Kosovo, where the Albanian majority greeted the news with fear, anger and a sense of betrayal. In July 1921 Kosovo Albanians submitted a 72-page petition to the League of Nations begging for union with Albania. It claimed that since 1918, Serbs had killed 12,371 people in Kosovo and imprisoned 22,000.[14] The petition failed to dent Serbia's heroic image and the Kosovo Albanians' plea was ignored.

In 1941 the occupying Axis forces assigned most of Kosovo to Italian-controlled Albania, while Germans occupied the north and a strip in the east went to Bulgaria. In the chaos of invasion, Albanians and Serbs burnt down one another's houses, and thousands fled. 'In early 1944 a Kosovar contingent of the Albanian nationalist Balli Kombetar as well as the Nazis' hastily formed Skanderbeg SS Division had conducted a reign of terror against any Serbs they found in Kosovo or Montenegro, forcing another 10,000 to flee,' wrote Lampe.[15] When the Axis forces withdrew in 1944 and were replaced by the Communist Partisans, the Yugoslav forces' actions against suspected collaborators degenerated into general persecution of Albanians. This treatment provoked a widespread Albanian insurrection that ran for six months and required 30,000 Yugoslav troops to quell. As usual, the fighting was punctuated by atrocities. In one of the worst incidents, Yugoslav soldiers herded several hundred Albanians into a tunnel in Montenegro and sealed it, asphyxiating them.[16]

The land of brotherhood and unity. After the war, Albanians in Kosovo found themselves living once again in a state whose Slav majority regarded them with suspicion and hostility. As Miranda Vickers notes, 'Kosova, therefore, emerged from the war into the new federal Yugoslavia under a state of siege, her population regarded as a threat to the new state.'[17] To remove this threat, Tito and Stalin had agreed that Kosovo should eventually be united with Albania. But Tito, much like Western statesmen today, was wary of offending Serbian nationalist sentiment. In 1946 Tito told Albanian leader Enver Hoxha: 'Kosovo and the other Albanian regions belong to Albania and we shall return them to you, but not now because the Great Serb reaction would not accept such a thing.'[18]

Tito never delivered on his promise, but he did slowly improve political conditions in Kosovo. In 1969 the University of Pristina opened, which for the first time in Yugoslavia offered university-level classes in Albanian. Institutes devoted to Albanian literature and culture opened, and cultural exchanges with Albania were permitted. Under a system of proportional representation, Albanians were heavily represented on managerial boards of state enterprises, the civil service and government. In an effort to offset 'Greater Serbian hegemonism', under the 1974 Constitution for the Federal Republic of Yugoslavia, Kosovo became an 'autonomous province' within Serbia. But while six different Slav groups within Yugoslavia were considered 'nations' and therefore entitled to their own republics, which at least nominally had the right to secede, Albanians were considered merely a 'nationality'. The overt political rationale for this designation was twofold: that Albanians already had their own republic in Albania; and that if given the right to secede the Albanians would actually exercise it. Albanian political leaders acknowledged that Kosovo in this period was a republic in all but name. But this *de facto* status was not good enough for Kosovo Albanians.

Though the Yugoslav authorities tolerated expressions of purely cultural self-assertion, during the 1970s many Albanians were convicted of plotting the secession of Kosovo from Yugoslavia. In addition to separatism, Albanians were increasingly accused of physically assaulting and threatening Serbs and damaging their property. Serbs further accused the Albanian police and other authorities of failing to prosecute crimes against them.

Despite receiving much greater economic development funding than other poor parts of Yugoslavia, Kosovo's unemployment rate — at 27.5 per cent — remained the highest in the country.[19] As prosperity rose in other areas, Kosovo's relative poverty became even worse. The contribution of economic frustrations to inter-ethnic antagonisms was exacerbated by the disproportionate representation of Serbs in the professions. This trend, in turn, was perpetuated by the University of Pristina's concentration on Albanian literature and culture rather than more vocational technical subjects. Indicatively, Kosovo's late president, Ibrahim Rugova, held a doctorate in Albanian philology, and its former Prime Minister, Bajram Kosumi, holds a master's in the subject. While some Serbs enjoyed privileges that grated with the Albanian majority, the reality was that the economic situation was bad for all but the best connected. Kosovo's economic problems were not primarily a consequence of neglect; the main explanation for economic frustration appears to be that improvements in education raised expectations faster than economic development could overcome Kosovo's historically impoverished starting point.

Against this background, on 11 March 1981, a student in the cafeteria at the University of Pristina found a cockroach in his soup and threw his tray on the floor in disgust, an act which sparked off the worst violence in Yugoslavia since the Second World War. Police arrested some leaders of a protest over conditions at the university, whereupon the protesters' focus switched to liberating their comrades. The protests, involving between 2,000[20] and 4,000[21] people, then evolved into a more general complaint about disparities in Kosovo. Tear gas finally dispersed the protesters the following morning. After two weeks, protests resumed in Prizren and Pristina, and this time they turned violent. According to the

Pristina daily *Rilindija*, 35 people were injured and 22 arrested. A few days later, the revolt spread across Kosovo with people from all walks of life pouring onto the streets. The federal government declared a state of emergency, while 30,000 troops backed by helicopters patrolled the province. Kosovo's boundaries were sealed, a curfew was declared, and schools and factories were closed. The protesters' demands included a Kosovo Republic, improved conditions for workers and students, freedom for political prisoners, and unification with Albania. When the news blackout was lifted, the media focused on this last, irredentist demand. The Yugoslav press reported that by the end of April eleven people had been killed. Amnesty International said the number could have been as high as 300. Some Albanians said it was closer to 1,000.[22] Relations between Kosovo's Albanian majority and the federal state never recovered. Among Albanians, the demonstrations are universally regarded as a key political watershed of the Yugoslav era. After 1981, sixty per cent of all political prisoners in Yugoslavia were Kosovo Albanians.[23] Many of Kosovo's leading figures were arrested for their roles in the protests.

Throughout the 1980s, Kosovo Serbs complained more and more about discrimination in employment, petty harassment and outright attacks by Albanians. The most celebrated such case in this period concerned a 56-year-old Serbian peasant, Djordje Martimovic, found bleeding and unconscious with a beer bottle up his rectum. Though the preponderance of evidence suggested that the injury was self-inflicted, the Serbian media blamed unidentified Albanian attackers. The seminal Memorandum of the Serbian Academy of Sciences and Arts said the Martimovic case was 'reminiscent of the darkest days of the Turkish practice of impalement'.[24] Equating the Martimovic case with an impaling and Kosovo Albanians with the Ottoman Turks had an enormous impact on Serbian consciousness. Worsening economic conditions in Serbia and the political and social uncertainty created by Tito's death had already made many Serbs feel victimised. 'The impalement metaphor worked well to further feelings

of endangerment and to propel the desire for historical revenge,' writes
Julie Mertus.[25]

Milosevic's vortex. If one had to trace the dissolution of Yugoslavia — the
most prosperous and permissive country in the socialist world, a regional power in southeast Europe, a founding member of the Non-
Aligned Movement, host to the 1984 winter Olympics and hundreds of
thousands of western European sun-seekers — to a single day, it would
be 24 April 1987.

On that day, Slobodan Milosevic met with a group of discontented
Serbs in Kosovo Polje, a suburb of Pristina. Milosevic, recently elected
president of the Communist Party of Serbia, had never before shown
any interest in Kosovo and in fact had a reputation as a hardline socialist
critic of anything smacking of nationalism. Milosevic's political patron,
Ivan Stambolic, then President of Serbia, had dispatched him to listen to
the grievances of a group of angry Kosovo Serbs who were complaining
about harassment and intimidation and threatening to come to Belgrade
to demonstrate. As he entered the building, thousands of the Serbs
seemed to be throwing stones at police, who were mostly Albanian;
the stones came from a truck parked just out of sight — the master
stroke of Milosevic's stage management of the whole event. When the
future supremo emerged from the building, he looked into a waiting
TV camera and declared: 'No one should dare to beat you!' As a Kosovo
Serb leader said later, 'This sentence enthroned him as a Tsar.'[26]

Inside the building, the Serbs demanded that Belgrade take steps to
protect their rights against the depredations of Kosovo's Albanian leadership. Milosevic answered:

'You should stay here, both for your ancestors and your descendents … But
I do not suggest you stay here suffering and enduring a situation with which
you are not satisfied. On the contrary! It should be changed, together with all
progressive people here, in Serbia and in Yugoslavia …Yugoslavia does not exist
without Kosovo! Yugoslavia would disintegrate without Kosovo! Yugoslavia and
Serbia are not going to give up Kosovo.'[27]

Milosevic had managed to change the focus of political debate in Serbia from socialist ideology to nationalism. Using Kosovo Serbs as his storm troopers, in the next two years Milosevic organised an estimated 100 'Meetings of Truth' all over Serbia involving a total of five million people.[28]

In order to deliver on his pledge to 'unite Serbia', Milosevic had to destroy the autonomy granted to Vojvodina (a region north of Belgrade and populated largely by ethnic Hungarians) and Kosovo under the 1974 Constitution. In October 1988, Milosevic's protesters pressured first the government of Vojvodina and then of Montenegro to resign, whereupon he replaced them with his own lackeys. His efforts to do the same in Kosovo provoked fierce resistance. In February 1989, 2,000 workers from the Trepca mining complex, now in the Serb-majority area of northern Kosovo, marched the 55 kilometres to Pristina, where they were joined by thousands of others to protest against Milosevic's manoeuvres. Some went on hunger strike, while industrial action and demonstrations erupted across Kosovo. Shkelzen Maliqi, a leading Kosovo Albanian political commentator, wrote: 'The whole of Kosova has risen — desperate, frightened and angry ... a kind of Albanian intifada has begun.'[29] When Milosevic's constitutional amendments were forced through the Kosovo Assembly in March,[30] the Belgrade Assembly exulted that Serbia was 'whole' again. In Kosovo federal police used tanks, helicopters, tear gas and automatic weapons against the widespread demonstrations. According to official reports, 25 people were killed. Other sources as usual place the number of casualties far higher.[31]

On 28 June 1989, Milosevic, recently anointed President of Serbia, climbed the rostrum at the memorial of the Battle of the Field of Blackbirds that Serbian epics tell us the Serbs had lost to the Ottomans exactly 600 years before. Speaking before a million Serbs bussed in from around Yugoslavia, Milosevic tapped into ancient myth and contemporary grievances to complete his transformation from faceless Yugoslav apparatchik to Serbian nationalist hero. In the process, he threw out the supra-national Yugoslav ideology expressed in the ubiquitous slogan 'brotherhood and unity' and replaced it with an unapologetic, vengeful Serbian chauvinism. The 80 per cent of Yugoslavia's citizens who were not Serbs trembled.

The leading Belgrade daily *Politika*, by then controlled by Milosevic's yes-men, was devoted entirely to coverage of the anniversary. The headline proclaimed 'Six centuries from the Battle of Kosovo, the time of Kosovo' while the subhead read: 'The Serbian people has glorified and still glorifies its heroes and recognises its traitors.'[32] Throughout Serbia, Kosovo was in the air. Serbs gloated over their reconquest of the province. Serbian bookshops filled their shelves with books about Kosovo. Musical artists dedicated their works to Kosovo. There was even a new perfume, 'Miss 1389'.[33]

Over the next several months, federal police arrested or detained hundreds of people accused of organising protests or believed capable of organising protests in the future. Objecting to this crackdown, Slovenia and Croatia withdrew their police units from Kosovo.

Kosovo society was by now almost wholly segregated, with Albanian and Serbian children attending school in different shifts or in separate rooms. This segregation set the stage for a bizarre drama that finally catalysed the exodus of Albanians from state institutions. In late March and early April 1990, the Yugoslav media reported that thousands of Kosovo Albanian schoolchildren had fallen mysteriously ill. Lines of cars carrying children complaining of drowsiness, headaches and light-headedness streamed towards the hospitals and clinics in Pristina. Two thousand parents of children who had allegedly been poisoned gathered at a sports auditorium in Pristina and declared that they would keep their children out of school until they had received a satisfactory explanation. At the same time, Tanjug, the official Yugoslav wire service, reported numerous incidents of Albanian students attacking their Serb counterparts, accusing them of administering the poison. Tanjug also said that no poisoning had actually taken place and that the entire affair had been contrived by Albanian separatists.

Immediately after the poisoning incident, Belgrade purged 2,000 Albanians from the police force in Kosovo and replaced them with 2,500 Serbs. Further purges and resignations of Albanians followed in hospitals, schools and state enterprises. By the end of the summer over 15,000 Kosovo Albanians had been dismissed from state jobs. The salaries of all 21,000 Albanian teaching staff ceased to be paid as of March 1991. Virtually all Albanian-language media were suppressed. Albanian gatherings were broken up.

In response to this crackdown, 23 Albanian activists, most of them academics, met in Pristina's Elida Café in 1989 and founded the Democratic League of Kosovo. Ibrahim Rugova, a mild-mannered professor of Albanian literature and literary critic, was elected president as a compromise candidate. A referendum on independence was organised in which 87 per cent of the 1,05 million eligible voters — that is, virtually every non-Serb — cast ballots. Of these, practically every single person voted for independence. On 19 October 1991, the Kosovo Albanian parliamentarians confirmed the result of the referendum and declared Kosovo an independent republic. In unsanctioned elections the following spring, Rugova (the sole candidate) was elected president and the LDK, running against at least 18 other parties, won three-quarters of the vote.[34] On the basis of this democratic if unrecognised political structure, the parallel government's representatives in Albanian émigré communities began collecting 'taxes' to support it and its education and health care systems back in Kosovo.

The non-violent character of this movement was largely inspired by the example of Solidarity in Poland and the belief that the US would not allow a democratic, non-violent movement to fail. In 1988 and 1989 Rugova and Surroi, an influential newspaper publisher, collected 400,000 signatures for a petition calling for 'Democracy without Violence'. Determined to defy the Serbs' portrayal of them as primitive,

Albanian leaders also tried to end the age-old practice of blood feuds. This campaign reconciled some 2,000 families and allowed 20,000 people to emerge from their homes.[35]

In July 1990, a two thirds majority of Kosovo's provincial assembly met on the steps of its building, which its Serb president had locked them out of, and unanimously approved a declaration of self-determination. In September they approved a constitution for Kosovo that declared: 'The Republic of Kosova is a democratic state of the Albanian people and of members of other nations and national minorities who are its citizens: Serbs, Muslims, Montenegrins, Croats, Turks, Romanies and others living in Kosova.'[36] Hereafter, Albanians set up schools which employed 20,000 teachers, established clinics in private homes and spurned state facilities wherever possible.

Albanians and Serbs were inhabiting parallel worlds: Albanians controlled the private sector while Serbs controlled the public sector. During the evening promenade, members of the two nationalities strolled along opposite sides of the street. Unlike a few years earlier, their kids no longer played together. Police harassed actual or potential troublemakers with arrests, weapons searches and shakedowns, while people considered more serious threats, including former policemen and would-be military personnel, were targeted in political trials. Records show that the Serbs generally went after the actual culprits but showed such contempt for the rule of law in their trials that they became valuable grist to the Albanians' propaganda mill.

As time went on, Albanian activists became increasingly factionalised. Those who had been part of the Communist structures before the repeal of Kosovo's autonomy became estranged from those who had always opposed the system, many of whom had been political prisoners. The great majority who favoured peaceful change became divided from militants committed to violence. These splits between Albanian activists have had a huge influence up to the present, particularly because many activists don't distinguish between what they regard as errors and acts of treason. Without a judiciary to issue sentences, militants have tended to administer capital punishment themselves through political assassinations.

The origins of the Kosovo Liberation Army are opaque. Tim Judah writes that the name was chosen and a four-man exploratory committee set up at a meeting of 100 activists in Drenica (in central Kosovo, 90 minutes' drive southeast of Pristina) in 1993. These four included the former student leader Hashim Thaci, who would go on to found Kosovo's second biggest political party, the Democratic Party of Kosovo (PDK), and a leader of the émigré community in Switzerland, Xhavit Haliti. [37] Other accounts argue that the nucleus of the KLA was formed by émigrés working in Europe and Albania, and that the movement was hijacked and handed to Thaci's clique by the CIA and Sali Berisha, Albania's president at the time. Whatever their origins, the number of armed militants was initially tiny, and they enjoyed no mass support inside Kosovo. Only occasionally did they kill Serbian police officers and Albanians they believed to be traitors. Rugova denounced such violence as acts of provocation by Serbian secret police designed to discredit the LDK's policy of peaceful resistance.

Support for using violence to pursue independence began to grow after the Dayton Peace Conference in November 1995. Dayton was focused on ending the war in Bosnia that had taken 200,000 lives and on formalising the borders of Croatia, which had recently reconquered territories previously lost to Serbs. Richard Holbrooke, the American diplomat who presided over Dayton, denies that it was a missed opportunity for resolving the simmering crisis in Kosovo, insisting that the leaders gathered there had enough on their plates sorting out Bosnia and Croatia. But Albanian media in Kosovo, all of which were controlled by the LDK, had encouraged the belief that Kosovo was far higher on the Western diplomatic agenda than it actually was. Rugova had been telling people for years that if they just remained patient and peaceful, the West would keep the pressure on Belgrade until it was forced to

give Kosovo its independence without the violence that had racked Bosnia and Croatia. Instead, Dayton resulted in the lifting of the embargo
that had been in place against Yugoslavia. The country was still blocked
from badly needed financial support from the World Bank and the IMF,
but this continuing pressure was little understood by Albanian activists.
Albanians were especially shocked when the EU recognised the rump
Yugoslavia as comprising Montenegro and Serbia — including Kosovo.
Germany even repatriated 130,000 Albanians to Kosovo.[38]

The embryo of the Kosovo Liberation Army then issued a commu-
niqué threatening to execute any Albanian advocating autonomy rather
than outright independence. This killed off compromise solutions in
the air at the time, such as the notion of 'Three Republics' in which
Kosovo would form a loose federation of equals along with Serbia and
Montenegro. The EU hoped that making Kosovo independent in all but
name might avoid fanning nationalism in Serbia while satisfying Albanians' aspirations, but this misunderstood the Albanian position: by the
mid-1990s, the advantages of separation from Belgrade had become
fused with sloganising appeals for independence. Most Albanians had
come to believe it was impossible to gain one without the other.

The catalyst that finally transformed the KLA from a group of angry
young men into a paramilitary force was not planned by anyone. In
the spring of 1997, pyramid schemes into which most Albanians had
poured their meagre life savings collapsed. Albania quickly descended
into chaos. Armouries were thrown open and suddenly the country
was awash in weapons. Albanian militants, who had never before had a
ready source of guns, now began buying up Kalashnikovs at $5 a piece.
Within weeks, the first uniformed KLA members appeared in villages
in the Drenica valley.

From this point, momentum swung quickly away from the LDK
and towards violent confrontation. In September, student protesters rejected Rugova's calls to cease their demonstrations and instead
sought out contacts with the KLA. Serbian police assaulted peaceful

demonstrators and stepped up detentions of activists. Later that autumn, men dressed in KLA uniforms began appearing at the funerals of their supporters, events that drew crowds of thousands. In the first two months of 1998 alone there were 66 skirmishes, up from just 55 in all of 1997.[39]

In late February 1998, Yugoslav forces undertook major actions against KLA-supportive areas around Kosovo. On 5 March, a heavily armed police contingent surrounded the Jashari family compound in Prekaze. The police shelled the houses with artillery and sharpshooters shot those who fled. In all, the action left 58 dead, including Adem Jashari, the KLA's first martyr. Armed Albanian militias appeared seemingly overnight and the KLA suddenly emerged as a significant political force. Expatriate volunteers streamed into northern Albania and from there moved over the mountains into Kosovo. Hit and run attacks against police stations increased. However, the KLA actions were already marked by a lack of unity and coordination that would continue to poison political life after hostilities ended.

Belgrade responded by sending in Yugoslav army units to support police and paramilitary units in large-scale operations. International observers recorded a pattern of the Yugoslav forces using excessive force and committing extra-judicial executions and abductions. As its presence grew, the KLA was observed committing the same kinds of offences though on a smaller scale. Yugoslav forces bombed villages in the Prizren and Gjakove districts, and killed many KLA members with ambushes along the borders. In July, the KLA overran Orahovac and abducted 55 Serbs, later releasing 35. The Yugoslav forces continued to shell villages and towns, driving civilians from their homes. The UNHCR estimated that in August 1998 there were 260,000 displaced people within Kosovo and another 200,000 outside it.[40]

The international community viewed these events with growing concern. The Organisation for Security and Cooperation in Europe (OSCE) deployed monitors along Kosovo's borders. The US-led Kosovo Diplomatic Observer Mission, with the participation of Russia and some European states, deployed in Kosovo and created a link between the international community and the KLA. In September, the UN Security Council passed Resolution 1199 demanding a ceasefire and the withdrawal of Yugoslav forces 'used for civilian repression'.[41] Three days later, Yugoslav forces mortared a village, 'killing at least 18 women, children, and elderly persons'.[42]

On 13 October 1998, NATO voted to authorise air strikes if security forces were not withdrawn from Kosovo within 96 hours. After negotiating with US envoy Richard Holbrooke, Milosevic agreed to pull back security forces, allow in aid groups and also allow the deployment of 2,000 monitors with a new OSCE Kosovo Verification Mission (KVM). The agreement also included provisions for the development of limited autonomy, elections within nine months and recruitment of an Albanian police force. While Milosevic at first honoured the letter of this agreement, state authorities found other ways to harass their enemies. By the end of the year, an estimated 1,500 Albanians had been arrested and charged with terrorist acts. For its part, the KLA had abducted an estimated 150 persons.[43]

At the same time, the KLA took advantage of the Yugoslav withdrawal to strengthen its own positions on the ground. 'According to the UN Secretary-General's 24 December report, "Kosovo Albanian paramilitaries have taken advantage of the lull in the fighting to re-establish their control over many villages in Kosovo as well as over some areas near urban centres and highways. These actions ... have only served to provoke the Serbian authorities, leading to statements that if the Kosovo Verification Mission cannot control these units, the Government would".'[44]

In January 1999, the Yugoslav Army deployed into Kosovo in large numbers. They took up permanent positions along the Macedonian border in anticipation of a NATO ground attack and also helped police to disrupt the KLA's supply routes. On 15 January, Yugoslav forces attacked the village of Racak and killed 45 Albanian civilians. The KVM investigated the massacre the very next day, reporting 'evidence of arbitrary detentions, extra-judicial killings, and mutilation of unarmed civilians'.[45] The head of the KVM mission, Ambassador William Walker, visited the site, publicly condemned the massacre and demanded the names of the officers responsible. Belgrade shortly thereafter declared Walker *persona non grata*.

Galvanised by the Racak massacre, on 29 January the Contact Group (ad hoc group comprised of France, Germany, Italy, Russia, the UK and the US) summoned the Yugoslav government and the Kosovo Albanians to Rambouillet, outside Paris. There the Contact Group presented both sides with an ultimatum: either accept a proposed settlement within 21 days or face the use of force. Challenged by political opposition at home, Milosevic dispatched a delegation but forbade it to accept infringement of Yugoslav sovereignty or the presence of armed troops in Yugoslav territory. The Kosovo Albanian delegation, by contrast, deployed a raft of arguments as to why the Kosovo Albanians constituted a territorially defined people with a right to self-determination. Rugova and Surroi, with backing from US Secretary of State Madeleine Albright, persuaded the KLA members to accept a three-year cooling off period before holding a referendum on independence. Key to their acceptance was the stipulation that Kosovo's final status would take into account 'the will of the people'. After holding consultations back in Kosovo, the Albanian delegation signed the accord on 15 March in Paris. Chief negotiator Christopher Hill travelled to Belgrade to try to persuade Milosevic to sign but the Serbian demagogue refused even to meet the American diplomat. Holbrooke tried to drive home the threat of air strikes one final time on 22 March. 'You know what will happen if I leave,' Holbrooke is reported to have said to the intransigent Milosevic. 'You will bomb us,' he replied. Soon after, Operation Allied Force began. For the first time in its history, NATO was at war.

UN peace operations

'Kumanovo for Kosovo', a piece of jingoism from the first Balkan War, referred to the key battle in which the First Serbian Army routed the Ottomans in northeastern Macedonia and opened the way for the conquest of Kosovo. With improbable symmetry, it was in Kumanovo in 1999 that NATO and the Yugoslav National Army signed the Military Technical Agreement ending hostilities and providing for the withdrawal of Serbian forces from Kosovo and the deployment of the multinational Kosovo Force. The next day the UN Security Council adopted Resolution 1244 mandating a civilian mission to administer Kosovo day to day while building democratic institutions and preparing the ground for eventual resolution of Kosovo's status.

But while the military had spent many years and billions of dollars preparing its planes, bombs and aerial maps, the civilian structures that would administer Kosovo had to be cobbled together in about a week. Though cross-border intervention is much older than most people realise — military operations to maintain peace have occured at least since the Delian League in ancient Greece — the UN had never before created a new political entity from the ground up.

Though military operations to maintain peace have occurred at least since the Delian League in ancient Greece, modern peacemaking began with the creation of the League of Nations after the First World War. In the 1920s the League successfully mediated territorial disputes between Germany and Poland, between Greece and Bulgaria and between France and Germany. Better known to posterity are the League's abysmal failures: to prevent Japanese aggression against China in Manchuria in 1931 and Italy's shamelessly imperialist invasion of Ethiopia, and its unenforced policy of non-interference in the Spanish Civil War. Outspoken Soviet delegate Maxim Litvinov compared the League 'to a community that formed a fire brigade "in the innocent hope that, by some lucky chance, there would be no fires." Now, however, fires had broken out, and the community wanted to disband the brigade — not forever, but just until the danger of fire had disappeared.'[46]

The creation of the United Nations was, like a second marriage, a triumph of hope over experience. As the Second World War had wrought even greater destruction than the First, so the architects of the new world body were determined to correct the weaknesses of the League of Nations. Chapter VI of the UN Charter called for the peaceful resolution of disputes; Chapter VII empowered the Security Council to call on member states to use armed force to preserve international peace. Secretary-General Dag Hammarskjöld joked that peacekeeping, which was not specifically envisaged anywhere in the charter, was 'chapter six and a half'.

The UN was employed early on to oversee the truce that followed the Arab-Israeli war in 1948. Peacekeeping missions became bigger and more ambitious during the fifties and sixties, but were always constrained by the polarisation of the Cold War. The Security Council mandate for a force to defend South Korea was a fluke resulting from the Soviet ambassador's boycott of the session where it was voted on. After the US, the Soviet Union and the Arab world declared their opposition to the British-French-Israeli invasion of Egypt to seize control of the Suez Canal, the UN deployed 6,000 troops to maintain a buffer between the armies. The UN dispatched an ambitious mission to administer the Congo after it descended into chaos following independence. This was followed by the still ongoing mission to observe the truce between Greeks and Turks in Cyprus. The last peacekeeping force to be created for a decade was the UN Interim Force in Lebanon, created to observe the Israeli withdrawal and help the government to reestablish control. 'Of the thirteen peacekeeping operations set up before Cold War tension began to fade, all but one were of the traditional Cyprus type, in which the Blue Helmets monitored a truce between warring sides while mediators sought a political solution to the underlying conflict,' according to Paul Lewis.[47]

The thaw of the Cold War created new possibilities and new demands. Until then, all the UN officials involved in setting up peace operations could share a taxi to New York's Kennedy Airport. The UN's Department of Peacekeeping Operations (DPKO) was set up only in February 1992. The great majority of conflicts since then, an average of about 28 per year, have been internal not international.[48] In response to this epidemic of civil wars and failed states, the world has become increasingly involved in complex and large-scale peace operations. The UN was credited with a number of successes in what became known as 'second-generation' operations in El Salvador, Nicaragua, Namibia, Mozambique, Eastern Slavonia and Cambodia — places where there was a reasonable degree of peace to keep.

The UN was notably less successful in places where local parties still had the will and wherewithal to continue fighting — Rwanda, Somalia and Bosnia, for example. In such difficult environments the UN was generally denied the personnel, equipment or mandate it needed to fight back. Secretary-General Boutros-Ghali pointed out that of the 19 countries that had pledged troops to potential peacekeeping missions when the Rwandan genocide erupted, not one of them would allow their soldiers to be sent to Rwanda. Boutros-Ghali resurrected the idea of a UN rapid reaction force; the powers all ignored the idea, while reserving the right to lambast the body for doing too little too late.

The hypocritical use of the UN as a scapegoat for great power dithering has itself created a new handicap for the world body. In Kosovo, the UN's mission was burdened by impossible expectations. Believing that the UN could do anything it wanted, many in Kosovo concluded that any shortcomings by the UN administration must have been deliberate. In reality, the officials who comprised UNMIK were pioneers making it up as they went along. It was their misfortune to plunge into a maelstrom of local animosities which had been stirred, not quelled, by many centuries of foreign intervention.

PART I

THE FOUR PHASES OF INTERNATIONAL ADMINISTRATION IN KOSOVO

EMERGENCY
JUNE 1999–OCTOBER 2000

On 10 June 1999 Kosovo became a ward of the international community. On that day the UN Security Council passed Resolution (UN-
SCR) 1244 establishing the UN Interim Administration in Kosovo,
or UNMIK. It mandated the mission to carry out all aspects of civil
administration, establish democratic institutions required for substantial self-government and create the basis for eventually resolving
Kosovo's disputed political status. In other words, UNMIK was to run
Kosovo and prepare it for what came next — whatever that might be.
What the UN Security Council resolution did not do was to address
the question at the heart of the war between Serbs and Albanians:
Who would be master in Kosovo?

The day before, NATO had signed the Military Technical Agreement
— a legal document that allowed the most powerful military coalition the world had ever seen to deploy unhindered within Kosovo. The
governments of both the Republic of Serbia and the Federal Republic
of Yugoslavia (which by then consisted only of Serbia — including
its formerly autonomous provinces of Vojvodina and Kosovo — and
Montenegro) had agreed to a staged withdrawal of all their forces from
Kosovo within eleven days.

Kosovo thus briefly turned into one of those post-war free-for-alls
with no legally constituted authority on the ground. The Yugoslav Army
and federal police (MUP) withdrew within a few days, snaking north in
long convoys. Thousands of Kosovo Serb civilians streamed after them

in cars, trucks and tractors loaded down with as many personal goods as they could carry. Some Serbs tried to stay, but many of those were intimidated into changing their minds when Serb corpses began appearing around Pristina, some of them headless. On 18 June the International Committee of the Red Cross reported that between 50,000 and 60,000 Kosovo Serb civilians had left Kosovo in the previous two weeks.

At the same time tens of thousands of Kosovo Albanians expelled during the war by state security forces were pouring back into Kosovo. Many lodged themselves in major towns because their homes in scattered villages had been destroyed or because they thought there might be more work in the cities. The streets were full of dogs (which are generally popular among Serbs but despised by most Albanians) that had been abandoned by their fleeing Serb owners. As there was no running water in Pristina, the Grand Hotel, which became the hub for foreigners including the 2,500-strong international press corps, stank of overflowing toilets.

Crowds of Albanians celebrated their return by driving along pot-holed streets devoid of traffic lights. They honked their car horns triumphantly, waved Albanian flags and greeted the incoming foreign troops. Meanwhile groups of armed Albanians all over Kosovo took advantage of the security vacuum to perpetrate a campaign of vengeance, score-settling, and plain apolitical crime. Hundreds of homes belonging to Serbs and other minorities were burned and looted. In the second half of June, Kosovo Albanians forcibly expelled an estimated 5,000 Roma from a neighbourhood in the southern part of the soon-to-be-divided city of Mitrovica. Dozens of people disappeared or were killed outright, most reportedly abducted by men claiming to belong to the KLA. The dead and disappeared included not only members of minority communities but also rival factions within the Kosovo Albanian community. Men claiming to represent the KLA took possession of various public buildings, houses and apartments (a practice that continued through to 2005). The same men also established administrative and security organisations, and asserted their authority as a *de facto* government.

This assertion of authority by anyone who had the audacity and weapons to try it was made possible by the fact that until the end of the summer the legal civil authority in Kosovo, UNMIK, consisted of just a couple of hundred civilians, nearly all of them concentrated in Pristina, where they devoted most of their time to setting up their operation and writing reports back to their respective headquarters in New York, Geneva and Vienna. This summer of no-holds-barred Hobbesian politics left a lasting legacy of contempt for legally constituted authority that UNMIK would struggle in vain to overcome in the succeeding years.

The emergency phase of the international administration began with several enormous challenges, but the most obviously urgent was the need to provide shelter and basic services to 900,000 people, most of them Kosovo Albanians, who had been internally displaced or become refugees before and during the NATO air campaign. The first Special Representative of the UN Secretary-General, Sergio Vieira de Mello (who was later killed by the bomb attack against UN HQ in Baghdad in August 2003), arrived with only a few days' notice with a skeleton crew of eight. For the first six months of UNMIK's putative authority over Kosovo, a self-appointed administration controlled by leaders of the KLA actually governed Albanian-inhabited areas. Serbs took their cues from Belgrade-controlled Serb-majority areas.

The first person to serve a full term as Special Representative of the Secretary-General, Bernard Kouchner, was a humanitarian icon. As a co-founder of the Nobel Peace Prize winning medical charity Medécins sans Frontières, Kouchner had spent years shaming governments and charities for failing to intervene in humanitarian crises. In Kosovo, he worked from early morning until late into the night, personifying the idealistic fervour of the mission in its early days. His pronouncements were always infused with the language of rights, ethics and justice; *Realpolitik* and logistics seemed less important. Kouchner was better at starting things than finishing them. Many of his initiatives, which he had conjured almost out of nothing, soon evaporated, as the commitments of local leaders and international bureaucrats proved hollow. But despite the lack of follow-through, under Kouchner UNMIK met the immediate humanitarian challenge, and the mission's focus shifted to political and economic development. Kouchner presided over the first political milestone with the reasonably successful conduct of municipal elections in October 2000.

Also in October 2000, Slobodan Milosevic was removed from power in Belgrade, and rump Yugoslavia, which retained formal sovereignty over Kosovo, overcame its pariah status. This made the relationship between UNMIK and Belgrade more potentially constructive and for that very reason more complex. To the international community, Kosovo became a different sort of problem from October 2000 onwards.

The first sixteen months of the mission, then, from June 1999 until October 2000, were a unique phase in Kosovo's development. It was an unscripted, chaotic time in which much was achieved, mistakes were made, and paths irreversibly chosen. It was post-war Kosovo's 'Emergency Phase'.

Security and the rule of law

The summer of 1999 was a season of vengeance and raw predatory violence. The OSCE collected dozens of horror stories. A deaf and mute Roma man was abducted from his home because his family had allegedly cooperated with the former authorities. A 44-year-old Serb man was 'beaten to death with metal sticks by a Kosovo Albanian mob and his throat was reportedly slit with a piece of glass'.[1] The burned body of a Roma leader was found inside his gutted house in the Roma neighbourhood just south of the Ibar river in Mitrovica from which his community had been forcibly expelled. Serbs were shot and killed while working in their fields. These attacks and dozens more like them were reported by field staff working with the OSCE. All these attacks occurred when NATO-led KFOR was responsible for security in Kosovo.

No one knows exactly how many people were murdered in Kosovo that summer. At a press conference in New York on 28 September, Zivadin Jovanovic, the FRY (Federal Republic of Yugoslavia) Minister of Foreign Affairs, put the number as high as 400. On 13 October a KFOR spokesman stated that the total number of killings in Kosovo since 12 June was 348.[2] KFOR claimed that when it had arrived in June 1999 the weekly murder rate was 50; by November 2000 this figure had decreased to four.[3] Overall estimates for the number of Serbs killed in the first year of international administration range from 600 to 800.[4] Kouchner felt powerless to stop the violence: 'I've been a human rights activist for 30 years and here I am unable to stop people being massacred.'[5]

While violence against ethnic minorities was the biggest security problem, criminal activity during the emergency phase ran the gamut from arson, seizure of property and smuggling to politically motivated kidnapping, torture and murder. Non-ethnic crime was fuelled by a number of complementary factors: the huge quantity of weapons available, the surprising resilience of the Kosovo Liberation Army in its various guises, the popular mistrust of legal authorities, and the sparseness of the international presence, especially at the local level. Antipathies between different Albanian groups, based on regional and political rivalries and past political alignments, also played a part, as did suspicions of collaboration with the Serbian authorities.

The anarchy that consumed Kosovo that summer was partly spontaneous, partly coordinated. The spontaneous part seems to have occurred in the earliest days of the mission, mostly in June 1999, when Albanian refugees returned to their homes, jubilant and furious. Thereafter, tell-tale patterns emerged in the violence, 'suggestive of a period of planning or of terror cells operating in certain areas'.[6] Victims tended to be clustered by their demographic characteristics — at one time, victims were almost entirely elderly, then middle-aged, then the victims of grenade attacks were almost entirely women. The patterns were so obvious that, according to one OSCE insider,[7] the official record of the attacks deliberately presented them in a random order so as to obscure their clear pattern. The radical Kosovo Albanian newspaper *Rilindija* may have inspired many of the killings. Several times, after the paper reported that 'Serb paramilitaries' were operating in a particular area, murders would occur in that locale. In 2000 an Orthodox priest was killed when his car was riddled by machine-gun fire after the paper 'outed' him by alleging that he had committed atrocities against Albanians.

Why didn't the international community stop these murders? KFOR arrived slowly, and the rest of the international community followed even further behind. More than six weeks after the end of the war, the obvious lack of troops needed to prevent inter-ethnic violence in Kosovo was a critical problem. KFOR stated that by late July there were 'already some 36,500 troops in Kosovo, and some 6,000 more in theatre'.[8] But these numbers were clearly insufficient to deal with the crisis at hand. Why this delay? There were many factors: insufficient logistical planning, concern for force protection, and a failure to anticipate the full extent of the violence that followed immediately after the war. But the most compelling explanation is that NATO misunderstood the environment and the nature of the threats it harboured.

Ironically, given that NATO had purportedly intervened to protect Kosovo Albanians from the Serbian government's abuses, neither KFOR nor UNMIK was configured to protect minorities. 'When we were deployed in theatre,' recounted one Dutch military adviser,[9] 'our main objective was to prevent the VJ [Yugoslav army] from reneging on the agreement. So, we guarded the ABL [the Administrative Boundary Line, which divides Kosovo from Serbia-proper] and watched out for the VJ returning — don't forget they had already broken their agreements before. Our mission was to create a safe and secure environment, not really to protect the Serbs, and our rules of engagement would have made that difficult anyway.'

This fundamental political misapprehension was augmented by that constant of military operations, the last-minute change of plan. A Swedish battalion was about to set up camp in Prizren in the south when it was ordered to proceed instead to Gracanica, one of the most important Serb enclaves and religious sites, just outside Pristina.[10] The British and French sectors were swapped, assigning the French to the crucial northern sector, centred on the flashpoint city of Mitrovica. In the months and years to come the very different approach to peace-keeping adopted by the French in this area came to be the subject of much controversy and criticism.

NATO's slow and messy deployment was a model of efficiency compared to its civilian counterparts. Three months after the conflict, UNMIK still did not have a presence in all of the then 29 municipalities in Kosovo. A year after the conflict, there were still fewer than 300 international UN staff to manage a province of two million people. Many of these were distracted by the numerous high-profile and VIP visitors, media relations, and other roles essential to maintaining political and institutional support but irrelevant to conditions on the ground. Only a minority were interacting directly with local people, or actively governing Kosovo. 'They were crazy times,' said one. 'We were very, very busy all the time, but it was mostly doing things with other internationals.'[11]

In the months when they were most needed, the international police (CivPol) were not there. CivPol's slow arrival became a running scandal during the emergency phase of the mission. None arrived for two months, the rest followed in small numbers, and it took a full year to deploy three-quarters of the anticipated strength (3,626 out of 4,718 had been deployed by mid-June 2000).[12] Local newspapers published weekly figures of international police on the ground compared to the number promised. The number of police became the yardstick for measuring the gap between the international community's promises and its actions.

Many police were ill-prepared for working in Kosovo. The requirements for employment with CivPol were a driver's licence, a very basic standard of marksmanship and an equally basic knowledge of English. The first CivPol officers took up their duties without any orientation whatsoever about the conflict that had occurred or the nature of the society. The policing that resulted could be sadly absurd. In February 2000, for example, a pair of American policemen were assigned to patrol the historic city of Prizren. Their approach was to drive their Toyoto-4Runner around the narrow streets, yelling out of the window — in English — at people to move out of the way. They had no idea what the local people had been through and were convinced that, despite their appearance of poverty, the Kosovans had grown secretly rich from American largesse.[13]

Without any effective local police force, the responsibility for normal policing fell to KFOR — a duty for which the soldiers were not trained or equipped. KFOR's approach to crime prevention consisted of fixed checkpoints and patrolling streets and roads. Their orders were to intervene if they happened to witness a serious crime occurring.[14] The international authorities' thinness on the ground (both KFOR and UNMIK) for the first several months permitted mass reprisals against Kosovo Serbs and the rise of thugocracy. Both left poisonous legacies that proved virtually impossible to cure.

The absence of credible security forces allowed those with guns and the willingness to use them — mostly former members of the KLA — to assert control in many spheres. Some became officials in Thaci's self-declared 'provisional government'; others joined the new Kosovo Police Force. KLA members were soon to make up the majority of the Kosovo Protection Corps. Many also engaged in various forms of crime. Though agreements with KFOR and UNMIK had already abolished all branches of the KLA several times, in March 2000 the KLA military police, the black-shirted PU (Policia Ushtarake), continued to operate. Among the activities they allegedly committed were the coercive extraction of 'contributions' from businesses and individuals, the burning of minority houses, and the expropriation of flats and businesses. In November 1999, five people were found killed in a five-kilometre radius around a KLA compound north of Pristina. Of the four who could be identified, three were Roma who had been 'executed' by gunshots and one was an Albanian woman who had been stabbed to death. All four had been accused of having collaborated with Serbian authorities, and were abducted from their homes or in the street by men claiming affiliation with the KLA.[15] During much of the emergency period, such crimes were committed with virtual impunity. Three hundred Serb houses were burned in Prizren; only two suspects were arrested. Several prominent members of Ibrahim Rugova's LDK, the KLA's only serious political rival, were abducted and killed.

KFOR's mandate required it to disband the KLA. On 21 June 1999, Hashim Thaci, commander of the KLA, signed an 'Undertaking of Demilitarisation and Transformation' according to which the KLA would cease to exist as a military organisation from 20 September, a deadline that was met. Despite being demobilised, throughout the summer and autumn of 1999 members of the KLA were flushed with a (questionable) belief in their central role in liberating Kosovo and consequent sense of entitlement to a privileged position. They were also armed and clearly prepared to use force to advance their interests. Unlike the Coalition Provisional Authority in Iraq, UNMIK and KFOR recognised that merely turning the fighters loose would be inviting trouble.

The challenge was to absorb the fighters and keep them in disciplined structures without creating a rival force to KFOR. UNMIK's major policy innovation for dealing with this dilemma was to create the 5,000-strong Kosovo Protection Corps or KPC, a civilian organisation that was to act as a 'civil emergency force'. An initial agreement signed by KFOR commander General Sir Michael Jackson described it as being something 'like the US National Guard'. The US was the KPC's most important foreign patron, providing $13 million in its first two years, over a third of its total budget.

From the beginning there was tension between, on the one hand, UNMIK and most of KFOR, who (officially at least) considered the KPC to be purely civilian, and, on the other hand, the KPC members themselves who did everything possible to preserve intact the military style and organisation of the KLA. Former KLA commanders who joined the KPC insisted on the organisation adopting a name in Albanian that is intentionally ambiguous about whether it was involved in 'protection' or 'defence'. General Jackson, then KFOR commander, was well aware of this ambiguity but accepted it in the interests of securing an agreement.[16] The KPC's commander, Agim Ceku, was a career officer in the Yugoslav Army and fought with Croat forces against Serbs in the early 1990s. Though widely respected by KFOR officers as an honest professional, Ceku made little secret of his vision of the KPC as the nucleus of a future army for an independent Kosovo. The commanders of each of the KPC's six 'regional task groups' (RTGs) were the very men who had commanded the KLA in the same zones. The red and black shoulder patch that KPC members wear on the shoulder of their green uniform is virtually indistinguishable from the now-outlawed KLA emblem. Each member of the KPC has a military rank. KFOR assigned a liaison officer to each RTG and a senior officer to the KPC's headquarters in Pristina. [17] One of these liaison officers is tellingly quoted saying, 'I am employed by [KFOR commander General] Reinhardt, but Ceku is my boss!'[18] In the summer of 1999, a huge arms cache — enough to equip two brigades — was found in what had been Ceku's sector as a KLA commander.[19]

Having created this entity, the question then arose as to what it should do. SRSG Kouchner initially said of their role: 'The Corps will provide disaster response services, including for major fires, and industrial accidents or spills; perform search and rescue; provide a capacity for humanitarian assistance in isolated areas; assist in demining; and contribute to rebuilding infrastructure and communities.' In reality, most of the tasks found for them tended to be more mundane, from fixing plumbing to clearing roads. They refused many of these tasks, on the grounds that they were not suitable for a victorious army. In the end, 'most of them just ended up drinking coffee all day.'[20] Subsequent reform of the KPC then became very difficult, even though the members were paid generous stipends.

Early on, KFOR and UNMIK found indications that membership in the KPC did not necessarily mean an ex-KLA fighter had been domesticated. According to classified NATO reports, informers claimed that KPC members not only attacked Serbs, but were involved in illegal trade in prostitutes, cigarettes, fuel, weapons and appliances. 'Many KPC members, in some cases high-ranking KPC officials, have ties with criminal organisations,' said one such report prepared in 2000.[21] KPC commanders profited personally from the seizure of vacant apartments and commercial properties, which they often doled out to cohorts as sources of income.[22] In February 2000, members of the KPC in Mitrovica fired weapons at French KFOR soldiers in protest at their failure to protect Albanians in the north. 'The KPC was composed almost entirely of former KLA fighters and when the UNMIK police arrested those KPC members firing and brandishing weapons, including AK-47s, the Kosovan Albanian judge released them the next day.'[23]

Christer Karphammar, a Swedish jurist who was Kosovo's first international judge, said he directly knew of several cases in which UN and KFOR senior officials opposed or blocked the prosecution of former KLA members, including some now in the KPC. 'That means some of the former [KLA] had an immunity. The investigations were stopped on a high level,' he said. Karphammar, who left the UN in May 2001, said that throughout his 18-month tenure there, the judiciary was not allowed to work independently. The reason, he said, was that NATO and

UN officials feared they 'would put their lives at risk' by acting against former members of the rebel group.[24]

According to police reports, a former KLA commander used the butt of his pistol to club an ethnic Albanian doctor sitting near him at a soccer game because the doctor criticised the performance of a player who happened to be his nephew. The beating fractured the doctor's skull. UNMIK police handed the case to the Minor Offences Court, which gave it to the Municipal Public Prosecutor before it was taken by International Prosecutor Michael Hartmann. An international was prepared to testify against the former KLA commander but UNMIK blocked his arrest, believing that if he were arrested, it could destabilise Kosovo on the eve of municipal elections and bolster hard-liners in Serbian parliamentary elections in December.[25] The need for stability ahead of impending elections in Kosovo or in Serbia became a stock excuse to avoid the prosecution of influential figures.[26]

Another example of politically driven interference occurred in February 2000 when international officials forced the release of more than a dozen former members of the rebel army, including a man who was wanted by Interpol. The ethnic Albanians had been detained by French forces for organising a riot in Mitrovica. But French intelligence officers refused to give information they collected in interviews to the regional court. According to Karphammar, who would have heard the case, all the suspects were released 'before the real court investigation started, because of a threat by rebel leaders that if they were not released, KFOR soldiers would come under threat.'[27]

Many cases were blocked by senior officials in KFOR and UNMIK. In the name of 'stability', the mission betrayed many of the brightest, most idealistic people in Kosovo in favour of the most thuggish. This handful of unpunished crimes had a far-reaching ripple effect: critics of the most powerful figures understood that if they confronted the hard men, the international administration would do nothing to support them. Karphammar believes this policy fatally crippled the mission from its first months.[28]

The failure to challenge veterans of the KLA effectively was mirrored by a simultaneous failure to enforce the rule of law in areas that did not welcome the KFOR intervention, principally northern Kosovo. Most Serbs had been instinctively hostile to KFOR and UNMIK. In northern Kosovo, where they were in a local majority and had the critical mass needed to be self-sufficient, they actively opposed the new order. The managers of local water and telephone utilities refused to talk to UN-MIK officials. Local Serb employees of UNMIK were intimidated. Even construction materials and equipment donated by charities, such as those offered to refurbish the heating system of Mitrovica's run-down hospital, were turned down or vandalised.

With the Yugoslav police and army gone, Serb paramilitaries tried to maintain control in areas with Serb majorities. From late 1999 the group that called itself 'the bridge watchers' — young men with walk-ie-talkies who based themselves in the seedy Dolce Vita cafe in north Mitrovica — kept a continuous watch on the main bridge to discour-age Albanians from crossing over. They were also known to harangue foreign journalists and to whip up crowds to intimidate international police into releasing suspects they had detained. Kosovo Albanians liv-ing north of the Ibar river were harassed and driven out. On 2 February 2000, a UNHCR bus transporting Serbs in Mitrovica was struck by an anti-tank rocket, killing two and gravely injuring five. The next day a grenade was tossed into an occupied Serb cafe in Mitrovica. These events sparked rioting among Serbs in the half of the city north of the Ibar river where they were in the majority, killing at least five Albanians and Turks. The Serb mob also burned UNMIK and UNHCR vehicles. Albanians retaliated by attacking Serb houses in northern Mitrovica. Bouts of lawlessness ensued in the city for several days.

KFOR's reaction to this was mixed. The French sustained 69 inju-ries while trying to stop the February killing spree. The French brigade commander, Brigadier General Pierre de Saquii de Sannes, admitted that he was lucky no troops were killed and made it his priority to ensure that remained the case — to the inevitable detriment of efforts to enforce the rule of law in the area. Danish troops assigned to work alongside the French complained bitterly, and some police patrols felt 'absolutely abandoned' as a result of the French emphasis on 'force protection'.[29] The soft French approach was denounced as 'cowardice' and 'appeasement' by some officials in Pristina. On one occasion in June 2000, an elderly American policeman was surrounded and attacked by a Serb mob less than ten metres from a French checkpoint. Even though the policeman was bleeding from head injuries, the French soldiers did nothing. Terrified, the policeman managed to escape by clambering down the river bank.[30] Establishing international authority in northern Kosovo remained an elusive goal ever after.

While KFOR and CivPol battled, with more or less effectiveness, to establish a modicum of public security, a handful of civilian officials laboured to create a functioning legal system from the ground up. It was a massive challenge. Many courtrooms had been mined or booby-trapped by the Serb forces as they left, records were missing or destroyed, and court offices ransacked.[31] UNMIK tried to establish a special 'Kosovo War Crimes and Ethnic Crimes Court', but it was blocked by UN budget officials in New York who said it would be too expensive.[32] Even UNMIK's efforts to establish a basic, reliable, impartial judiciary in Kosovo ran up against severe difficulties.

Kouchner had to decide which laws to apply in Kosovo. In his first legislative act he asserted that 'applicable law' would be the Yugoslav laws in place before NATO commenced the air war on 24 March, excluding wartime emergency powers. Though none of these laws had been discriminatory in themselves, the Yugoslav authorities had applied them in a discriminatory fashion throughout the 1990s when there were few Albanians in the judiciary. After the arrival of UNMIK, many Albanians expressed intense hostility to the laws that had operated under Milosevic, and many Albanian jurists refused to apply this body of law, deciding cases instead on the basis of the laws — which in any case were often identical or very similar — that had been in force when Kosovo was stripped of its autonomy in March 1989. In practice, judges, virtually all Albanian, applied a double standard, using whichever laws best served the interests of their community.

In the face of continuing public pressure, five months after adopting the laws in place during the 1990s, UNMIK reversed itself and made the March 1989 law applicable in Kosovo. This restored the federal Law on Criminal Procedure which provided for investigative judges before indictments were filed and jury panels for trials, usually made up of two professionals and three laypeople.

Though UNMIK's charter, UNSCR 1244, specified the use of international police, it was silent on the question of who should replace the judges and prosecutors who fled with other Serb state officials. Foreign jurists had served before in special war crimes tribunals such as those in Nuremberg and Tokyo, as well as the tribunals in The Hague and Arusha, and foreign lawyers and judges had monitored legal systems in intrusive international administrations such as that in Bosnia. But foreign judges and prosecutors had never served alongside local colleagues in a post-conflict environment. Since institution-building was at the heart of 1244, there was no question of foreign jurists staffing all of the courts *instead* of locals. The OSCE, which had expected to have responsibility for the courts, had planned to have foreigners working alongside Kosovans. But less than two weeks before the cessation of hostilities, the UN was given the lead in Kosovo. 'Instead,' said the International Crisis Group, 'the early UNMIK administration rejected that OSCE proposal, fearing that gaining additional power through the appointment of international jurists who were UN staff would leave it open to charges of neo-imperialism, especially since the United Nations already held executive and legislative power through the SRSG.'[33] The SRSG duly appointed 55 Kosovo judges and prosecutors to the Emer-

gency Judicial System. Most were retained by regular courts when the
emergency system was replaced in October 1999.

The problem was that the handful of Albanian or Serb jurists who
remained in Kosovo and had worked in the court system during the
1990s were viewed by virtually all Kosovo Albanians as collaborators
in an oppressive system. Most of the Kosovo Albanian judges and prosecutors appointed by UNMIK, therefore, had never before worked on
the bench or in a prosecutor's office; the minority who had judicial
or prosecutorial experience had been pushed out of their positions in
1989, and had no experience working in a legal system free of the heavy
hand of Communist 'telephone justice'. Moreover, since all Serb judges
and prosecutors had either fled or honoured their community's policy
of not working with the UN administration, the jurists were nearly all
Kosovo Albanian.

The hundreds of inter-ethnic attacks against Serbs and Roma required
judicial investigations to take testimony. The lack of judicial personnel
resulted in few indictments, while many suspects — for all crimes, not
just interethnic ones — were held for months in pre-trial detention.
Applicable law only allowed six months' pre-trial detention, and in
December 1999 this resulted in a crisis, as many war crimes cases were
not ready to be tried. The SRSG overcame this problem by extending
the limit to one year. But Kouchner failed to sanction this change in a
new regulation, which given his dual role as legislature and executive
would have given it the force of law. Nor did he announce that he was
derogating from the European Convention on Human Rights. Consequently, executive detention was extra-legal, reinforcing the prevailing
local view that raw power trumps the rule of law.

At the same time, KFOR and UNMIK officials noted a huge dispar-
ity between Kosovo Albanian judges' and prosecutors' handling of cases
concerning Albanians and those concerning Serbs. When former KLA
members were arrested by KFOR or CivPol for attacks on Serbs, the
Albanian prosecutor would propose the suspect's immediate release

and the Albanian judge would approve it. Serbs facing the same charges, on the other hand, would languish in prison for months. KFOR responded to the premature release of Albanian suspects with an extra-legal detention practice known as a 'COMKFOR hold', the authority for which derived not from applicable law or UNMIK's regulations but from KFOR's mandate to provide a safe and secure environment. OSCE and human rights officials protested against this as a violation of judicial independence. A British colonel defended the practice as necessary in the biased environment that then prevailed, citing the release by a Kosovo Albanian judge of an Albanian suspect despite eyewitness accounts by KFOR soldiers that he had thrown a hand grenade into an occupied Serb store, injuring three.[34]

Michael Hartmann, a senior prosecutor with UNMIK, cited three explanations for Albanian jurists' biased behaviour: 'personal prejudice, community pressure and fear of ostracism, and threats or fear of harm against self or family'.[35] Many of those working in the court system would have experienced various forms of abuse under the Milosevic regime, culminating in crimes against humanity. Even if they managed to suppress whatever bias might naturally result from such trauma, many Albanian jurists feared negative social and professional consequences if, in the words of extremists, they 'went easy' on Serbs or seriously prosecuted former KLA fighters described as 'war heroes'. More direct intimidation took the form of phone calls from powerful figures or actual threats of bodily harm to the judge or his family. As Hartmann put it, 'One could not reasonably expect the Kosovan jurists to overcome these life experiences immediately, and become independent and impartial jurists, even if they sincerely desired to be such.'[36]

One of Kouchner's responses to the Mitrovica violence of February 2000 was to appoint one international judge and one prosecutor to the city's district court, one of five such courses in Kosovo. Initially no international prosecutors or judges were assigned to Pristina, where 35 per cent of crimes were committed, to the other district counts in

Prizren, Gjilan or Peje or to the Supreme Court. The pioneer 'IJPs' (international judges and prosecutors) in Mitrovica, initially on renewable six-month contracts, had the same powers and functions as their Kosovan counterparts except that they were limited to criminal cases and had the authority to 'select and take responsibility for new and pending criminal investigations and cases'. [37]

In May, Serb prisoners launched a hunger strike to protest against having been held in pre-trial detention for ten months 'and counting'. [38] Most had not even been indicted. The hunger strikers and their supporters in Kosovo and Serbia demanded that they be tried immediately and that the international prosecutor and judge be assigned to each of their cases. The SRSG recognised the sense of this demand, and enacted a regulation [39] which extended the IJP programme to the remaining four judicial districts and added international judges to the Supreme Court.

On 28 May 2000, a terrorist fired on a group of Serbs socialising outside a grocery store in Cernica in the Gjilan district, killing three people, including a four-year-old boy. One of two wounded survivors identified the gunman as Afrim Zeqiri, a former KLA fighter whom KFOR had already arrested three times, twice for threatening Serbs. After each of these previous arrests, a Kosovo Albanian judge had released him after the Albanian prosecutor abandoned the charges. This time, the SRSG assigned an international judge to Gjilan, a Finnish riparian (pertaining to rivers) rights expert, and he exercised his right to select the case. Despite this, the case was derailed when the Albanian prosecutor and the international judge both failed to question the witnesses that Zeqiri's lawyer proposed in order to provide him an alibi. The judge managed to lose key evidence, including the cartridge casings from the murder scene and the photos of the now buried bodies. The prosecutor dismissed the case as not grounded in fact. This was despite eyewitness testimony by one of the wounded Serbs who had seen Zeqiri shooting and two other witnesses who said they had seen Zeqiri in Cernica just before the attack, thus contradicting his claim to have been in Gjilan at the time.[40] Under the applicable law, the international judge had no option but to confirm the prosecutor's abandonment of the case. The SRSG countered this move by assigning the Mitrovica international prosecutor to the case in Gjilan. Kouchner also asserted, for the first time, the extralegal prerogative of 'executive detention' to keep Zeqiri in custody while the attack was being reinvestigated.[41]

By the end of 2000, international judges had been assigned to each of Kosovo's five district courts and one had been assigned to the Supreme Court. Two more international prosecutors were hired and assigned to Pristina and Prizren. Having only one international on the Supreme Court meant that he was regularly outvoted by the two Albanian members of the panel, a situation made worse by the fact that no international prosecutor was appointed to the provincial public office that presented a written opinion to the highest court.

Under the applicable law, trials for all crimes carrying a punishment of ten years or more were presided over by a five person panel of whom only two were professionally trained lawyers and three were lay people. This guaranteed that internationals would always comprise a minority on panels hearing war crimes cases. No Serb lay judges were ever assigned to trial panels. Not surprisingly, therefore, the pattern of biased judgements continued. Almost all convictions of Serbs on genocide and war crimes charges during this period were subsequently reversed by the Supreme Court after it had acquired an international majority.[42]

'The first and most important lesson to be learned from Kosovo,' Kouchner told a journalist as he ended his tenure as SRSG, 'is that peacekeeping missions need a judicial or law-and-order "kit" made up of trained police officers, judges and prosecutors, plus a set of potentially draconian security laws or regulations that are available on their arrival. This is the only way to stop criminal behaviour from flourishing in a post-war vacuum of authority.' He acknowledged that his own staff had repeatedly spurned proposals to bring in foreigners who could prosecute crimes impartially. On this, his staff were 'absolutely wrong,' he said, adding that 'Kosovo needs more such foreign judges and prosecutors now'.[43]

Inter-ethnic relations

Following the agreements of June 1999, the international community was overtaken by a succession of events that dramatically changed the face of Kosovo and the surrounding region. The displaced Kosovo Albanians who had fled to neighbouring countries, principally Albania, Montenegro and the Former Yugoslav Republic of Macedonia (some 848,000 had been registered in camps established for them during the bombing campaign[44]) rushed back into Kosovo. Although in itself this quick return was a great success, it had catastrophic consequences.

Most immediately, Kosovo's Serb population and other Serb-speaking minorities, who had numbered 200,000 before the war, felt extremely threatened. Hundreds were killed. The rate of ethnically motivated crime, including murder, subsided quickly during the second half of 1999 and into 2000. By the end of the emergency phase, in the autumn of that year, inter-ethnic murder had declined to just a few each week. But most Serbs and many of Kosovo's other minorities were still very fearful of venturing into Albanian-dominated areas, and many blamed the international community for failing to protect them. Much of the decline in inter-ethnic murders can be attributed to Serbs having moved into more compact, less vulnerable areas or having left Kosovo altogether. Referring to UNMIK's claims to have dramatically improved security for Serbs, one of the Kosovo Serb community's most visible figures, Father Sava, would quote Tacitus: 'They made a desert and called it peace.'

UNMIK did not, in fact, pretend that conditions for Serbs were peaceful. Kouchner said: 'Now a sinister reminder of that oppression [by Milosevic] is re-emerging as the remaining minorities, particularly the Serbs, find themselves the victims of the severest forms of discrimination and reprisal, including murder.'[45] At the same time, Kouchner, as his successors would, clutched at ephemeral indications that trends might be improving. UNMIK's hopeful optimism made Serbs worry that their plight was being misrepresented to the outside world. The Serbs' determination not to reinforce the impression that their situation was acceptable or even improving contributed to their boycott strategy over the succeeding years.

Security was not the Serbs' only concern. Many lost their jobs as the old Belgrade-backed institutions in Kosovo dissolved along with Yugoslav power in Kosovo.[46] For its part KEK, the electrical utility, produced a calendar for 2000 featuring photos of alleged Serb atrocities. To add injury to insult, it would often send Serbs bills for 2,000 DM while not billing many Albanians at all. Electrical and communications connections to enclaves were continuously being cut by vandals. Some KFOR contingents went to extraordinary lengths to provide links that were less vulnerable — the Swedes buried a cable in the enclave of Gracanica and the British installed a microwave relay.[47] Facing physical threats, unemployment, forced eviction and continuous harassment, at least 100,000 Serbs abandoned Kosovo to live elsewhere, generally Serbia proper.[48]

Some Kosovo Albanians sought to justify this modern-day exodus. A few of the Serbs, they say, were individually responsible for the ethnic cleansing of Kosovo that led to the bombing. Many, perhaps most, they argue, were complicit in the oppressive regime of the 1990s. Thus their forcible expulsion was seen as merely payback, a form of collective punishment worthy of the unprovoked collective punishment they had inflicted on the majority population before the war.

The departure of more than half of Kosovo's Serb population, including many of the most economically active and talented, left Kosovo without many of the skilled people needed to restart key industries, such as the deeply troubled power sector. Within the first few months of the international administration, this movement of people

made the objective of a genuinely multi-ethnic Kosovo much harder
and perhaps entirely unattainable. This took place while KFOR was at
least nominally responsible for security (even though the NATO-led
force did not yet have the capacity to stop most of the persecution).
In its first months, the international administration was unwittingly
but effectively aiding and abetting the very ethnic cleansing that it had
been created to prevent — though now the positions of the Serbs and
Albanians were reversed.

Animosity between the international community and the Milosevic
regime, which continued to hold power in Belgrade for the first fifteen
months of the UNMIK mission, reinforced the tension between Serbs
and Albanians. Milosevic ordered Serbs not to cooperate with UNMIK,
threatening to cut 'collaborators' off from pensions and other benefits.[49]
Many Serbs reported physical intimidation by state representatives. Although UNMIK could offer large salaries and other payments to try to
entice the minority population, few Serbs accepted. Why risk a lifetime
pension for a few months' pay with UNMIK, which they expected to be
a very temporary institution?

Some of the international community's reflexive policies exacerbated the Serbs' predicament. Everybody knew Pristina, Kosovo's putative
capital, was too dangerous for Serbs, and thus an extremely unpromising centre for a new multi-ethnic society; UNMIK established itself
there anyway. Many of the areas inhabited by Serbs were declared 'no-
go' areas for internationals for 'security reasons'.[50] Some internationals
took on the prejudices of the community they lived among. Since many
more internationals interacted with Albanians than with Serbs, this was
a distinctly lopsided phenomenon.[51]

Although it was official UNMIK policy, some parts of the mission
made no effort to enforce the use of both the Serbian and Albanian
languages. UNMIK tried to find Serbs to employ, but few would defy
the order from Belgrade to have no dealings with what the Serbian government regarded as a hostile occupation. As a result, some of the new

institutions created in 1999 and 2000 were the most ethnically pure ever seen in Kosovo — the apartheid had not been dispelled, merely reversed, and sometimes strengthened in the process.

International staff members became engaged in fierce disputes about the ethnic homogeneity of the new institutions. Those tasked with creating a multi-ethnic Kosovo condemned them; many others argued from the utilitarian line that helping the majority community should be the priority. Multi-ethnicity was unworkable, the utilitarians argued, and insisting on it would just make institutions unworkable too.[52]

There were a few deliberate efforts to bring the Serbs and Albanians together in Mitrovica, where, despite the unpromising record of violence and provocation, the demographics were more amenable to progress, because both communities were represented in significant numbers. French KFOR had employed tactics used in Bosnia, acquiescing in a straightforward partition of the city along the line of the river Ibar. Serbs controlled the north of the city, and Albanians controlled the south. Although this meant that the Albanians were more numerous than the Serbs and controlled a larger area, it meant that politically the two sides could be treated as equals.

Kosovo's first municipal assembly elections were scheduled for the end of October 2000; the rules under which the new municipal assemblies were to be elected, meet and conduct themselves had not been drawn up with Mitrovica in mind. International officials in Mitrovica offered local leaders a customised arrangement modelled on Northern Ireland's Good Friday Agreement: each community would be recognised, have a veto on proceedings, and have an incentive to use that veto only wisely. The Serb leader, Oliver Ivanovic, feared that the likely Serb boycott of the forthcoming elections would leave his community isolated and so was prepared to sign up. Bajram Rexhepi, who was later to become Kosovo's Prime Minister, was more hesitant. With the election law already laid out in terms favourable to the Albanians, Rexhepi understandably saw no reason to make concessions. Suggestions that both he and Ivanovic might qualify for the Nobel Peace Prize failed to convince, and the chance was lost. Thus, when the Mitrovica municipal assembly was elected, it was devoid of Serbs. A chance for a multi-ethnic Mitrovica had been squeezed out by the one-size-fits-all template imposed by Pristina.[53]

If multi-ethnicity could not be implanted in the whole of Kosovo, or in the city of Mitrovica, there was still a hope that it might be viable in a thin central belt in Mitrovica, where the two communities confronted each other. This was the 'confidence area', made secure by barbed wire and a high troop presence after the riots of February 2000. It was extremely small: less than one kilometre long, and less than half a kilometre wide, much less in places. But it contained some of the key civic buildings of the city: the cultural centre, municipality building, sports centre, and former bank building, and some old factories. The idea was that if Serbs and Albanians could be encouraged to mix here, then their cooperation might eventually spread elsewhere. Put the other way, if multi-ethnicity was not possible in the confidence area, then it was doomed throughout the whole of Kosovo.

Intensive efforts were made to refurbish the buildings in the confidence area. A new bank, set up by young Dutch entrepreneurs, was sited in the area, opposite the main police station. The sports centre, cultural centre and main bridge were revamped. Even the dusty brown soil was planted with new grass and shrubs in an effort to make the area more appealing.[54] Mitrovica's infamous main bridge, the site of several riotous clashes between the two communities, was at the very centre of this confidence area. The bridge was refurbished with a futuristic design meant to express creativity and reconciliation.

Under the bridge was the water pipe which linked the two parts of the city. The Serbs had alleged that the supply to the north was being cut back by the Albanians, so they could keep more water for themselves; the Albanians denied this. A 'Mitrovica Water Committee' was formed, and, in return for a retraction of their main allegation, the Serbs won the right to inspect the stopcock whenever they chose. Through this Committee internationals won one of the first real agreements between the two communities since the war. Unfortunately, it proved an isolated case.

Essentially, the confidence area failed to overcome Serb suspicions. Serbs who had been evicted from their flats in the area were not persuaded that it was safe or sensible to return, and were wary of the new bank and the other facilities. Although, some three years later, it would be possible to arrange a rock concert in the middle of the bridge, playing to separate but adjacent Serb and Albanian audiences, the only confidence that the confidence area could engender concerned the dividing line between the two communities. Instead of becoming multi-ethnic, most of the confidence area became Albanian-only territory; rather than eroding divisions, it helped to entrench the dividing line between the two communities under the eyes of KFOR.

Political development

Although the Western Alliance ostensibly 'won' the Kosovo conflict, NATO's bombing campaign did not end in an unconditional surrender by the rump Yugoslavia but in a negotiated compromise reflected in UNMIK's mandate. UN resolution 1244, agreed by the US, Russia and the rest of the Security Council in June 1999, did not tackle the most substantive areas of disagreement: whether Kosovo should become a new sovereign state; the exact role of Belgrade and Kosovo Serbs in the administration of Kosovo; and how long the 'interim' arrangements should last. Instead, this disagreement was passed down to the operational level and left to the bodies responsible for implementing the deliberately vague new settlement. As in Bosnia, many of those tasked with reconstructing Kosovo felt that the blueprint they had been given described a holding operation, not a building programme.

Some people involved in the negotiations process remark that it was a success to get any sort of agreement at all. James Rubin, a senior US negotiator at the talks, remarked: 'There was still no agreement on how the post-war peacekeeping force would work or about the Russian place in it, but all three sides believed that they still had time to deal with this.'[55] The fact that the agreement didn't settle the exact future of Kosovo was unavoidable. The lack of agreement between the great powers reflects, in part, the difficulty of the issues at hand — years later, it is still unclear whether or not Kosovo should be independent. But it also shows a lack of willingness by senior figures to grapple with all the major issues. Once the immediate crisis was tackled, the other problems were postponed rather than resolved. If there had been a determination to tackle these problems later, it would have been excusable. But the incomplete agreement of 1999 has not been completed since, and Kosovo suffers today as a direct result.

Kosovo was to be a new sort of mission: international institutions would actually govern a territory as a fully fledged administration. Unlike the administration of post-war Germany and Japan, where great national powers — the US, UK, USSR and France — had taken a share of power, this time it was international institutions which would take the lead. Nation states would only be given responsibility for security through KFOR, learning from Bosnia where multinational control had blurred lines of authority and handicapped the UN's military force.

In addition to these conflicting international pressures, UNMIK faced strong-willed rivals for political power within Kosovo. KLA commander Hashim Thaci began organising a provisional government at Rambouillet, established in exile in the second week of the NATO bombing campaign, and by June 1999 was able to deploy would-be civil authorities to the 27 out of 29 municipalities in Kosovo where Albanians constituted a majority.[56] The head of each, appointed by Thaci, called himself the 'President of the Commune'. The typical mayor had been active in the LDK and had joined the KLA late, usually serving in an administrative capacity. Each municipal administration was divided into several departments — administration, health, economy, property, urbanism, planning, judiciary, public order and defence — headed by local people who usually had some degree of technical expertise. As the town halls had little or no income, the self-styled officials officially received no income from their political activities.[57] Meanwhile, Ibrahim Rugova and Bujar Bukoshi, respectively President and Prime Minister in the pre-war parallel government, continued to insist that they represented Kosovo's legitimate political authority.

Facing these well-entrenched local rivals were a very small number of international civilian staff, few of whom knew Kosovo in any depth. The first Special Representative of the Secretary-General, Sergio Vieira de Mello, arrived with a team of eight people. By the end of June their number had grown to 24 and by mid-autumn to a couple of hundred. Most of these civilian officials, however, were based in Pristina.[58] UN-MIK had managed to appoint regional administrators in each of Kosovo's five regions, but each had just a handful of staff to administer several municipalities. They tended to concentrate on the towns where they lived.[59] By September, UNMIK had assigned civilian officials to each municipality, though at first they had no office or place to live and would commute from the regional centre. By June 2000 — a year into the mission — UNMIK had just 292 professional staff out of an authorised strength of 435, leaving one out of three positions unfilled.[60] The staffing rate in the regions was just 42 per cent. Civil registration, an essential prerequisite to holding elections, was conducted during the summer of 2000 by some 700 UN Volunteers. In October, a report by the respected international think tank, the International Crisis Group, opined: 'A painless takeover, which might have been possible in mid-June without opposition, is no longer possible now that the UCK structures [Thaci's KLA-based "provisional government"] have gained strength and confidence.'[61] Moreover, many officials in UNMIK at the time believe that the US State Department had advised Kouchner not to pick a fight with Thaci.

While Albanian leaders asserted the authority of the rival provisional governments as co-equals of UNMIK, Serbs instead did their best to ignore the international administration. They continued to use the public services — schools, hospitals, post — supported by Belgrade. While this directly contradicted 1244's description of UNMIK as the sole administrative authority in Kosovo, UNMIK's slowness to staff municipalities made it difficult to object. As one international employee working in Kosovo at the time explained, 'The Serbs' parallel structures were the only way they survived in the beginning since Albanians denied them access to electricity, phones, etc. It was uncanny how the electricity would be cut only in the enclaves. The Kosovo mobile phone service, operated from Pristina, would often cut out in Serb areas.'[62]

Salaries of doctors, nurses and teachers as well as pensions continued to be disbursed by Belgrade, giving many people a direct cash incentive to remain loyal to the Milosevic regime. The administrative structures of the three Serb-majority municipalities north of the river Ibar remained intact even after the establishment of UNMIK municipal administrators in the north and municipal elections in October 2000, which the Serbs boycotted. Until Milosevic was defeated and then forced from office in Belgrade, virtually all Serbs refused to work with UNMIK, making it very difficult to staff offices in Serb areas.

The confused lines of authority inspired a new configuration in Kosovo. The UN, which had been neglected in Bosnia and sidestepped during the Kosovo war, was to be first among equals. Not only was the UN given responsibility for civil administration in Kosovo, it was given clear primacy over its coalition partners. There were three of these — the United Nations High Commission for Refugees (UNHCR), which dealt with the humanitarian emergency; the OSCE, which led the Kosovo Verification Mission before the war, and was now mandated with fostering human rights, democracy and modern social institutions; and the European Union (EU), responsible for the economy.

This pyramidal hierarchy brought many benefits. But each of the four pillars still took different approaches. The EU Pillar, for example, planned to rely almost entirely on locally recruited staff.[63] So afraid was the EU of creating a colonial presence in Kosovo that the Pillar's operational budget for the first year was just 6 million euros - little more than 1 per cent of the $435 million budget allocated to the UN.[64]

The OSCE struggled to assert its control over the portfolios assigned to it. Although it was officially charged with building functioning democratic institutions in Kosovo, in practice it was the UN that created the political institutions, the new municipal structures, and most of the new administrative agencies. The UN approach to administration, understandably, was to either do something itself or create a local institution to do it instead. This left the OSCE with the softer stuff — helping the emerging media, organising elections, nurturing political parties, and promoting human rights. The most substantial institution created by the OSCE was the successful police training school. But this is the exception which proved the rule: the Pillar responsible for institution building was generally shut out of the major institutions, especially in the early days.

All these international institutions were bombarded by events. Some long-term planning was done, often by outside consultants, and short-term decisions were usually made with at least some awareness of their longer-term consequences. But most international staff found themselves just struggling to keep up with daily demands. The immediate and the urgent often displaced longer-term needs of central importance. The nature of the urgent problems meant it was often easy to see quick results. This flurry of activity had the benefit of keeping morale high.

Despite the dedication displayed by most international staff, turnover was high. Many people pushed themselves too hard and burned out. The environment, especially the chilling winter of 1999-2000 during which many homes had no heating, also wore them down. Record low overnight temperatures of -36° C were recorded in Pristina.[65] 'I left a glass of water beside my bed one night, and when I woke up, it was all ice!' recalls one.[66] Few internationals seem to have left because they found Kosovo too violent, but the general anarchy and the physical discomforts were disorienting for many.

The high turnover meant that many employees spent much of their time learning about the ever-evolving international structures rather than engaging with local challenges. New staff needed to be welcomed, catered for, and trained up into the workings of the international community in Kosovo. This all took time, and diverted people from the main task.

Staff efforts were often hindered by feeble administrative support. While it would seem sensible to equip an international mission before it started, many of Kosovo's staff members only got the necessary tools after they needed them. Some items, such as computers, cars, and office furniture, suffered particular logjams; others were merely distributed poorly. Administrative support generally followed, rather than led, the main work of the missions. The lack of tools, and the difficulties in overcoming it, certainly reduced overall effectiveness.

Despite these problems, the international presence in Kosovo enjoyed a massive moral authority among Kosovo Albanians during these early months. Dedicated staff working hard in chaotic and often unstable environments achieved a great deal. With hindsight, a more rapid deployment of staff and equipment would have helped UNMIK achieve even more at this time. Loss of opportunities in this early phase became much harder to remedy later.

The slow arrival of the government and international organisations contrasts with the rapid entry into Kosovo by non-government organisations. A diverse range of these organisations queued at the border into Kosovo to be allowed in at the earliest opportunity.[67] Some were vying for the accolade of becoming the first NGO into Kosovo, but most were genuinely driven by the scale and urgency of the humanitarian need before them. Although most of these NGOs had simpler tasks than KFOR and UNMIK, and needed fewer resources to do them, they demonstrated just how swiftly organisations new to Kosovo could act.

Hearts and minds

The rubric for Kosovo's post-war administration, UNSCR 1244, left unresolved the underlying cause of the armed conflict — the question of who would rule Kosovo. Given this enormous handicap in building a sustainable peace, one might have expected the mission to place enormous emphasis on using all available means — an intensive public information effort, sensitivity to the effect of various actions on public confidence, education reform, careful regulation of the media, and various efforts to facilitate the non-violent resolution of disputes — to change the attitudes that had led to and resulted from the conflict. But direct efforts to win hearts and minds or to build public confidence in the new order generally turned out to be desultory.

'The international military campaign rode on a wave of popular sentiment — the Kosovo Albanians widely interpreted it not only as a humanitarian intervention, but also as an opportunity to reaffirm their long-held aspiration to independence,' said Blanca Antonini,[68] who in 1999 and 2000 was deputy head of civil administration in UNMIK. 'In this climate, the difference between peaceful aspiration and hatred of the Serbs and everything associated with them was blurred. From the very beginning, UNMIK engaged the Kosovo Albanians and was particularly keen on establishing a close relationship with the potential "spoilers", mainly the former KLA leaders.' In practice that meant KFOR and UNMIK were more concerned with placating those who opposed inter-ethnic tolerance than defending those few who supported it.

More generally, it meant a hands-off approach to the local political culture, which was widely based on bullying. In post-war Germany and

Japan (which involved radically different circumstances but are never-theless regarded as paragons of post-conflict international administra-tions), educational reforms, control of the media, public symbols and propaganda were all used to foster pacific attitudes. In Kosovo, though, most of UNMIK and KFOR regarded the local Albanian population as the aggrieved party in a one-sided conflict, and good-willed partners in the territory's reconstruction. Operating from such assumptions, the international authorities naturally regarded measures to purge the media, educational system and public sphere of noxious influences as inappropriately intrusive. Says Antonini: 'The international commu-nity — and UNMIK in particular — did not have as a priority the question of culture, and made little or no effort to integrate the expe-rience that both major communities in Kosovo had accumulated prior to the international intervention. By failing to do this, it sidelined as irrelevant an issue of enormous sensitivity in the context of a conflict in which the symbols of cultural identity were often more powerful than weapons.'[69]

Like every experienced political figure, Kouchner understood the importance of pressing the flesh. He made frequent visits to the re-gions. Sergio Vieira de Mello had created a Kosovo Transitional Coun-cil to consult local political and religious leaders in decision-making, and Kouchner's political advisers had frequent contact with their lo-cal counterparts. Kouchner created special task forces to try to tackle especially urgent and conspicuous problems, such as refuse collection (large mounds of garbage were to be found in all of Kosovo's cities and towns) and the security of minorities. When such initiatives foundered on operational limitations, they bred disappointment and cynicism among the public.

In the summer of 2000, it looked as though there might have been a chink in the otherwise uniform Serb boycott of UNMIK institutions in Leposavic, Kosovo's northernmost municipality. In the summer of 2000, local mayor Nenad Radoslavljevic was threatening to defy the Milosevic line by cooperating with UNMIK and encouraging his electors to take part in the vote. UNMIK recognised the opportunity and made an extraordinary effort to help Radoslavljevic by delivering swift and tangible benefits to the local community. Half the regional headquarters staff were deployed to the town and told to make themselves busy. Donors were asked to fund special projects in the town of Leposavic. For some three weeks, it looked as though Leposavic could be won over. But then the pressure from Belgrade proved too much, and Radoslavljevic felt his support slipping away. The episode demonstrated how, even when the international community tried to be fast, smart and well-organised, its efforts could still be scuppered by the man in Belgrade. This flurry of activity, like some of the other taskforces, yielded few lasting results.

For the first year of the international administration, the Albanian media were generally friendly to UNMIK while Serb media were hostile. Susan Manuel, UNMIK's longest-serving spokesperson, recalls having been treated 'like a queen' while serving in Belgrade before the NATO intervention and 'like a witch' thereafter.[70] In Pristina the local media appreciated UNMIK press officers' accessibility and Kouchner's volubility.

Only when the media were used to incite murder did UNMIK assert its authority to regulate this influential sphere — and even then only rhetorically. In October 1999 the SRSG created the office of the Temporary Media Commissioner (TMC), an independent office under the aegis of the OSCE, but gave it no powers of enforcement. To introduce a measure of regulation into the chaotic and often vituperative media environment, the TMC first suggested establishing a 'media policy board' composed of eminent citizens. The initiative which was modelled on the Bosnian example was shot down by criticism in the international media as censorship by another name. The TMC then tried to encourage local media professionals to draft a code of conduct for themselves, but this failed for a lack of consensus.

During this period, it was common for both Albanian and Serbian media to denounce individuals, without evidence, as criminals or traitors. Sometimes this led directly to killings. On 27 April 2000, the Pristina-based newspaper *Dita* published an article about Petar Topoljski, a 25-year-old Serb employee of UNMIK, along with a photo, accusing him of complicity in war crimes. On 15 May Topoljski was found murdered.

The Topoljski case prompted Bernard Kouchner to give the TMC teeth. In a controversial decision to stop media from propagating violence, Kouchner issued an executive order closing *Dita* for eight days. Kouchner's move caused consternation among the Albanians. Veton Surroi, editor of the popular *Koha Ditore* paper, allowed the paper to be printed on his presses in Macedonia and brought in over the border into Kosovo. 'Once they did that, there was no way we could check every car or lorry coming into Kosovo, to check it didn't have any of the banned literature,' admitted someone involved in media regulation at the time.[71] 'We just had to let it go.' Sales of the newspaper soared; an attempt to clamp down on hate media had backfired spectacularly.

This conundrum prompted Kouchner to issue two new regulations, 2000/36 and 2000/37, creating stronger controls on broadcast and print media respectively. 2000/37 gave the TMC the right to impose sanctions on the publishers and editors of newspapers, like *Dita*, that incited violence. All defendants had the right to appeal to a three-person Media Appeals Board comprising an international human rights expert, a local media representative and an international judge. In its first 18 months, the office of the TMC imposed sanctions three times against three different papers - *Dita* again, the LDK newspaper *Bota Sot* and the PDK paper *Epoka e Re*.

The KLA tried to take over Kosovo's state broadcaster, Radio Television Kosova (RTK), in the summer of 1999. KFOR evicted them. But the men with guns were able to use every other means for propagating their militant message. Even staunchly pro-independence intellectuals who preached ethnic tolerance were not immune to KLA-sponsored retribution. *Koha Ditore's* publisher, Veton Surroi, wrote a commentary in his paper in August 1999 condemning 'the organised and systematic intimidation of all Serbs simply because they're Serbs,' calling such attitudes 'fascist'. He went on to write, '[From] having been victims of Europe's worst end-of-century persecution, we are ourselves becoming persecutors and have allowed the spectre of fascism to reappear ... Is this what we fought for?'[72]

On 2 October, the KLA-funded news organisation of Hashim Thaci's provisional government, *KosovaPress*, launched a vitriolic attack and a thinly veiled death threat against Surroi and *Koha Ditore's* editor, Baton Haxhiu. The article said that the two had a 'Slav stink', and were supporters of Slobodan Milosevic. It said that they risked 'eventual and very understandable revenge' for the Surroi comment. It concluded that, 'such criminal and enslaved minds should not have a place in the free Kosovo'.[73]

The effect of such malevolent media was amplified by the fact that the UN administration itself had few means with which to put across its own point of view. While Bernard Kouchner evinced a Clintonesque need to be loved, especially by the Albanian majority, UN headquarters allocated scant resources to the mission's division of public information. Whereas NATO arrived with a full press office included 32 press officers, and a stage and sound system for press conferences, UNMIK, by contrast, arrived with two press officers. The pair were equipped with just single a cell phone and a UN flag borrowed from the UN office in Macedonia.[74]

As a wealth of experience in conventional wars and counterinsurgency operations attests, propaganda is only helpful when it amplifies and interprets observable facts on the ground. A number of actions early in UNMIK's administration, both overt and covert, helped cement the impression, especially among Serbs, that the US was biased in Albanians' favour and would allow well-placed former KLA members to literally get away with murder. When US Secretary of State Madeleine Albright made a triumphal visit to Pristina on 15 July 1999, she ostentatiously kissed Hashim Thaci on world television. Given that virtually all Serbs viewed Thaci, aka 'the Snake', as a war criminal, and he was then defying UN authorities by asserting the legitimacy of his 'provisional government', Albright's kiss sent a strong signal that alignment with the US trumped all other considerations.

Beyond such demonstrations of impunity, the international administration's loudest message was the one created by its failure to provide security for minority communities. 'Michael Jackson [the first commander of KFOR] let 100,000 Serbs leave Kosovo,' said Karin von Hippel, who advised Kouchner on minority affairs. 'This, along with the violence in Mitrovica, showed Albanians that they could get away with anything, and Serbs that they wouldn't be protected.'[75]

UNMIK and KFOR's efforts to control provocative nationalist symbols were desultory. When it came to the issue of nationalist symbols, UNMIK did not have a uniform policy throughout the territory. At the headquarters level the mission was reluctant to issue regulations that would ban the use of Albanian flags in public buildings, and left the issue in the hands of regional and municipal administrators. The advice that the head of the civil administration gave to his staff in the field was: 'If an activity is not openly criminal, let it happen.' As a result, the policies applied differed from municipality to municipality. In Pristina and Kamenica, rules were more strict; in Pec, the Albanian flag was hoisted alongside the UN flag. The relationship with the KFOR commander in each case was, of course, of paramount importance to the decision.[76]

In October 1999, the International Crisis Group opined: 'By no means all of the UN administrators have yet succeeded in flying the [UN] flag. Those who have did mostly not attempt to enforce the original policy of flying the UN flag instead of the Albanian double-headed eagle. One understands the reason for this policy — the eagle is for Albanians but not the other peoples of Kosovo — but it does

seem unwise to offer needless provocations to a 95 per cent majority population.' Needless? If KFOR and UNMIK's top priority was
to minimise the chances of a backlash by members of the Albanian
majority, they could have saved themselves the trip to Kosovo. If, on
the other hand, it was to create physical and psychological security,
the failure to enforce a ban on nationalist symbols was negligent in
the extreme. Moreover, concern about a violent public reaction to a
crackdown on vestiges of the KLA was belied by results of the first
election in October 2000, when Thaci's and Haradinaj's parties lost
badly to the purportedly pacific LDK.

International control was even more conspicuously absent in the field
of education. Kouchner often visited schools, but UNMIK rarely used
other means to intrude into the formation of the next generation of
Kosovans. Under Kouchner, there was no systematic effort to prevent
inter-ethnic hatred fermenting in the education system, or distorted
versions of history from being taught in schools. Albanian members of
an educational advisory group set up and closed in the mission's first
year were dismayed that UNMIK made no effort to depoliticise the
school system, instead leaving it in the hands of political party bosses
who used it as an enormous patronage network.

At bottom, the education system was ignored, like so many other
critical spheres, for two reasons: first, because the international community lacked the capacity to intervene properly; and second, because
the international community misunderstood the nature of the conflict
in which it had intervened. Unlike their predecessors in occupied Germany and Japan after the Second World War, UNMIK officials didn't see
reforming education as vital to achieving its mandate. Instead of harnessing education as a vehicle of progressive change, UNMIK's priority
was simply to get the schools back to work. Donors, seeing reopened
schools as a photo opportunity, were happy to oblige. There was a sense
that the surviving school system was a success story of the pacific Alba-

nians, and that 'if it's not broken, don't fix it'. Education became one of the first areas turned over to local control.

The economy

At the end of the conflict in June 1999, Kosovo's economy was derelict and threadbare. The Yugoslav dinar had collapsed. Most, but not all, Albanians used German marks. 'I remember paying for something with Deutchmarks, and getting change in Swiss Francs,' recalls one international adviser there at the time.[77] 'When I pointed out that the change he had given me was worth more than I had paid him, he said it was the only coin he had!'

Despite this confusion of currencies, Kosovo was still a cash economy — bank accounts had been plundered in the past, and savings were generally thought safest kept under a mattress. As the Serb-dominated administration withdrew from most of Kosovo, taxes ceased to be collected,[78] and most Kosovo Albanians lost whatever pensions they were due. So the post-war economy had no standard currency, no functioning system of taxation, no official government services, no proper benefits system, few private services except importing, and no banking system. Apart from the many decrepit factory sites scattered around Kosovo, the territory had many characteristics of a pre-industrial society.

Yugoslav economics, Milosevic's policies, the social dislocation of the 1990s and war damage had all contributed to making this economic wasteland.

Yugoslavia's economy was already in decline when Milosevic came to power, but the trend accelerated rapidly under his regime — GDP fell by a third between 1978 and 1990 and then fell by more than half again during the 1990s.[79] As Yugoslavia's outmoded economic system shrivelled, crippled by unsustainable debts, the Croatian and Bosnian wars, and the UN sanctions imposed in 1992, Kosovo suffered particularly badly. Already the poor relation, it saw its share of the shrinking pot become even smaller. Infrastructure investment gave way to asset stripping. Hyperinflation eroded the real value of earnings. Any fledging firms which might have emerged to replace the outmoded socialist industries were choked by bureaucracy, taxes and other costs.

On top of this, there was massive dislocation of skilled labour. Many Kosovo Albanians had been forced out of their jobs during the 1990s. This meant that few had the fresh technical, financial or managerial skills needed to revive large institutions. The public utilities and government sector became mere shells when almost the entire qualified Serb workforce fled after the war. The few Serbs who stayed were usually excluded from senior positions they had held during the 1990s. Skills cleansing was a side-effect of ethnic cleansing.

Material destruction added to this gloomy situation. Approximately 120,000 houses were destroyed in the war, and twice as many damaged. Some of the military targets which were bombed, such as the telephone exchange, were important for the economy. But the physical damage was small compared to the wider impact on business: most production stopped altogether during the 78 days of bombing, never to restart.

The institution charged with tackling the calamitous economic situation was the European Union, principally because it was to become the main donor to Kosovo (about two thirds of the funds infused into Kosovo came from EU states). Compared to the other main institutional actors - NATO, the UN and the OSCE - the EU was a newcomer to nation-building. When the EU had disbursed aid in other places, it had done so slowly and deliberately through delegations working with local administrations. This model was unfeasible for Kosovo, where there was no proper government to work with and the funds needed to be delivered fast. So it created two new institutions: the European Agency for Reconstruction, an on-the-ground outfit designed to refurbish Kosovo's infrastructure quickly; and the EU Pillar of UNMIK. The Head of the EU Pillar was made deputy to the UN Special Representative, giving the EU its most direct executive role in administration anywhere at that time.

The EU Pillar took a market-based approach. It decided it should not attempt to prop up socialist enterprises. Instead, it focused on creating a framework in which private enterprise could flourish. Hence, the most urgent priority was to institutionalise a sound currency, and in August 1999 the EU legitimised the deutschmark in Kosovo. This economic measure had the added political benefit of wresting monetary control away from Milosevic and preventing him from printing money to hijack the new funds coming into Kosovo.[80]

Kosovo could not survive on donor funds forever. The easiest way to collect revenue locally was to charge duties on non-charitable imports. The Customs Service had the advantage of being relatively easy to set up, spreading the burden widely and — in theory anyway — encouraging Kosovo-based firms which could operate without paying tax.

A new banking and payments authority was created to oversee a new banking sector and supervise government transactions. The Department of Reconstruction was formed to coordinate the massive international donor effort.

EU officials believed it would be counterproductive to target employment specifically. This, they argued, had been tried under Milosevic, who subsidised many thousands of jobs to buy political docility. Milosevic's subsidies had been funded by printing money to hyperinflationary levels and through taxes on 'productive' firms. By scrapping the old system, the EU hoped to clear away the inefficient legacy of socialism and allow entrepreneurs, who were assumed to exist in Kosovo, to catch up with the rest of the continent. Indeed, the private sector began to flourish in Kosovo even before the reforms took place.

The EU Pillar did launch a few small initiatives to generate jobs. The UNDP and EU worked together on some 'quick impact' projects, which employed low-skilled workers to do menial tasks for a few weeks of reasonable pay. These schemes were very popular, could be targeted for political effect and helped participants to refamiliarise themselves with work. But they also exposed some of the deficits that would stymie growth — of skills, work-orientated training, and economic leadership. People in Kosovo needed more than a free market to find work; they needed employers, and these the international community could not create without reverting to socialist models. Hence, most of the employment opportunities unleashed by Kosovo's new free market were small-scale — hairdressers, taxi drivers and small shopkeepers. Kosovo's manufacturing and agricultural sectors remained largely moribund.

Local vested interests blocked other efforts to 'rationalise' Kosovo's economic dinosaurs. Some of Kosovo's largest firms, such as KEK (the electrical utility), employed perhaps five times as many staff as they should. Fearing that sacking 80 per cent of the workforce would provoke riots, the EU sought to reduce the payroll incrementally. Local trade unions opposed these efforts with legal moves and direct action.

Nine months into the mission, the EU still had only 13 international staff — clearly insufficient to redress the endemic skills shortage or restructure firms. Although many Kosovo Albanians demonstrated entrepreneurial flair in family businesses, work culture in larger organisations was exceptionally slack. Employment for many involved simply having one's name on a list, arriving at work to drink coffee all day, and sometimes receiving a salary. These work attitudes, ingrained during the old socialist days, proved very hard to change. According to one local UN staff member, in the Yugoslav era a worker in a socialist enterprise prided himself on how little he could get done each day; now they were genuinely aggrieved that that they actually had to work.[81]

Under Milosevic, most of the large firms had been 'socially owned'— a socialist form of ownership unique to former Yugoslavia, famously but unhelpfully described in law as 'owned by everyone and by no-one'. These could not be restarted legitimately because nobody knew who owned them. Lawyers suggested that anyone who made one of these socially owned enterprises productive could be sued by Belgrade, or by various creditors. Consequently, most either lay idle or were taken over by local mafias.

Water and electricity were also the responsibility of the EU Pillar. Both utilities performed significantly worse than they had done before the war: again, the skilled managers and technicians had gone, and the new workforce did not know how to make the decrepit infrastructure function. Electricity, vital for heating in the harsh Balkan winter, suffered particularly, as Kosovo ceased to be subsidised by inflows of power from Serbia proper even as demand soared.[82] The increase in demand was exacerbated by the inability to enforce the payment of utility bills. Most people knew they would not have to pay for their power, so they consumed as much as they could.

What the international community had to meet these challenges was plenty of money. Representatives of donor agencies roamed Pristina looking for worthy causes to invest in. Some were inevitably more popular than others: while several countries wanted the credit for funding Kosovo's new Albanian-language television broadcaster, mending the decrepit sewerage system was far less popular.[83] As the head of the Department of Reconstruction, Roy Dickinson, acknowledged, everybody favoured donor coordination in principle, but no one wanted to be coordinated.[84]

Nevertheless, donor coordination in Kosovo may have been better than in previous missions, notably Bosnia. Dickinson's department enlisted KFOR support to compile accurate data on projects planned, undertaken and completed. This enabled him to spot trends and help donors avoid being overcharged. It also meant that when, for example, the Islamic Development Bank spent ten times more than other donors to repair each school, the reason could be investigated: it turned out it was installing a free Wahhabi mosque in each new school they built.[85] Meanwhile, the US Congress had stipulated that no more than 15 per cent of all donor funds should come from the US. The Department of Reconstruction was able to calculate what this amounted to, and inform Washington accordingly.

Different donors approached Kosovo differently. The European Agency for Reconstruction, responsible for about half of all donor spending in Kosovo, often took on the most thankless work, including the deeply troubled energy sector. It tended to move more slowly than bilateral agencies, and often went through two levels of sub-contractors, each of whom would take a substantial cut, to get work done. USAID, on the other hand, tried to compensate for its relatively small share of total funding by quickly delivering on high-profile and often politically important projects. Other bilateral donors tended to target their funds towards municipalities where their nationals held senior appointments.

Donor funding did not necessarily translate into political loyalty. This was most sharply felt in northern Kosovo, where UNMIK's authority was most brittle. In August 2000, a new 'development strategy' was launched for northern Kosovo. Foreign-funded projects worth several million deutchmarks were highlighted — a very considerable disbursement, in view of the area's relatively small population. Serbs, though, generally refused to be bought. Many took pride in their refusal; others simply enjoyed the largesse without becoming any friendlier toward the donors. The majority, who either were receiving funds from Belgrade or had other financial ties to Serbia proper, did not want to jeopardise them by becoming involved with the international community. Hence, money generally proved an ineffective lever where the mission was unpopular.

Despite the almost complete absence of production, at the end of his eighteen-month tour as SRSG Kouchner was upbeat about economic progress. 'The power plants, roads and schools are all functioning. The shops are full. Building is booming. Kosovo begins 2001 with a solid economic framework and a balanced budget,' he said.[86] Although this claim is perhaps more positive than the real situation would justify, there were certainly some important economic advances made in the first year and a half of the mission. Over time, though, many of these achievements would come to be viewed as superficial and tenuous.

CONSOLIDATION
OCTOBER 2000–JUNE 2002

Bernard Kouchner, the charismatic doctor, administered emergency life support to Kosovo, but left before curing any of its crippling maladies. The contrast between him and his successor could hardly have been more extreme. Hans Haekkerup, a former Danish Defence Minister, must be among the most private public figures in Europe. Yet working with quiet determination (and determined quietness), during his truncated tenure Haekkerup achieved three landmark political developments: the adoption of a constitutional framework laying out the architecture for new provisional institutions of self-government; province-wide elections for a parliament with substantial responsibility for domestic affairs; and a working relationship with the new regime in Belgrade.

Under the taciturn Dane UNMIK's presence finally became ubiquitous throughout Kosovo, apart from the Serb-majority north. Over a million inhabitants of Kosovo were issued with UNMIK travel documents — the non-state equivalent of a passport — that were recognised by a growing list of countries. Kosovo benefited from a degree of monetary stability that other poor and politically turbulent societies can only dream of when the euro became its official currency. New amenities — cash machines, modern grocery stores, skiing in the Serb enclave of Brezovica, a booming café culture and Italian and Indian restaurants — gave Kosovo a deceptive veneer of normality.

But the superficial and inchoate nature of Kosovo's apparent progress was symbolised by the abortive construction of hundreds of buildings across Kosovo: slapped up in a hurry with no permission and often no clear title to the land, then left half-built and unoccupied, most ended up as nothing but unsightly piles of breeze blocks in fields of mud. KEK, the electrical utility, continued to be unable to satisfy Kosovo's fast-expanding demand, the result being daily power cuts that severely complicated life and sapped public confidence. Meanwhile, successors to the KLA in various guises continued to flex their muscles, with the murder and harassment of LDK officials and clandestine support for fresh insurgencies on Kosovo's borders.

Despite these dark undercurrents, UNMIK's theme from early 2001 until mid-2002 was consolidation. Priorities had changed since the early days. The humanitarian agenda had been overtaken by a political one. When UNMIK began a second drive to prepare for the coming Balkan winter, it had lost the sense of urgency of the first year. With no recorded deaths as a result of the winter cold, it seemed that the Kosovans were more self-reliant than many in the international community had imagined.

It was a time when Haekkerup and his successor, Michael Steiner, were able to devise and implement plans to build on the haphazard achievements of the emergency period. Kosovo was now seldom in the headlines, which gave the the mission a bit of breathing space. UNMIK officials had time to plan the political structures to which local people would be elected; scope for rapprochement with Belgrade; and an opportunity to rationalise the structure of UNMIK itself, which had so far grown spontaneously in a series of ad hoc responses to crises, and thus reflected the chaos of the circumstances in which it had evolved. This new orientation towards deliberate design began at the top levels in Pristina and slowly filtered down through the rest of the mission.

As Kosovo calmed down, dramatic developments altered the surrounding region. Belgrade went through a series of major changes — a democratic coup in October 2000; a watershed parliamentary election in December 2000; major power struggles within the new regime; and last, in June 2001, the extradition of former President Slobodan Milosevic to The Hague on war crimes charges. To the south in Macedonia and to the east in southern Serbia, new Albanian militant insurgencies supported from Kosovo complicated both the security and the diplomatic environment. Observers could be forgiven for concluding that Kosovo, the main troublespot in the region during 1999, had become an oasis of calm and order. And then, in September 2001, terrorist attacks on the US abruptly pushed the whole Balkans to the margins of the world's agenda.

Kofi Annan, Secretary-General of the United Nations, hoped that the new 'war on terrorism' would not distract the world away from Kosovo. 'Although the terrorist attacks took place in New York and Washington,' wrote the Secretary-General the following month, 'they were attacks against all humanity and against the values of peace, democracy and human rights on which the United Nations was founded. Never has there been a greater need for resolution in confronting the forces of violence, bigotry and hatred. In this context, the success of the UN mission in Kosovo matters now more than ever.' After noting that 'in terms of the world's ability to hammer swords into ploughshares at the dawn of the third millennium, UNMIK is the state of the art,' Annan concluded: 'For the sake of people throughout the world, in this small corner of it the forces of tolerance and peace must prevail.'[1] Despite such ringing rhetoric, retaining the attention and resources needed to finish the job in Kosovo became an ever increasing challenge.

Security and the rule of law

Kosovo remained violent and volatile. In the first week of February 2001, exactly one year after the last bout of deadly violence, Mitrovica erupted again. As before, a minor provocation from one side was more than reciprocated by the other, and the spiral escalated dangerously. This time, it was Albanians who exploded in rage. An Albanian child had been killed in an incident in north Mitrovica and many Albanians were certain that it was a deliberate act of provocation by the Serbs.

Angry mobs of Albanians routed the French troops guarding the checkpoint on the south of the small buffer area, the 'Confidence Zone', which kept the two communities apart. Two KFOR armoured vehicles were torched (although the crowd considerably moved an UNMIK police car away from the flames), and the mob massed threateningly near the UN regional headquarters. The French, in an effort to keep the rioters away from the building, fired tear gas into the entrance. The building filled with tear gas and the UN staff, who had no respirators, were soon in distress. 'We could barely breathe, people were crying, vomiting, panicking. Trapped inside, we were all scared, especially for the Serb staff,' recalled one person trapped in the building.[2] The UN Regional Administrator, Tony Welch, a British general-turned-development expert, tried to summon help from Pristina but was met with a stone wall of bureaucracy. Haekkerup refused to speak to him and only a military officer, US Marine Colonel Tom Tyrell of UNMIK's planning unit, showed any interest in the crisis.[3]

All but essential UN and OSCE staff were told to keep away from the city centre, although the UN Headquarters remained open. After thirty-six hours, the exhausted French troops guarding the confidence zone were replaced by Italians and the violence immediately moved from the bridge area to the French headquarters in the centre. It became clear that the target for this wave of violence was not primarily the Serbs but the French troops stationed in the town.

At the height of the rioting Dr Bajram Rexhepi, who was to become the first Prime Minister in Kosovo's Provisional Institutions of Self-Government, led a band of medical staff into the crowd and administered aid to those who were injured or suffering from the effects of tear gas. The Mayor of Mitrovica, Faruk Spahia, was forced to take refuge in the UN Headquarters, only to be caught there in a second wave of tear gas.

Two more days of rioting followed, causing some thirty military and over a hundred civilian casualties. The French military headquarters was burned and abandoned, but the UN Headquarters was never attacked. Rioters attempted to burn the Serbian Orthodox church in the south of the city and overturned Serb gravestones in the nearby cemetery. A Serbian OSCE staff member was seriously beaten by the mob but escaped with his life. Other Serbian UN and OSCE staff members fled to the north of the city and remained there until the violence was over.

Finally, the new SRSG, Hans Haekkerup, was persuaded to come to Mitrovica where he performed what the regional administrator, Tony Welch, described as 'a remarkable act of appeasement'.[4] Haekkerup signed a declaration that the confidence zone would be extended into the Serb side of the city, the Serb 'bridge-watchers' would be disbanded, and non-French troops would be rotated through Mitrovica. The first two promises proved to be unachievable and the third politically unacceptable. No Serb representative was invited to the meeting. The rioting, however, stopped immediately and an uneasy calm descended on the city.

Despite occasional attacks on ethnic minorities, in other parts of Kosovo the security situation appeared to have improved dramatically during the first 18 months of the protectorate. But like so much in Kosovo, progress came at a cost. 'Security' was achieved only at the price of effectively allowing nationalists to achieve their aims without violence. In practice this meant that UNMIK came to accept as normal the *fait accompli* of ethnic cleansing.

The protectorate's failure to provide security was epitomised by a deadly terrorist attack on a bus carrying Serb civilians, and even more dramatically in the failure to convict anyone for the crime. On 16 February 2001, five buses carrying 250 Serbs, mostly young people going to visit friends and relatives, escorted by seven KFOR armoured per-

sonnel carriers, set out from Nis in southern Serbia for Kosovo. When
the convoy had reached a point about a mile into Kosovo, Albanian extremists waiting on a hill a mile away detonated a pipe bomb under the
road containing 200 pounds of TNT. The explosion blew the lead bus
high in the air. It landed 45 feet away. Eleven people died, including a
two-year-old boy, and 18 were injured.

Three months before the attack, NATO had collected evidence that
a terrorist incident was likely on this stretch of highway, in a sector
within the British area of responsibility. On the basis of this intelligence,
the British intensified surveillance of the highway, first by men hidden in
roadside bushes and then by visible patrols. The patrols usually checked
27 culverts and 35 other vulnerable places twice a day. On the day of
the attack, a Serb holiday when people visit the graves of their relatives,
the passengers pushed those guarding the boundary with Serbia to let
the bus pass quickly so that they could reach cemeteries by noon, as
tradition required. Consequently, the bus entered Kosovo 55 minutes
earlier than expected and before the British soldiers had checked four
of the culverts. Because of a technical problem with their communications equipment, the soldiers manning the boundary were not able to
warn the search team that the buses were on their way.

The perpetrators of this terrorist attack were identified by KFOR
almost immediately. NATO intelligence officers, privy to powerful eavesdropping systems and information from hundreds of paid
informers, had concluded months before that a 'Kosovar Albanian
terrorist cell, approximately nine in number' had been responsible
for the attack. The bombing was carried out by three people to create 'personal insecurity in the Serb population'.[5] Intelligence reports
stated that the group's leader and some of its members belonged to
the Kosovo Protection Corps.[6]

Though four suspects were detained in March in well-coordinated
raids supported by hundreds of KFOR troops and helicopters, none
were convicted. Police and the international prosecutor were ham-

strung by several factors. NATO refused to share information on the attack obtained from human informants and from wire tapping, fearing it would compromise its sources, while the UN did not pay informers or use wire tapping (these policies were later reversed). On top of these limitations, some aspects of the investigation appeared to have been undermined deliberately.

British Royal Air Force Squadron Leader Roy Brown, KFOR's chief spokesman at the time, said in response to questions about the bus case that the peacekeeping force was willing to 'act against high-profile individuals' and frequently shared information with police. But, said Brown, KFOR must also follow 'constraints imposed by the national security considerations of the 39 nations that contribute to KFOR.' He did not detail those constraints.[7] KFOR and UNMIK officials worried privately that challenging Albanian militants would provoke them to turn against KFOR itself. Protecting his soldiers was top priority for every KFOR commander.

Immediately after the Nis Express bus was bombed, NATO paved over the crater in the highway — thereby destroying potential evidence, according to the police. The suspect against whom police had collected the most damning evidence was Florim Ejupi, a 23-year-old. Ejupi's cell phone, seized during his arrest, indicated that he had spoken with one of the other suspects believed to be involved at the time of the bombing. DNA from a cigarette butt found near the hilltop tree stump where the bomb was detonated (a wire ran from the stump to the site of the explosion) matched the DNA sample in Ejupi's police file in Germany.

Ejupi and the four other suspects were transferred without explanation from a police detention facility in Pristina to a stockade at Camp Bondsteel, the US's main army base in Kosovo. On 15 May, Ejupi became the latest of about 30 defendants, many of them facing charges of ethnically motivated violence, to escape from various detention facilities in Kosovo in 2000 and 2001. Ejupi reportedly used a wire cutter passed to

him in a spinach pie baked by his family. US army officials say the escape
required about ten minutes' work cutting through two wire fences. 'My
opinion is he did not escape,' said Detective Stu Kellock, former head of
UNMIK's regional serious crimes squad. 'I thought a prisoner could not
just walk away from Bondsteel. In my opinion he was taken elsewhere
for questioning or something and I still do not understand why we, the
police in the investigation who held jurisdiction, were not involved.' UN
sources believed Ejupi had worked for the CIA and that his trial would
have caused serious discomfort to the Americans.[8]

Even if the international community had been pulling in the same
direction, the police would still have faced the challenge of getting
local people to help them solve serious crimes. Baton Haxhiu, editor
of *Koha Ditore*, wrote a scathing editorial about the Nis bus massacre,
saying the police had been 'castrated' by the case and condemning Albanian leaders for imposing a 'code of silence'. Indeed, the widespread
code of silence was the criminals' greatest advantage over law enforcement. Most Albanians simply refused to talk. Many tacitly supported
the attacks on Serbs, and regarded them as fair retribution for the
atrocities committed under the Milosevic regime. Those who opposed
them were often afraid to speak out or loath to betray friends or relatives to the police. Political leaders would recite platitudes against violence when pushed to do so by their international interlocutors but,
with only a few exceptions, they appeared conspicuously half-hearted.
The number of inter-ethnic murders was falling, but the hatred that
fuelled them remained.

Kosovo Serb leaders complained that not one Kosovo Albanian was
convicted of the murder of a Serb in Kosovo in the first two years of
the protectorate. In February 2002, UNMIK police were unable to provide Amnesty International with statistics on the number of interethnic
crimes for which a perpetrator had been convicted, pleading that they
did not as a matter of practice systematically differentiate between
interethnic and other categories of crime. The fact is that in the first

years of the protectorate, only one crime against Serbs resulted in a conviction, and that was *in absentia* after the suspect escaped prior to his trial.

After almost three years of virtual impunity, moderate progress in prosecuting ethnically motivated crimes was finally made in the spring of 2002. On 15 April, Shefket Maliqi and Ismail Jahiu, both Albanian, were sentenced by an international panel of judges in the Gjilan district court to 15 years' imprisonment for murdering a 17-year-old Serb, Aleksandar Dodia, and causing serious bodily harm to an Albanian passer-by during a drive-by shooting in the ethnically mixed town of Vitina. On 14 May 2002 Roland Bartetzko, a German citizen married to a Kosovo Albanian and a former member of the KLA, was sentenced to 23 years' imprisonment following his conviction for the murder of Aleksandar Petrovic, who was killed in a car-bomb attack outside the Serbian Ministry of the Interior in Pristina, as well as the attempted murder of four other men and 'terrorism' the year before. Also on 14 May 2002 an Albanian, Artan Hasani, was sentenced to 15 years for the murder of a 70-year-old Serb woman in Prizren in March 2000; Hasani had repeatedly tried to drive her from her home before finally attacking her and leaving her body in the street. Two Albanians were indicted on 27 May 2002 on two counts of murder, six counts of kidnapping and 'terrorism' against Serbs in Gjilan in June 1999. On 26 September 2002, UNMIK police arrested two Albanian men for the murder of a 50-year-old Serb woman three years earlier.

Amnesty International, though, was not impressed. 'Despite recent improvements,' they wrote, 'Amnesty International is concerned that UNMIK police were both insufficiently prepared and under-equipped to investigate the majority of ethnically motivated crimes which took place between July 1999 and 2001. As a result, the majority of such cases remain unresolved.'[9] Amnesty's critique was valid as far as it went. But even the best prepared and equipped police force in the

world would have little success investigating serious crimes as long as
the population adhered to such a rigid code of silence.[10]

The deck was stacked against law enforcement from the beginning.
Criminals and extremists were effectively given a head start of more
than a year over the police. Within UNMIK, a central office responsible
for policing and the justice system, a re-designated Pillar One, was not
established until May 2001. The first class of officers in the newly established Kosovo Police Service (KPS) graduated from the academy in
Vushtrri in October of 1999, but it took years to come close to training
enough officers for all of Kosovo. Many of those who trained the new
officers, both in the academy and on the job, were impressed by their
dedication and idealism. At the same time, academy director Steve Bennett said the quality of the recruits was undermined by the 50 per cent
quota for former KLA members.[11]

Kosovo Police Service officers set about enforcing traffic regulations, in particular speed limits. Some took particular pleasure in
penalising internationals; others were more lenient on internationals
than on others. Even with irregular enforcement, the number of road
traffic accidents in Kosovo fell by a third between 2001 and 2003 (from
8,731 to 5,402), even though more people were driving.[12] Meanwhile,
many Kosovans viewed anyone in law enforcement with contempt.
Local people were particularly dismayed by the KPS's adherence to
legal procedures. Because the UN refused to pay informers and the
law forbade the use of electronic surveillance (until early in 2002), the
KPS were exceptionally dependent on public goodwill and cooperation. For complex cultural and political reasons, such cooperation was
not forthcoming. For all their hatred of the Serbian police, most Kosovo Albanians couldn't imagine how police could be effective without
beating witnesses and coercing confessions. The Kanun Lek Dukajini,
the traditional Albanian legal code that still exercised considerable
influence in Kosovo Albanian society, prohibited Albanians from ever
cooperating with police. A Canadian-Albanian restaurant owner had his

establishment vandalised in Canada because he'd been seen offering a cup of coffee to the local cop.[13] In a single week in July 2001, the international police who oversaw the KPS recorded seventeen incidents of death threats or assaults on KPS officers while on duty. Many of these incidents of violence erupted from trivial events, a traffic ticket issued to a speeding car, a vehicle towed for blocking a road, or the questioning of suspects in a case of assault. 'The immediate reaction by some people was to shout obscenities, threats or abuse and, in some cases, to physically attack the officer involved,' wrote police spokesman Derek Chappell. 'In some cases criminal suspects had sought out the officers off-duty to threaten them for arrests they had made while on duty.'[14]

The failure to prevent interethnic violence and prosecute those who perpetrate it cannot be laid at the doorstep of the international police or the judiciary alone. A fractious political culture forged by years of conflict also played a role. During this period, for example, an alternative explanation for attacks on Serbs began to emerge in the Albanian community: that Serb security services were behind them, in order to discredit Albanians (much as Bosnian Serbs had accused Bosnian Muslims of firing rockets into a central Sarajevo marketplace to attract international sympathy). With no convictions following in the wake of inter-ethnic murders, it is hard to say whether this claim has any basis. There is some circumstantial evidence suggesting a complex motive for some of the crimes. Murders often preceded high-profile visits. Visits by UN Secretary-General Kofi Annan and European Commissioner Chris Patten in 2002, for example, were both overshadowed by attacks against Serbs or Serb churches immediately before their arrival in Kosovo.[15] Atrocities against Serbs in the hours leading up to the VIP visits meant that during Kosovo's brief moments in the media limelight, the victimisation of the Serbs loomed large. Such stories made the case for denying Kosovo independence more effectively than any statement from Belgrade ever could. In the conspiratorial world of Balkan subterfuge, it is entirely possible that these apparently inter-ethnic murders were in fact committed by Serbs to renew their claim to victimhood. It is also possible that the murderers were Albanians who were either very cunning or very stupid in the pursuit of their objectives. Without convictions, it is hard to draw even the most basic conclusions about the motives of the perpetrators.

The inevitable focus on interethnic violence often overshadowed the worrisome level of violence within the Albanian community. Feuds were played out between the various political factions within the Kosovo Albanian community, often with lethal brutality. On 17 January 2002, Smajl Hajdaraj, a 50-year-old member of the Assembly for the LDK, was shot to death outside his home in Peje. He had been a senior commander in the KLA during the war. Two LDK members died and another was wounded in a drive-by shooting in Skenderaj. Police believed the incident was part of a feud and not politically motivated. In early October an Albanian politician alleged to have collaborated with Slobodan Milosevic was gunned down in front of his family.[16]

While various forms of violence and other crime continued to challenge law enforcement within Kosovo, KFOR had to divert significant resources to help prevent spillover from two insurgencies that erupted on Kosovo's eastern and southern borders. On 5 April 2001 the *Dnevnik* newspaper in Skopje, the capital of the cumbersomely named Former Yugoslav Republic of Macedonia (Macedonia) immediately south of Kosovo, reported that four Macedonian soldiers had been captured near the border with Kosovo by what the Macedonia government described as 'Kosovo militants'. This was the first act in a new insurgency by a group of Albanian militants in Macedonia who called themselves the National Liberation Army (NLA). About a third of Macedonia's population is ethnically Albanian and they are concentrated in the west and north of the country, along the Albanian and Kosovo/Serbian borders. Albanian grievances in Macedonia included the country's designation of 'Macedonians', meaning Slavs speaking Macedonian, as the country's primary nationality; not being allowed to use Albanian in official business; and being denied a university that taught in Albanian.

Until 90 years earlier Pristina and Skopje had both belonged to the same administrative district, the Ottoman vilayet of Kosovo. Serbia captured most of the vilayet in the First Balkan War of 1912, just as the Ottoman government had finally acceded to Albanian demands to form a cohesive and autonomous Albanian region within the empire. During and after the Yugoslav period, Albanians on both sides of the Kosovo-Macedonia border maintained close links. Hundreds of thousands of Kosovo Albanians found refuge in Macedonia during the 1999 war. Many Macedonian Albanians with long-standing ties to Kosovo took up arms to fight alongside the KLA. After the insurgency began in Macedonia, some former KLA fighters returned the favour. NATO officials believed that the KLA and NLA were linked less by fighters moving from one territory to another than by common financial and political supporters among the Albanian diaspora.

The insurgency in Macedonia was also linked to one in the Presevo valley in southern Serbia. During the NATO air war, Albanians in southern Serbia had been subject to arbitrary arrests and other forms of violence and harassment from government security forces, particularly after the notorious Pristina Corps relocated to the region in June 1999. Some 15,000-17,000 Albanians moved from southern Serbia to Kosovo during this period. At the same time the Military Technical Agreement between NATO and Belgrade created a five-kilometre-wide demilitarised strip along the Kosovo boundary but inside Serbia proper. The purpose of this strip, the Ground Safety Zone (GSZ), was to prevent accidental clashes between KFOR and the Yugoslav Army.

Ethnic Albanian rebels calling themselves 'the Liberation Army of Presevo, Bujanovac and Medvedja' (UCPMB in Albanian) soon began exploiting the GSZ to launch hit-and-run attacks on Yugoslav police and other state targets. They could strike in southern Serbia, then rush back to the GSZ where Yugoslav forces could not retaliate. Uniformed men identifying themselves as partisans of the UCPMB first appeared at the funeral of two Albanian brothers in June 2000 (the brothers had allegedly been killed by Serbian security forces while driving a tractor). The UCPMB pledged to protect Albanians in the region and agitate for autonomy for the three municipalities in the region in preparation for eventual unification with Kosovo. Many also profited from collecting tolls along the boundary with Kosovo. Nebojsa Covic, who later headed the Serbian government's successful effort to negotiate a political solution to the crisis, said that between 21 June 1999 and 21 November 2000 Albanian guerrillas launched 296 attacks, killing 11 Serbs (five police and six civilians), injuring 38 (33 police, three Serb civilians and two UN staff), kidnapping two civilians and destroying a significant amount of state and private property.[17]

Serbian officials also asserted that UCPMB guerrillas were linked to the Nis bus bombing. On 18 February 2001, Serbian and Yugoslav officials held a meeting where they agreed on unspecified retaliation against the terrorists. Fortunately, the cooler heads within the new post-Milosevic regime prevailed and Covic was mandated to seek a negotiated settlement. He asked NATO to take the lead in negotiating with the rebels. Meanwhile, he put together a plan to reintegrate the Albanians of southern Serbia into state structures, demilitarising the region and creating a multi-ethnic police force. NATO, persuaded that the plan was viable and anxious to break the UCPMB's links with the simmering insurgency in Macedonia, agreed to a phased reoccupation of the Ground Safety Zone by the Yugoslav Army. In coordination with KFOR, between 14 March and 31 May the Yugoslav Army flooded the area with 15,000 troops, thus peacefully regaining effective control over 1,200 square kilometres of territory. Despite a couple of violent incidents, KFOR was pleased with the measured pace of the deployment. In Kosovo, Hashim Thaci and Ramush Haradinaj were prevailed on to express publicly their support for the peace plan. After the ceasefire, however, there remained an estimated 2,000 former Albanian militants in the area along with huge caches of arms. KFOR offered an amnesty to those who entered Kosovo, and the Serbian government offered the same for those who stayed in Serbia.

During this period, many former UCPMB fighters turned to smuggling arms from southern Serbia through Kosovo to the National Liberation Army in Macedonia.[18] Many Serbian officials believed that fighting erupted around Tetovo in Macedonia because supporters of a 'Greater Kosovo' project among the Albanian diaspora had realised that the game was up in southern Serbia and so shifted their focus to the more vulnerable state to the south. While pleased with the result that Covic and NATO achieved in southern Serbia, these Serbian officials faulted the West for responding to Albanian insurgency in an ad hoc fashion while the insurgents themselves pursued a coordinated, long-term strategy.[19]

The judiciary. Despite the introduction of international judges and prosecutors, ethnically-based bias continued to prevail in Kosovo's judicial system. Kosovo Albanian prosecutors charged Serbs more severely than their alleged crimes warranted, while Albanians were often treated more leniently. International judges were regularly outvoted on five-person panels. One KPS officer arrested a Roma man for 'war crimes' whom he had seen punch an Albanian during an argument. In another case, a local judge issued an arrest warrant for five Serbs based on a 'witness' having heard in a café that one of them was a war criminal. In yet another, the evidence providing the basis for a war crimes charge against a Serb amounted to just two pages: one was a letter from the local prosecutor requesting the arrest; the second was a form signed by the accused when he had worked as a policeman in 1999 to the father of a young Albanian who had been murdered, saying that the family could come to claim the body. When an international prosecutor questioned the charge, the local prosecutor replied that if the accused hadn't committed the crime himself he must know who had.

Quick turnover of international personnel in the Department of Justice impeded effective measures to remedy such bias. There was no institutional memory built up, no record of lessons learned, and the sparse new recruits were thrown into action with virtually no preparation. Two Canadians, one judge and one prosecutor, stepped off the plane on a Thursday and were presiding over war crimes trials the following Monday.[20] For all their Common Law expertise, the Canadians were applying a body of law — essentially the Yugoslav Criminal Code of 1989 — with which they were entirely unfamiliar. The average international judge stayed in Kosovo for just nine months.

Despite these weaknesses, UNMIK did eventually move against the systematic bias by enacting two groundbreaking reforms. The first was regulation 2000/64, the 'Assignment of International Judges and Prosecutors and Change of Venue',[21] which allowed the SRSG to petition for a particular case to be heard by a panel composed of three professional judges, with a minimum of two international judges, instead of a five-judge panel with a local majority. Unlike special panels in East Timor, Sierra Leone and Bosnia, these '64' panels were formed on an ad hoc basis and applied the same laws as other Kosovo courts. UNMIK explained the need for international majorities on these panels in terms of 'recognising that the presence of security threats may undermine the independence and impartiality of the judiciary and impede the ability of the judiciary to properly prosecute crimes which gravely undermine the peace process and the full establishment of the rule of law in Kosovo...'[22]

Nevertheless, even this measure was limited. Although the Department of Judicial Affairs tried to assign local judges to each '64' panel, in some controversial and high-profile cases of war crimes, organised crime, or terrorism, the Albanian judges either refused to sit or made excuses to avoid sitting with the internationals on the panel. Also, if a '64' panel was not assigned before a trial started, and Kosovans quickly formed a trial panel — or if a Kosovan prosecutor failed to give notice of an indictment — international oversight could be locked out. Even when a '64' panel sat on a case, its verdicts could still be overruled.[23] For example, a Kosovan prosecutor managed to abandon the case of Afrim

Zeqiri, who had been accused of raking a group of Serbs with machine gun fire. When a '64' panel granted an international prosecutor's motion to reopen the case, the all-Albanian Supreme Court trumped its decision by ordering the defendant to be released.

Gradually, UNMIK was able to inject international oversight into the judicial process. The SRSG overruled the Supreme Court's decision in the Afrim Zeqiri case. He also required any Kosovan prosecutor abandoning a case to notify the international prosecutor in that judicial district within fourteen days, to allow the international prosecutor time to file a resumption of the prosecution. By the end of 2001, there were approximately 80 ongoing court cases assigned to or selected by international judges and prosecutors; there were more than 90 by October 2002.[24] There was also a significant number of cases being investigated by the police and being supervised by the international prosecutor.[25] Meanwhile, recruitment improved, reaching a high-water mark of seventeen International Judges and eleven international prosecutors.

The focus on how to prevent local judges from issuing biased decisions distracted attention from developing the capacity of the local judiciary as a whole. According to international prosecutor Michael Hartmann, UNMIK's plan for developing local judicial capacity at this point was based on the 'tea bag theory' — that local jurists would learn to adjudicate impartially by osmosis. But because the international judges and prosecutors were all overworked, none had any time for mentoring their local counterparts. On the contrary, under the '64' system, a local judge would be lucky to get one or two war crimes trials per year — not enough to learn how to conduct them professionally. Local prosecutors never worked alongside their seasoned international counterparts. The only local jurists whose skills were dramatically improved by contact with the internationals were the defence attorneys, who spent years sparring with top international trial lawyers.

While the courts struggled to come to terms with international legal norms, the rule of law was not pervading wider Kosovo society. For example, licensing was introduced for activities like extracting gravel from river beds to make construction material, but lorries carrying gravel were almost always filled up more than the licences allowed; the few filled level, as the new law required, sold very poorly at market.[26] Standards were being set, and order was returning to Kosovo, but the two did not match up.

Parts of UNMIK, meanwhile, swung to the extreme of legal scrutiny. Even though there was not yet an effective court system in Kosovo and no outside agency seriously challenged UNMIK's actions, the mission became increasingly cautious about the legality of its own actions. The UN headquarters in New York, wary of legal challenges from Belgrade, reinforced the conservative approach. Within UNMIK, Haekkerup sought approval for every substantial move from his legal adviser, Alexander Borg-Olivier.[27]

Inter-ethnic relations

Eighteen months after the end of the war, inter-ethnic relations in Kosovo had calmed down considerably. By far the greatest improvement was the sharp decline in the inter-ethnic murder rate. In the long summer of 1999, the first four months of UNMIK and KFOR's existence, there were 348 ethnically-motivated murders; in the first four months of 2002 there were none.[28]

However, this was not so much progress for multi-ethnicity as for segregation. Serbs and Roma had become clustered and confined to their own separate and less vulnerable areas. In January and February, 2001, the last two Serbs in Podujevo, both elderly women who had been living under round-the-clock KFOR protection for two years, finally left. Their departure was accompanied by 'ugly scenes of jeering and verbal abuse'.[29]

Unlike apartheid South Africa, where the government had determined where different communities would live, in Kosovo the driving force was informal intimidation and harassment. Serbs and other threatened ethnic groups clustered together, terrified by knowledge of crimes actually committed against other Serbs and scared further by rumours that exaggerated their scale. The few Albanians remaining in Serb-dominated areas did the same. The boundaries between the two areas often became eerily quiet. Most people, who were victims of the segregation process rather than instigators of it, felt they were better off separated from other groups.

The international response to this was mixed. With multi-ethnicity so clearly an objective of the UN-led mission, there were a number of deliberate efforts to combat the drift towards segregation. Desperate to show some sign of progress on returning displaced Serbs to Kosovo, the UNHCR organised the return of 83 Serbs to the village of Osojane in August 2001. The Albanian majority in the region was exceptionally hostile to the Serbs and the returnees' safety depended on a level of protection that KFOR could not sustain for long. Several NGO officials involved in the project felt UNMIK was reckless in encouraging people to return to such a dangerous area just for the sake of political grand-standing. It was a danger acknowledged by Haekkerup: 'We do have the first returnees. We must go step by step. We must do it in accordance with the security we can provide.'[30]

One of the biggest problems for Serbs living in the enclaves south of the Ibar was not being able to travel in safety outside their small communities. KFOR and special police units escorted Serbs and members of other minorities in protective convoys. Albanian employees travelling to the courthouse in North Mitrovica, for example, were transported to work in armoured personnel carriers. Throwing stones at the military vehicles became a cruel local sport, made only more challenging by the presence of KFOR foot soldiers in the best places to throw from, and the high speed of the convoy.[31] In less hostile places, Serbs rode in normal vehicles, with a military escort driving in front or behind.

KFOR generally resisted escorts while UNMIK pushed for more. Sometimes they merely highlighted the fact that minorities were present, and that they were so vulnerable that they needed extreme levels of military protection. One military adviser considered them counterproductive: 'We're trying to normalise Kosovo; repeated requests from UNMIK for special protection are a step backwards.'[32]

In another way, the escorting system took responsibility away from internationals for trying to overcome the segregation. If an escort was needed but not available (often they took several days and much paperwork to prepare), this became an excuse for allowing a meeting to be mono-ethnic.

Different nations took different approaches to the problem of segregation. In the American-led sector, around Gnjilane in the east of Kosovo, an area with relatively modest levels of violence before the bombing campaign, KFOR actively tried to encourage interaction between Serbs and Albanians. Special shopping days were organised to enable the Serb minorities, generally living in isolated rural areas, to enter the Albanian-dominated town centre. An EU development expert working in the town at the time said of the scheme, 'It didn't really make Gnjilane multi-ethnic, but it was good. It allowed the Serbs to shop, and it helped the shopkeepers. It was a good effort.'[33]

In northern Kosovo, which had seen much harsher conflict, French forces were much more complicit in the segregation process. In an effort to instil order, reduce possibilities for attacks, and safeguard their own troops (French KFOR suffered more attacks than other brigades in the first two years after the war), the two main communities were kept apart. The result of virtually complete segregation was that the number of inter-ethnic attacks fell at a faster rate than in other areas, but the segregation was almost total.

Political developments generally made little impact on this picture. At least one of the deputies of each municipal assembly president (mayor) was supposed to be a member of a different ethnic group, but international monitors often had to exert strong pressure to compel compliance with the rule. When an international official prevailed, the small victory was mainly symbolic: Serbs and their interests hardly figured in the decisions of Albanian-majority municipalities.[34]

The Provisional Institutions of Self Government, which came into being from the middle of 2001 onwards, were all based in Pristina. Given that Pristina had been virtually cleansed of non-Albanians, this further exacerbated the problem of creating a multi-ethnic Kosovo. A contemporary OSCE report said that only 2.3 per cent of civil servants in Kosovo were from ethnic minorities. Procurement and other subcontractors were almost always from the Pristina area, reinforcing the segregation still further. The international administration had spawned institutions which were retarding its primary objective of ethnic integration.

Much of the most effective ethnic cleansing was achieved without actual acts of violence or even overt acts of coercion. UNMIK observed that when Albanians managed to buy one or two pieces of property in an area that had previously been homogeneously Serb, further property sales from Serbs to Albanians tended to follow in a torrent. Closer scrutiny revealed that many of those who sold had done so only under physical intimidation and threats. 'When you visited these places,' said Tania Mechlenborg, a UN employee who worked on the issue, 'you just knew something had to be done. The Albanians had a clear strategy of buying out the Serbs.' In an attempt to stem this practice, Haekkerup signed Regulation 2001/17, which required the sale of property in predominantly minority areas to be vetted by the local municipal administrator before finally being approved by the local court. 'It didn't work perfectly, but it did slow down the process,' said Mechlenborg. 'It meant people who were facing huge pressure, sometimes physical pressure, who previously thought they had no option but to sell, had something to turn to.'[35]

After Michael Steiner arrived in February 2002 he made it clear to Albanian leaders that the parlous condition of Kosovo's Serbs was

the greatest obstacle to the territory's majority realising its ambition
— independence. Prime Minister Bajram Rexhepi, who had gained experience with interethnic dialogue after the war as mayor of Mitrovica,
made the boldest overtures. Rexhepi visited the Serb enclave of Strpce,
delivered a speech in Serbian at the opening of a youth centre in the
Serb enclave of Kamenica and attended Easter services at the Serbian
Orthodox Patriarchate in Pec. Ordinary Albanians were sceptical of
such outreach efforts. Several interviewed by Kosovo's prime broadcaster, RTK, expressed disapproval of the PM's Easter visit.[36]

There may have been an opportunity to change the zero-sum logic
that plagued relations between Serbs and Albanians, but if so, it was
squandered. The downfall and subsequent arrest, extradition and trial
of Milosevic, a long process that began in October 2000 and ran for
many months, could have been cathartic for inter-ethnic relations in
Kosovo. Milosevic personified the abuse and oppression of the 1990s;
his trial could have facilitated reconciliation between Kosovo Albanians and Serbs. But the way it was handled by Serbs, Albanians and
internationals robbed the occasion of any healing properties. The new
Belgrade regime, worried about a backlash from Milosevic supporters and its own internal divisions, was tardy in deporting the fallen
tyrant. No words of humility or regret trickled towards the Kosovo
Albanians. The Kosovo Albanians, meanwhile, were angry that the
whole process had taken so long. 'Thank you — who's next?' was
the attitude of one very senior Kosovo Albanian politician.[37] The international community, meanwhile, failed to force contrition from
the Serbs and acceptance from the Albanians. 'Something went wrong
with Belgrade,' said EU Pillar chief Andy Bearpark. 'Once the regime
changed in October 2000, we should have been able to get them be-
having better towards Kosovo than they did.'[38] Consequently, many
Kosovo Albanians simply transferred their hostility to Milosevic's successors. The new leaders in Belgrade often found it easier to reinforce

the idea of Serbs as victims than to distance themselves entirely from the failed past of Milosevic.

When electoral defeat and well-orchestrated street demonstrations finally forced Slobodan Milosevic from power in October 2000, Kosovo lost perhaps its most valuable political card. Very few Albanians voted in the election that precipitated Milosevic's downfall — polling stations were not organised in their areas. Some cynics speculated that if Albanians had voted, they would have supported Milosevic to ensure that Serbia remained isolated. More thoughtful Albanian leaders acknowledged that Kosovo was better off with Vojislav Kostunica as Serbia's president, but many also worried that he was as nationalistic as Milosevic himself while being much more popular among the Western powers. The ICG warned, 'Kosovo Albanians were willing to be treated as wards of the international community as long as Belgrade was an international pariah. As Belgrade becomes an accepted member of the international community, Kosovo Albanians will also demand a seat at the table.'[39]

The fall of Milosevic in October 2000 at first made many hard-line Serbs more receptive to UNMIK. Gang leader Milan Ivanovic, one of the hard men of Mitrovica, feigned contrition about his obstructive behaviour. He called a meeting of international donors, and came close to apologising for the vandalism of heating equipment installed in the North Mitrovica hospital the previous winter by a French NGO.[40] However, as the months moved on, he reverted to his previous recalcitrant stance. In April 2002, he allegedly played a leading role in riots during which a grenade was thrown, injuring twenty-two Polish troops.

Milan Ivanovic's equivocal and wavering relationship with UNMIK was typical of the Serbs at this time. They were split fairly evenly between those who believed they should participate politically in the emerging institutions to fight their case from within, and those who favoured boycott and abstentionism. The most widely accepted compromise was to accept places in the new institutions, but frequently not attend, in protest at one or other recent event.

Political developments

While struggling to assert a minimum of authority in the north, UNMIK was attempting to create new political structures that involved local leaders in decision-making without giving them much actual authority. The first such structure, the Interim Administrative Council (IAC), included the two leading Albanian politicians, Rugova and Thaci, along with the Serb representative, Rada Trajkovic, who sometimes boycotted. From late 2000 they were joined by AAK leader Ramush Haradinaj, whose party had done well in the first local elections. The body did little to cut across any of the three divisions that bedevilled Kosovo's political development: local-international, Serb-Albanian and LDK-PDK.[41] Neither locals nor internationals tended to have much influence on the actions of the other; UNMIK didn't push interethnic collaboration aggressively, partly out of fear of creating political martyrs in the eyes of a population that bridled under outside control. Nevertheless, UNMIK officials regarded the very existence of the IAC as an achievement. 'You have to remember how difficult it was at that time,' recounted EU Pillar Chief, Andy Bearpark. 'Rugova and Thaci especially — getting them into the same room was serious progress.'[42]

In parallel with the IAC, 36 members of the Kosovo Transitional Council discussed more general issues in a televised discussion forum. As with the IAC, the members of the KTC were appointed in line with their perceived electoral strength. It was a powerless talking shop but also a precursor to properly elected institutions.

In 2001, these ad hoc bodies were superseded by the much more formal arrangements set out in the Constitutional Framework. This was a blueprint for political structures which gave elected local politicians significant powers — although the internationals kept control of the most sensitive areas, including security, most economic policy, and 'external relations' (what would be called foreign relations if Kosovo were a sovereign state).

The Constitutional Framework was a serious undertaking. The meetings in which it was drafted stretched over four months. A Dutch constitutional expert, Johan van Lamoen, who had drafted a similar document for the UN mission in East Timor, was flown in specially for the purpose. Kosovo Serbs, fearing it would be a stepping stone to independence, boycotted the drafting process. Kosovo Albanians, by contrast, intent on securing as many powers as possible, participated intensively in the drafting process and succeeded in generating a much longer and more detailed document than international officials had originally envisaged.[43]

The Constitutional Framework blueprint provided for a 120-seat Assembly of which 100 seats would be based on the fraction of the vote won by each party or coalition — roughly one seat for each one per cent of the popular vote. Another twenty seats would be set aside for minorities, ten for Serbs and ten for Kosovo's other ethnic communities (Roma, Ashkali, Egyptians, Turks, Bosniaks and Gorani). For reasons that would become clear later, Albanians did not raise strong objections to this positive discrimination in minorities' favour.

Albanians were, however, left dissatisfied with the circumscription of their authority and various features of the electoral system that tended to undermine traditional sources of power. The name of the document itself reflects a compromise in the face of effective Albanian lobbying. UNMIK had originally planned to call it simply 'the legal framework'. Albanian participants in the drafting sessions pushed for the political blueprint to be called a 'constitution', reasoning that Kosovo had already had a constitution of its own under the Yugoslav constitution of 1974 and anything less would represent a step backwards. As this appeared to conform too closely to a feature of statehood, which was proscribed by 1244, UNMIK settled instead on the compromise name 'Constitutional

Framework'. Albanian representatives pushed for competencies in the field of foreign affairs, but UNMIK rejected this out of hand as incompatible with its obligation not to prejudge Kosovo's final status.

All three major Albanian political parties preferred a system of multiple electoral districts so that those elected to the Assembly would represent local constituencies. The OSCE, which was responsible for organising elections, opted instead for treating all of Kosovo as a single electoral district, meaning that representatives would be elected on the basis of their party's performance throughout Kosovo. Although the OSCE's main argument for the single district was that it was much simpler to organise, it had the added value of deterring the establishment of local political fiefdoms.

Another controversial feature was the requirement that every third candidate in the top two thirds of each party's list must be female. To prevent voters from removing women from the lists, as had occurred during the municipal elections, the candidate lists were closed, so voters could not pick and choose candidates from the party list. Some Albanian politicians complained that the closed list system infringed their democratic prerogatives, and that the quota on women candidates held Kosovo to a higher standard than virtually any Western country (which, with the exception of New Zealand and some Scandinavian countries, was true).

The closed list system also gave party leaders great power: they alone (or their hand-picked apparatchiks) decided who appeared towards the top of the list, and were therefore virtually guaranteed to be elected. Party leaders could push opponents towards the bottom, and keep them out of the Assembly. The closed list system, together with Kosovo being treated as a single electoral constituency, meant that people elected to the Assembly were answerable only to their party leadership. They had virtually no incentive to interact with ordinary voters, address their concerns or help them with real day-to-day problems. The hope was that this would enable the party leaderships to push through a historic compromise, perhaps a grand accommodation between Albanians and Serbs, relatively safe from internal party criticism. The danger was that politics in Kosovo would become introspective, and detached from the concerns of real people.

Though the Constitutional Framework provided for elections to create a new Assembly with nine ministries responsible for most aspects of internal affairs, it did not endow its democratically members with ultimate authority in any area. On the contrary, its preamble reasserts the primacy of 1244 and also affirms that 'the exercise of the responsibilities of the Provisional Institutions of Self-Government [PISG] in Kosovo shall not in any way affect or diminish the ultimate authority of the SRSG for the implementation of UNSCR 1244'. Several independent international observers concluded that the new Assembly's authority was 'in fact very limited'.[44]

The validity of this interpretation depends on what one means by 'authority'. True, the Assembly could always be overruled by the SRSG. But the SRSG was under strong pressure from New York to avoid interfering in the affairs of the PISG except where they impinged on security, interethnic relations or Kosovo's political status. The international community had a strong interest in seeing the PISG succeed.

Nevertheless, tensions between UNMIK and the PISG were inevitable because most of the Albanians' political interests lay in the restricted areas. Kosovo's political leaders might have applied themselves energetically to the areas for which the Constitutional Framework gave them responsibility, including education, trade, public services, finances, health and environment, social welfare, agriculture and rural development. But these substantive areas of public policy — the bread and butter issues of Western politicians — were not what got Albanian leaders up in the morning.

Haekkerup signed the Constitutional Framework into law on 15 May 2001. Elections to the new bodies took place on 17 November. The election campaign itself had a dissonant, unreal quality as every party campaigned on promises which the election would never allow them to fulfil. Although the winner might be able to change education, revolutionise healthcare, or dramatically improve Kosovo's third-world transport system, none of these issues was discussed during the campaign. The three main Kosovo-Albanian parties, each dominated by the personality of its leader, invested little energy in developing a distinctive political agenda. Instead, they all struck nuanced positions on how they would pursue the priority that had dominated Kosovo Albanian politics for over a decade: independence.

This was demonstrated in all three main parties' strategies for attracting voters, which surpassed the superficiality of some of the most banal election campaigns in countries more weary of democracy. The LDK launched its campaign with a meeting in the sports hall in Pristina which resembled a folk festival more than a political rally, and organised demonstrations of traditional Kosovo Albanian dances on Mother Teresa Street running through the city centre. One international passer-by likened the display to the Eurovision song contest. At a rally in Klina, Rugova stated the party's core position: 'As you know, we declared independence in 1991 and we have built our state for more than ten years. Therefore we ask for the official recognition of Kosovo's independence by the United States, the EU and the international community.'[45]

The PDK and AAK emphasised their war records, often in rallies where AK-47s were enthusiastically fired off into the sky. Hashim Thaci's PDK had seemed to hold an enormous advantage over its rivals when it seized control of the administrations of all twenty-six Albanian-majority municipalities in the chaotic months after the war. The PDK's high exposure became a huge political liability when many Albanians came to blame chaos, crime and corruption that marked this period. After its disappointing results in the municipal elections, the party had tried to improve its image, most notably by recruiting Florina Brovina, a paediatrician, poet, former political prisoner and women's rights campaigner, as its presidential candidate. The PDK was most critical of the Constitutional Framework, which Thaci argued 'will hold hostage the aim of the people of Kosovo, which is political independence.'

Ramush Haradinaj, leader of the AAK, distinguished himself from Thaci's PDK by not only avoiding political issues like his rivals but actually declaring his alliance party to be 'above politics'. Under the slogan 'Neither Left nor Right but Straight Ahead', the AAK presented itself as more pragmatic than its rivals. As the PDK had recruited Florina Brovina, the AAK recruited a highly respected former Communist official, Mahmut Bakalli. Ramush Haradinaj told a rally: 'If anyone asks you why you think that the AAK is the best, I would ask you not to say that we are patriots because we are all patriots and we all love Kosovo. Say that the AAK works more than other parties, that AAK members wake up earlier than members of other parties and that they will do more for you than the others. I can say that personally I work more than Thaci and Rugova.'[46] The AAK was sanctioned by the Election Complaints and Appeals Commission because one of its members in Decani was found to have intimidated LDK officials.

Apart from the mammoth logistical job of organising the elections, which was successfully managed by the OSCE, the greatest part of UN-MIK's efforts in connection with the election was devoted to trying to persuade Serbs to participate. Since UNMIK understood that Serbs in Kosovo still for the most part took their cues from Belgrade, it concentrated on securing the encouragement from the Serbian government necessary for Kosovo Serbs to stand for office and to vote.

The Kosovo Serbs had two principal concerns about participating in the elections. Some Serbs worried that participating in the elections would imply that their physical security and freedom of movement were less restricted than they felt them to be. They also worried that their involvement would confer greater legitimacy on the PISG and on the campaign for independence that the new bodies would inevitably wage. For Serbs living in the areas north of the Ibar where they constituted the overwhelming majority, these two arguments carried the day. Serbs living in isolated enclaves elsewhere in Kosovo, however, had much stronger incentives to find a way to work with UNMIK and the Albanian majority. Their leaders, Bishop Artemije and Rada Trajkovic, recognised that by not participating they would effectively marginalise themselves and lose what little power they had to help shape Kosovo's future.

For politicians in Belgrade, Kosovo was an issue that could hurt them if mishandled but with which they couldn't expect to score any points with voters in Serbia. Serbian Prime Minister Zoran Djindjic delegated responsibility for Kosovo to Nebojsa Covic, a popular former mayor of Belgrade. Many saw the assignment as a poisoned chalice. Much as Churchill declared that he hadn't become His Majesty's first minister in order to preside over the dissolution of the British Empire, Covic felt a political imperative to at least create the appearance of doing something other than presiding over the steady erosion of Serbian authority in Kosovo. Vojislav Kostunica, the newly elected President, had to avoid alienating nationalists among the ranks of his own Democratic Party of Serbia (DSS) or the hardline nationalists among the Serbs in Kosovo. All this meant that UNMIK had to create a cover that would allow Covic and Kostunica to claim that they had wrung some concessions from Haekkerup in exchange for their support for Serb participation in the elections.

The cover was duly produced in the form of 'the Common Document', which Haekkerup and Covic signed in Belgrade on 5 November, less than two weeks before the crucial vote. The document affirmed that the new institutions would have no authority to take any steps towards resolving Kosovo's final status. It also committed UNMIK to work to improve the lot of Kosovo Serbs and established 'a High-Level Working Group' under the SRSG to bring together officials from Belgrade, UNMIK and the PISG to discuss minority issues. Covic immediately heralded the document as an enormous achievement of Serbian diplomacy that would dramatically increase Belgrade's leverage in Kosovo.

With equal predictability, Kosovo Albanian leaders were outraged. The PDK and AAK declared that they wouldn't recognise the new working group. Rugova and Haradinaj boycotted the 6 November meeting of the Interim Administrative Council in protest. Thaci appeared at the meeting only to denounce the agreement and left.

In reality, the Common Document was nothing but a reaffirmation of 1244 and UNMIK's responsibilities toward the Serb community. The 'High-Level Working Group' was just a fancy name for meetings that would naturally take place now that Milosevic had been replaced by more moderate and pragmatic leaders. Albanians were eventually mollified by statements to this effect by UNMIK officials and a commentary in *Koha Ditore*.[47] But the incident illustrated UNMIK's challenge in having to deal with two communities who each considered any gain for the other as automatically implying a loss for itself. It also illustrated how easily Serbian officials could wind up Albanians, even though Belgrade had no real power.

The Kosovo Serb candidates stood as a single electoral block, Coalition Return, but barely campaigned. Although those Serb leaders who opposed participation muted their criticism in public following Kostunica's pronouncement that Kosovo Serbs should participate, there were many reports of Coalition Return supporters being harassed as they worked to turn out Serb voters. To the Serbs' credit, they did base their coalition around a policy issue: the return of displaced people. But they had little idea of how to actually achieve this, other than by banging the table and maintaining strong links to Belgrade.

With the go-ahead from Belgrade coming so late and mixed signals from local leaders, the Serb participation rate was well below that of the Albanian majority. A high turnout could have won Coalition Return, the single Serb entity fielding candidates, 15 seats in the new Assembly which, alongside the ten seats set aside by the Constitutional Framework as a safeguard for minority rights, would have made it the second largest party in parliament. In the event, a turnout of about 46 per cent in Serb areas meant that Coalition Return won only eight seats in addition to the ten set aside.

Across Kosovo, the overall turnout rate was 64 per cent — a large drop from the 78 per cent participation in the municipal polls in 2000. But because many more people registered for the Kosovo-wide vote, including the Serbs, the lower percentage nevertheless reflected a higher absolute number of voters. Overall, neither community saw the elections for what they could have been: a chance to choose a governing administration for Kosovo. Instead, both regarded the polls solely as an incremental step towards resolving Kosovo's final status.

When the votes were counted, the LDK was the single largest party in the Assembly, with 47 out of 120 seats. But this was well short of the 61 seats needed to form a government. The PDK and AAK finished with 24 and eight seats respectively. Although their share of the vote was about the same as in the municipal elections, which disappointed both, the two KLA parties gained at the LDK's expense. While the PDK had been punished in the municipal elections for its perceived links to thuggery and its usurpation of municipal administrations in the chaotic months after the war, a year later some voters withdrew their support from the LDK because it was perceived as being passive and complaisant.

There were various possibilities for a coalition: with the small AAK, and some of the smaller parties, the LDK could have led a majority in the Assembly, but the AAK leader, former KLA war hero Ramush Haradinaj, refused to go into government without the PDK. Stalemate persisted for three months, made worse by the sudden and unexplained departure of SRSG Hans Haekerrup in the last week of 2001.

UNMIK faced a dilemma: how to give the parties enough direction to ensure an effective government without being so heavy handed that Kosovo political leaders could avoid hard choices and later blame the mission for its own shortcomings. In the end, it was the diplomatic of-fices, principally the US Office backed up by the rest of the Quint (UK, France, Germany and Italy), that brokered a coalition agreement.

Some candidates for high office were clearly unsuitable: the leader of Kosovo's new government had to be both 'clean and competent'. This stipulation ruled out Thaci's favoured candidate, Fatmir Limaj, who was later indicted by the war crimes tribunal in The Hague. (Thaci proposed the name, and Steiner rebuffed him with a theatrically delivered 'Never!') The PDK refused to line up behind the veteran LDK leader, Ibrahim Rugova. A deal finally was settled at the end of February 2002 — an all-party coalition with Rugova as President and the PDK's Bajram Rexhepi as Prime Minister. Ironically, this unity government left the Kosovo Albanians as divided as ever. Nobody had the mandate needed to drag the Kosovo Albanians towards a workable compromise final settlement. Rugova assumed a shrunken presidency, having bartered away many of his most important presidential duties in return for the position itself. Rexhepi, a former surgeon from Mitrovica who had little popular following, became a capable and energetic prime minister. But Rexhepi knew his powers were also limited by his own political party. The PDK allowed the international community to shoe-horn him into the top post, but Thaci remained firmly in control.

As it created increasingly substantial self-governing institutions, UNMIK also evolved. The dynamic structures born under Kouchner gradually calcified into much more static fiefdoms. As the average length of service for staff increased, employees became more familiar with the region, but the intensity of work slackened. Haekerrup insisted on being in the office no longer than 9am to 6pm[48] (in contrast with the round-the-clock commitment of Kouchner). The passion and morale of other staff began to slip. Many people who had been attracted to Kosovo by idealism were encouraged to stay by the lure of money. It is telling that the four UN officials killed in Baghdad in August 2003 who had previously worked in Kosovo — Jean Selim, Fiona Watson, Nadia Younes and Sergio Vieira de Mello — had all served UNMIK in its first months. Under Haekkerup, Kosovo had become too pedestrian for them.

As the political dust began to settle in Kosovo, it became clear that some of UNMIK's problems were a result of structural deficiencies. Many functions were duplicated, which lead to turf wars and confusion. For example, in an effort to compensate for the EU Pillar's lack of manpower in its first year, USAID had seconded many staff to work for the institution, but without relinquishing line management of them. Kouchner had also set up his own 'Economic Policy Office'. This meant that some early decisions regarding the economy were being made without coordination in three places — USAID, the EU and the SRSG's Office. There were other overlaps in UNMIK's structure: the distinction between the office of the UN Chief of Staff and the SRSG's office was often blurred. Both the OSCE and the UN had established their own departments for monitoring the media and dealing with political parties. UN regional administrators had the trappings of authority but little influence on policy making in Pristina. Most critically, they lacked the wherewithal to make good on promises made to local people.

There also remained questions about the mission's ultimate political master. 'It still wasn't clear who UNMIK was accountable to,' explained Andy Bearpark. 'The UN Security Council - yes - but also the UN Department of Peacekeeping Operations? The UN Department of Political Affairs? The Contact Group? The [European] Commission?'[49] All of these were offering advice to the mission and much of it was contradictory.

In 2001 UNMIK often resorted to extralegal executive action to clear away obstacles. By the middle of 2002, the use of such measures had become much rarer. There were still a few notable examples, such as the elite unit of Irish KFOR, sent in at night to retrieve garbage disposal lorries from striking workers near Pristina. The soldiers managed to 'hotwire' many of the vehicles and drive them away before the strikers could react.[50] But generally, a legal route was preferred.

UNMIK's emphasis had shifted from ad hoc problem-solving to creating more durable policies. A major conference on combating cigarette

smuggling held in May 2002, for example, focused on legal memoranda
and cross-border cooperation rather than simple direct action as the
most effective means of enforcement. The reason for this shift was
partly institutional, partly psychological. As KFOR deliberately scaled
back its operations, it became increasingly reluctant to help with civilian
administration. The non-military administration, both international and
local, was far less effective at removing obstacles from its path. 'KFOR
know how to get things done — they don't always think through the
consequences, but they do it. We are usually better at the thinking part,
but not so good at actually doing it,' acknowledged Bearpark.[51]

Hearts and minds

As the UN mission matured, it found that most of the easy problems
had already been cherry-picked. This was not driven by imprudence on
the part of the first generation of international officials. Rather, the pre-
dilection to focus on relatively apolitical humanitarian crises emerged
from the perennial problem, common to all organisations from private
corporations to governments, of allowing the *urgent* to overtake the
important. The relatively straightforward business of humanitarian relief
had been virtually completed; the international administration was fully
established. What then? Issues like the *de facto* division of Mitrovica,
growing Albanian hostility to UNMIK, how to rein in the former KLA,
and relations with Belgrade were much more difficult than providing
emergency shelter had been in the first year. The common feature of
these post-emergency priorities was that they were not merely logistical tasks, but political challenges that involved persuading local people
to change their behaviour.

Faced with harder problems, UNMIK's success rate naturally began
to fall. To the consternation of the wider international community,
which was bankrolling the exercise, performance was falling while
the resources being invested were at a maximum. Then the terrorist

attacks of September 11 occurred, adding a host of new contestants to what SRSG Michael Steiner would later call 'the international beauty contest'.

UNMIK's impotence in the face of local opposition was made clear when Steiner, immediately after taking the reins as SRSG early in 2002, determined to do something to clean up Kosovo. Rubbish had been a serious problem in Kosovo since the war, when the previous system of garbage removal had broken down. Many Kosovans simply left rubbish in the streets. Every spring, as the winter snows melted, large mounds of festering waste created a terrible smell and led to a few isolated deaths caused by endemic diseases thriving on the poor hygiene. Efforts to tackle the rubbish problem were not new: there had already been a 'rubbish task force' in Kouchner's time, and the municipal authorities elected in October 2000 were meant to have addressed the issue (although they did not have direct control of the new waste management firms).

Steiner tried to enlist senior local politicians to help his drive to clean up Kosovo, but they declined. After years of engagement in a life-and-death struggle of national wills, Kosovo politicians didn't think of politics in terms of helping their constituents with such quotidian problems as getting rid of garbage. Their constituents didn't realise they had a right to demand such service from their elected representatives, and in any case, garbage collection was low on their long list of priorities.[52]

UNMIK approached international donors for money to help with a clean-up, but none had any money which could be mobilised in the timeline required (most donor funds take at least twelve months to allocate, often longer). KFOR, haunted by the spectre of 'mission creep', refused to take part. Hence, the new SRSG, at the height of his powers, determined to tackle a high-profile and symbolically significant issue, could mobilise neither local nor international support for his initiative. In the end, the best that could be managed was to take the rubbish collection machines from Gjilan and move them to Pristina for four weeks. The SRSG's overwhelming legal authority barely enabled him to keep the streets clean. As with so many problems in this part of the world, Pristina could only be cleaned at the expense of another city.[53]

The increasingly apparent gap between the public's expectations and realities on the ground in all spheres undermined UNMIK's credibility. Even as UNMIK's logistical ability finally started to reach a peak some two or three years after the beginning of the mission, its moral author ity was already declining. Many Kosovo Albanians grumbled that the UN mission had done little for them, often underestimating the results that actually had been achieved or how much work was required to accomplish small steps because of the intransigence of their own leaders. Also, as Kosovo Albanians began to settle down to their rebuilt homes, their psychology became less pliable. They were less receptive to persuasion and publicity. Hostile attitudes to Serbs, instead of fading, began to harden.

Local media continued to foster antipathy against Serbs and rival political parties. As with local judges who faced intense pressures from their community to base their decisions on ethnic loyalties, the local media reflected the agendas of their owners and the prejudices of their audiences. This was particularly marked in coverage of the fall of President Milosevic. The day before Milosevic fell, a senior PDK official said: 'No matter which party wins in Serbia, it will be a matter of complete indifference to Kosovo.'[54] RTK planned not to cover Milosevic's fall until urged to by a foreign adviser. Even so, it still resisted a live interview with Kostunica, at time when Kostunica was in huge demand by the international media. All prominent politicians other than Ramush Haradinaj refused to appear on TV to discuss events in Belgrade. On the same day the LDK newspaper, *Bota Sot*, refused to mention the democratic revolution that was taking place in Serbia, instead running on its front page a tribute to Albanian martyr Adem Jashari, who had died more than two years before.[55]

UNMIK's biggest concern was the need to prevent hate speech, and for this it created the Temporary Media Commissioner (TMC). The

TMC was granted the authority to impose fines on newspapers and broadcasters who it decided had incited violence.[56] But in evaluating complaints, the TMC applied a very restrictive definition of hate speech. Although many articles published by print media in Kosovo incited hate and intolerance, and would normally be considered 'hate-full', they did not necessarily amount to 'hate speech' in a strictly legal sense. Legally-defined 'hate speech', punishable by up to ten years in prison, had to be 'hatred, discord or intolerance... publicly incited or publicly spread... between national, racial, religious, ethnic or other such groups living in Kosovo... likely to disturb public order.'[57] Of the fourteen complaints formally made against various media organs in 2002, the TMC decided that none had fulfilled all these criteria. The TMC restricted itself to cases against newspapers which it believed had violated sections of the Code of Conduct[58] designed to prevent vigilante journalism, a much less serious offence.[59]

The TMC tried to tackle articles like the piece entitled 'The Baton Haxhiu syndrome', which appeared in *Bota Sot* on 18 April 2002. It accused the respected editor of the *Koha Ditore* newspaper of 'acting in accordance with orders he received from the UDB [Serbian Secret Service], ... he produced only poison against his colleagues and Albanian politicians, causing fear and threats.' The article went on to say: 'Baton Haxhiu, even when the Serb regime left Kosovo, continued to cut Turkish heads with the sword of Stanisic.'[60] Also in April 2002, *Bota Sot* published a slightly less extreme diatribe against Blerim Shala, the editor of *Zeri* newspaper, entitled 'Miserable People of Journalism — Today's Patriots'. It said: 'These miserable people of journalism who, today, with their false "patriotism" pretend to be "more Catholic than the Pope" in Albanian opinion they are known as people who have always been in the service of anti-national forces.' It goes on to say: 'If there were any court institution in Kosovo, both these journalist 'patriots' should have provided explanations but also they should have been imprisoned, for all their anti-national injustices that they committed while cooperating with the Serb regime of Belgrade during their (sic) occupation of Kosovo.'[61] The TMC tried to sanction *Bota Sot* for these remarks. But internal obstacles within the OSCE and UNMIK, including exaggerated caution on the part of UNMIK's Office of the Legal Advisor, meant that three years into the protectorate there was still no mechanism for enforcing the sanctions the TMC imposed. 'Without the possibility of enforcing decisions, the law is ineffective and the institution loses credibility,' stated the TMC's annual report.

Despite the expenditure of considerable energy and even innovative thinking, the regulation and cultivation of independent media continued to fall short of expectations. Largely unreconstructed, the media further distorted and magnified actual failings of the protectorate. The Temporary Media Commissioner's annual report for 2002 noted matter-of-factly:

1. The Kosovo press is extremely politicised and doesn't hesitate to target individuals with violent campaigns, oblivious of their rights to privacy and safety;

2. Violence continues to affect the society, in a post-conflict climate of reprisal and settling of old scores;

3. The court system has not matured as fast as hoped and there is still no civil law on defamation;

4. Self-regulation of the press does not exist, despite the recent formation of a Professional Association of Journalists; the Association has not adopted its own code of ethics yet.[62]

The economy

Two years after the war, Kosovo's economy was growing — and being distorted — at an extraordinary rate. The rapid influx of thousands of international employees, most of whom were being paid at least fifty times the average Kosovan wage, provided a huge boost to certain sectors of the economy — particularly restaurants, bars and bootleg CD sellers. Property prices became inflated by the rents offered by internationals. On top of this, donors and the diaspora were pumping millions of euros into a tiny economy.

Predictably, this infusion of cash created an economic bubble. Many Kosovans flocked to Pristina, looking for work or 'investment opportunities'. According to one estimate in 2001, the population of the city had trebled since 1998. The distorted prices for property provided opportunities for some, but a housing problem for many. Lots of Kosovo families rented out apartments or rooms and squeezed up into the remaining space. Many of these people had been oppressed by the Serbs during the 1990s. Now they found themselves compressed by their rescuers. Many villages and distant towns, meanwhile, remained practically unchanged.

Growth rates well in excess of 10 per cent per year were reported. The IMF estimated growth in 2001 (the peak year) to be 14 per cent. This was one of the most impressive growth rates in the world, but it was not real growth; the surge in activity was merely bringing Kosovo back to its level before the war — when it was already the poorest part of Yugoslavia.

Poverty remained widespread. Average income per person was barely $3 a day — just three times the internationally recognised level of absolute poverty. A majority of people, concentrated in the poorer areas, were below this level. A World Bank survey living standards found that '40% of the population is poor and 12% extremely poor'.[63]

Bringing Kosovo above pre-war levels of development required a number of serious changes. The workforce needed new skills, the infrastructure needed to be revamped, and systems for reassuring investors that their money would be recoverable had to be put in place.

Some of these developmental leaps could be kick-started by the surge of donor money. By the end of 2001, donors had pledged about $2 billion for budget support, reconstruction and recovery activities, and already committed about nine-tenths of it. This was an extraordinary amount relative to Kosovo's size: more than one thousand dollars for every man, woman and child.

Tax and Customs officers were employed, and taxes gradually introduced, but revenue collection was hindered by the widespread evasion of taxes and utility bills. Many Kosovans had refused to pay bills under Milosevic as an act of civil disobedience, or because they were simply too poor to do so. During 1999 and 2000, when donor money paid for everything, the habit of paying taxes and utility bills broke down even further. By the time bill collection restarted, the stigma conventionally associated with not paying had disappeared entirely.

The process of re-establishing a bill-paying culture was made particular difficult with respect to electricity bills because of the problem of arrears, and incompetence among the bill collectors. In Peje, for example, a bill for 36,000 euros, stretching back three years to previous occupiers of a property, was written out in pencil. When the customer refused to pay, he was cut off.[64] Incidents like this were common. Ethnic minorities, concentrated in poorer villages, were generally less able to pay electricity bills, and also less likely to receive favours from the bill collectors. But they often played up the issue to make a wider political point: some Serb vigilantes destroyed payment meters and refused to allow bill collectors to enter their village.

Electricity bills were not the only economic issues to exacerbate inter-ethnic tensions. Following the demise of the Milosevic regime, the international community removed economic sanctions from Serbia. This allowed lorries to cross into Kosovo from the north, bypassing the Customs checkpoints on the border with Macedonia. The resulting hemorrhage of Customs revenue threatened to undermine the whole budget.

UNMIK resolved to establish tax points along the boundary with Serbia proper to stop the tax evaders. This move sparked a massive uproar within the Serb community, who again felt penalised and threatened a campaign of civil disobedience. Previously, many Serbs in the north had been paying taxes to Belgrade, and receiving generous subsidies in return; they now feared they would be taxed twice. Some Serb political leaders, despite being bitterly opposed to all things Albanian in public, were secretly conspiring with Albanians to evade the tariffs. Smuggling was profitable. There was also a symbolic dimension: since 'Customs' are collected on international borders, collecting them on the boundary between Kosovo and Serbia-proper seemed tantamount to making Kosovo independent by stealth.

In the face of Serb anger, UNMIK hesitated. Erecting the tax points was delayed, while an extensive publicity campaign was undertaken. Sensing weakness, and advised by some international staff members working in the area that the Customs points would not be introduced if they protested fiercely enough, the Serbs rioted.[65] Grenades were thrown at tanks (one bounced off back towards the person who threw it, blowing off his foot). One elderly Serb woman died from a heart attack probably triggered by the violence. Barricades were erected on the main routes into north Mitrovica. International staff were evacuated. Customs points were eventually introduced at Easter. the most important Orthodox holiday, a provocation that further fuelled the riots.

The tense situation persisted for several weeks, and the mission became divided over the issue. The EU Pillar, which had pioneered the policy to protect the budget, remained in favour. Many in the UN argued that the policy was unfair to Serbs, who were generally poorer and benefited less from the Customs revenues than Kosovo Albanians. French KFOR, who were responsible for security in the area, said the Customs points made their work impossible and strongly favoured conciliating the demonstrators — a view backed by the French Foreign Ministry.

The Serb blockade of the routes north out of Kosovo coincided with the insurgency in northern Macedonia. In early March 2001, the Skopje government had closed the border with Kosovo, which disrupted imports. Now, with the insurgency in Macedonia more violent, they threatened to close the southern border again. There was a real prospect of Kosovo becoming completely isolated.

Various contingencies were investigated — if the worst happened, could food be airlifted into Kosovo? Could the tracks into Albania be widened to allow them to support heavy traffic? Meanwhile, staff within UNMIK calculated how many days' supply they had left of various vital commodities — particularly worrying was the supply of chlorine. The most important resources were stockpiled, and, to prevent panic buying, little was said publicly about the potential crisis.

In the end, high-level diplomatic pressure on the Skopje government ensured that the road south was kept open, even in the worst days of the insurgent violence, which petered out towards the end of spring 2001. After more than three weeks of crisis, the situation in northern Kosovo gradually resolved itself too. UNMIK won the Kostunica regime's support with a promise to find a way to eliminate double taxation. Protesters in Mitrovica were won over by word play: the new posts were not 'Customs' points, as one previous UNMIK announcement had declared, but 'tax' points.

With the Customs stations finally collecting money and goods flowing normally again, tax revenues recovered rapidly. The money flowed into a new institution, the Central Fiscal Authority (CFA), Kosovo's new treasury, created by the EU Pillar with considerable US help. The CFA provided an effective fiscal backbone to Kosovo's rapidly burgeoning government services. It managed to handle very large sums of money without any scandals or inefficiencies. Staffed with relatively few internationals, the CFA relied mainly on educated young Albanians.

By 2002, the CFA had transformed Kosovo's budget from being totally donor-driven to being almost entirely domestically funded. This process was faster and smoother than much else that went on at the time. But it also created a danger for the economy, that a large government sector would emerge, leeching money from the struggling private sector with an unsustainable tax burden.

Kosovo's government had particularly strong temptations to over-tax. Not being a sovereign country, Kosovo could not use credits from the World Bank or other international lenders; its budget was required to balance. The CFA brought in a procurement process to ensure that no government department spent money it did not have. It also kept a tight lid on government spending — basic civil service pay was fixed at 300 euros a month — even though private sector pay and local UNMIK salaries were often several times higher. The budget strictures meant that every year there was a sizeable surplus that needed to be spent in a few short days. This was better than having a deficit, but hardly the most efficient way to run a budget.

CONFRONTATION AND STAGNATION
MAY 2002–FEBRUARY 2004

'Landing here on a chilly April evening in 2003 in the company of a contingent of Bangladeshi peacekeepers,' read the best piece of reportage on Kosovo from the period, by *The Guardian's* Jon Henley,[1] 'there are a couple of early hints that all is perhaps not quite as it should be. The first is the airport clock, which says it is 11.47am on Sunday 22 December. The second is the sign saying: 'No long-barrelled weapons beyond this point.' (You get used to signs like that in UN-land.) The road into Pristina is long and littered with half-built houses sporting unnecessarily large balconies. There's plainly something of a construction boom under way, which should be encouraging, except that nobody seems to know — or wants to ask — where the money's coming from. In front of every building is a throbbing diesel generator, because the mains electricity is never working. (That's another thing you get used to.) Along Bill Clinton Boulevard packs of small children hawk smuggled cigarettes, pirated CDs, and fake Nokia mobile housings. The Grand Hotel, the town's biggest, is a 20-storey Tito-era monster with octogenarian staff and an unreliable supply of hot water even in the rooms that have allegedly been renovated. It does not take credit cards. Every other established business here appears to be a car wash, or one of those places where you take your Balkaned-out tyres to get them approximately retreaded. And every other vehicle is a big white four-wheel drive with big blue letters stencilled on the side: UN, UNHCR, WHO, OSCE, K-For, EU, Unicef, WFP.'[2]

The problem with this surreal, tragicomic picture was that it was accurate. Nearly four years after the war, people had hoped for much more. By the spring of 2003, everyone in Kosovo was becoming painfully aware of the yawning gap between expectations and reality. The heady post-war days were long gone and normal life was still nowhere in sight. Tempers frayed. Rot set in.

As they drove around a gutted, lawless landscape and froze through their first winters, the early international officials in Kosovo could not have known that UNMIK's first months would come to seem like a paradise lost. Physically tough as this early period had been, politically it was straightforward. The need to erect tents and restore utilities and to take the first steps in organising the administration allowed UNMIK largely to avoid confronting the deeply controversial issues at the heart of its mission. In terms of the relative absence of political conflicts over core goals, the first three years of the protectorate were a honeymoon. By the time Michael Steiner had settled into the job of SRSG, that honeymoon was well and truly over. 'This is a place of centrifugal forces, of many and old contradictions,' he said in May 2003. 'The truth is this: now the chaos of 1999 has been resolved, they're all coming back to the surface... There are no short and quick fixes here.'[3]

In the face of these 'centrifugal forces', UNMIK tried to project an air of masterful self-assurance. 'All of Kosovo's friends agree,' explained an article in UNMIK's policy magazine in August 2002, 'that its future depends on progress in three broad areas: institutionalising the rule of law; the return of displaced people and their integration into a multiethnic Kosovo; and the generation of a new economy based on the private sector. The rule of law is the indispensable foundation for progress in the other two areas. Until now Kosovo's leaders have expressed broad support for the steps required to move forward. But the process of translating words into deeds will provide ample potential for friction between UNMIK and Kosovo's institutions. When this friction appears, to some degree it represents a necessary and inevitable step in bringing actual practice into harmony with professed ideals.'[4]

Institutionalising the rule of law would mean finally bringing to book the malefactors who had taken advantage of the post-war chaos, even those who had been senior figures in the KLA. Though UNMIK did not crack down on criminals strongly enough to break their power decisively, the steps it did take provoked denunciations and protests. In the sphere of inter-ethnic relations, a democratic government was in power in Belgrade and a system for supporting the return of displaced people was in place in Kosovo; the next step was for Kosovo representatives to commence a dialogue with Serbian officials and for members of the Albanian majority to welcome back their Serb neighbours. Economically, the bubble created by diaspora remittances and the international presence didn't pop; instead it began to deflate slowly. Meanwhile, the EU-led agency responsible for running public enterprises and privatising socialist ones proved that a small army of Western technocrats and consultants was just as able to preside over a dysfunctional mess as any socialist apparatchik.

Steiner was like a circus performer spinning plates on poles to keep the audience from panicking as the tent burned down around them. He devoted enormous energy to trying to maintain a sense of forward momentum even as substructures calcified under the mission's feet. He was the most ambitious of the SRSGs. Those who came before him had relatively clear cut, uncontroversial tasks. Those who came after operated in the context of dramatically lowered expectations. His temperament, and the phase of the protectorate over which he presided, meant Steiner was the only SRSG who attempted to do the hard things that were necessary to transform Kosovo fundamentally into a law-abiding and peaceful society.

During his eighteen months in office, he launched no fewer than ten major initiatives to revive UNMIK and restore confidence in the international mission. 'I always wanted to maintain control of the public agenda,' said Steiner, 'to give people some issue to talk about so they wouldn't start focusing on the status question.'[5]

His list of efforts was exhaustingly energetic: Mitrovica, decentralisation, Pristina-Belgrade talks, returns of displaced people, transfer of authority to local institutions, economic and social normalisation, UNMIK reform, promoting integration into Europe and, the mother of all initiatives, 'the Standards'. Each drive made some progress, then seemed to disappear into a local political crevasse or a bureaucratic black hole. Steiner's initiatives succeeded for some time in giving the impression of progress, but few were able to overcome the zero-sum logic of Albanian versus Serb or the lack of consensus in the international community.

As UNMIK matured and gained wisdom, it also lost vitality. Staff morale dropped and so did the intensity of work. Some began to see their duties in Kosovo as periods of penance between weekends in Greece. UNMIK's capacity to persuade local people was eroding. As the basis for its moral authority — the 1999 war — became more distant, Albanian politicians became less afraid to criticise and mock the institution. When UNMIK tried to respond, its message was filtered through increasingly sceptical and hostile local media.

Steiner struggled to animate the bureaucracy beneath him, but often the organisation's inertia was greater than his considerable energy. Those charged with implementing policy could always find excuses for not doing it. Steiner cites the example of a plan to paint the fire engines in Mitrovica red. 'We talked about this every morning for six weeks, but then we finally dropped it because you can't justify focusing on painting fire trucks red every day for two months.'[6]

Steiner tried to reform UNMIK. He offered a more significant role to the OSCE, hoping that, as the mission moved from administering Kosovo to monitoring the local government, the OSCE would be well suited to this new observation role. But the OSCE was reluctant to take up the challenge. He tried to motivate UNMIK staff with a series of intimate messages, which he dubbed 'Pillar Talk', emailed to every staff member. Staff members enjoyed them, but the growing malaise was hard to shake. When UNMIK came up against Kosovo's new, emboldened government — finally sworn into office in June 2002 — the era of 'stagnation and confrontation' had begun, a phase which would culminate in a violent showdown in March 2004.

The value of Steiner's continuous flurry of activity can be gauged by what happened under his successor, Harri Holkeri. Since the next stage of the mission would entail establishing the basis for resolving Kosovo's status, Kofi Annan wanted an SRSG who had led a European government and also had close ties to the UN. No senior politician who was still active would be willing to leave his own country for over a year. So Annan turned to Harri Holkeri, who had been Prime Minister and President of Finland and President of the UN Assembly. The trouble was, Holkeri was ready to retire from public life and this was not a retiring job. Early in his tenure he explained to senior aides that he had told the Secretary-General that he had a number of commitments that he would have to fulfil despite his post in Kosovo, among them a series of lectures on a Mediterranean cruise ship.[7]

Security and the rule of law

In April 2003, two young Albanian members of the Kosovo Protection Corps, working for the previously unheard of Albanian National Army, tried to lay explosives on a bridge in northern Kosovo. If they had succeeded, they would have severed the rail link with Serbia-proper, and perhaps murdered many Serbs in the process. But the charges went off prematurely, blowing their body parts across the area and leaving the bridge intact. To discourage similar acts by others, their efforts were ridiculed as much as they were condemned — they were mockingly described as 'the first suicide bombers to target an inanimate object'.[8]

Such incidents were becoming rare. The murder rate was down — only 68 in 2002, compared with nearly 250 in 2000,[9] and only a handful of these could be described as ethnically motivated. Crime was declining, thanks in large part to the increasing size and effectiveness of the local Kosovo Police Force (KPS), one of Kosovo's best institutional success stories. A steady stream of eager recruits was trained by veteran policemen from around Europe and North America at the OSCE's police academy in Vushtrri. By the summer of 2003 there were 6,000 local police officers working alongside 4,472 international ones. Salaries of three to four hundred euros a month were better than those of teachers or government ministers. The institution blossomed, assuming increasingly important roles. Gradually, KPS officers were allowed to take over stations previously run by CivPol and to join the staff of units investigating the most sensitive crimes.

Other crime fell quite dramatically as well. In one report, the overall crime rate was said to be 'less than Stockholm's'. But such statistics were deceptive. Even if overall rates of violent crime neared European norms, the actual form of criminal activity exercised a far more pervasive and toxic influence on Kosovo society. Unlike in Western countries, where crime is usually segregated from normal life, the threat of violence in Kosovo continued to influence politicians, business people and even how ordinary individuals approached resolving disputes. Many high-profile figures accused of heinous crimes, largely against fellow Albanians, successfully cultivated an air of untouchability.

Indictments of former KLA fighters. The apparent impunity of high profile figures took a blow with the first indictments of former KLA fighters by the ICTY (the International Criminal Tribunal for the former Yugoslavia). In February 2003 the Tribunal indicted three men (a fourth was originally arrested but charges were later dropped), the most prominent of whom was Fatmir Limaj, spokesman for the PDK. The men were charged with four to five counts each of crimes against humanity and violations of the laws or customs of war for running a prison camp in 1998, where they allegedly held captive and tortured both Albanians and non-Albanians accused of being collaborators with Serbian forces. Limaj was further accused of ordering the shooting of twelve captives, ten of whom died.[10]

Two of the men were arrested in Kosovo; Limaj was on a skiing holiday with party leader Hashim Thaci when he heard about the indictment and turned himself in to Slovenian police. The Hague's Chief Prosecutor, Carla del Ponte, was angry at KFOR for allowing Limaj to slip out of the protectorate when the military knew he was about to be indicted. Steiner, in turn, was angry with del Ponte for not giving him a chance to honour his promise to Kosovo's Assembly to allow Limaj to return to Kosovo before being transferred to the Netherlands. Limaj was prepared for the indictment. He told reporters in Ljubljana: 'Everything I did was in the service of my people. The fate of the individual isn't very important. I see this as the price of Kosovo's independence and I am ready to pay it.'[11] About 7,000 people demonstrated in Limaj's hometown of Malisevo. Limaj himself appealed for calm in a statement broadcast by RTK, and there were no other demonstrations. The government, however, immediately set up a legal defence fund and local commentators expressed confidence that Limaj would soon be able to establish his innocence.

Further ICTY indictments of former KLA fighters were delayed because witnesses were 'targeted by extremist groups'.[12] A case in point was the pre-trial investigation of the former KLA chief for the Pristina region, Rustem Mustafa, better known as Commander Rremi. Along with three others, Rremi was accused of illegally detaining, torturing and murdering people — again, mainly Albanians accused of collaborating with the Serbs — in the spring in 1999. A former captive of Rremi's who survived, Fehmi Potera, was mentioned in the indictment against the warlord and the media described him as a potential witness. Soon afterwards, he was attacked and wounded outside his home. Not surprisingly, after the attack Potera not only refused to speak but denied even knowing Rremi.

The evidence prosecutors were finally able to assemble against Rremi was weak. Nevertheless, he was convicted — some who knew the case suggested it was politically vital that he be found guilty.[13] For the crime of detaining and torturing 11 Albanians and one Serb, and of executing six Albanians alleged to have collaborated with the Milosevic regime, he was sentenced to 17 years in prison. This was two years longer than the heaviest sentence given to a Kosovo Serb for participating in the Racak massacre of 45 civilians in January 1999.

On 17 July 2002, the day after Rremi's conviction, a hand grenade exploded outside a police station in Podujeva, the home town of the four men convicted. That same day, fifteen police vehicles were vandalised in Pristina and Peje, where they were daubed with the Albanian word for 'occupier'. Kreshnik Gashi, a student from Pristina told the Institute of War and Peace Reporting (IWPR), 'No one disputes UN-MIK's authority to stage war crimes trials. However, the length of the sentence given to Rremi and his group shows its bias, because no Serb has ever been sentenced for such a long term by international judges, even though they have been tried for crimes which have exceeded the allegations against Rremi, both in the number of people killed and the means used to do those killings.'[14] Days after the verdict was handed down, a rocket-propelled grenade was fired at a district court building in Pristina and a second bomb was detonated outside a police station. While UNMIK officials and police denounced these acts of low-level terrorism as attacks on the rule of law, the protestors were at least partly correct in thinking that they smelled a rat.[15]

In the twelve months to the end of August 2002, more than sixty former KLA fighters were detained. This politically-driven sentencing set the stage for violence and political confrontation in the following weeks. Albanians became especially exercised by these KLA arrests after UN Police failed to indict Milan Ivanovic, a Serb leader in northern Mitrovica accused of throwing a grenade in a melee with Polish peacekeepers.[16] A series of protests demanding the release of ex-KLA fighters resulted in the injury of 52 civilians, 11 police officers and 3 soldiers. Instead of condemning the violence, Prime Minister Bajram Rexhepi issued a statement describing the former KLA suspects as 'political prisoners'. It went on to say: 'Whoever thinks that these arrests will discipline the personalities that led the war for Kosovo's freedom and that are today engaged body and soul for the independence and democratisation of Kosovo is deceived.' The leader of Rexhepi's PDK party, Hashim Thaci, called for his supporters not to confront KFOR — repeating a familiar pattern of playing the moderate after provocative statements by someone in his own circle. The LDK, anxious to avoid conflict with the international community over anything other than stubbornly repeating its demand for independence in every public statement, declined to support Rexhepi's position.[17]

When political protests failed, militants had other ways to undermine the court system. Another such case involved the so-called Dukagjini Five, which included Daut Haradinaj. In November 2002 a '64 panel' (a judicial panel with an international majority, established under UNMIK regulation 2000/64) convicted Daut Haradinaj and four others of torturing and murdering four members of a rival Albanian armed group at the end of the war in June 1999.[18] A defector from the group, Ilir Selimaj, agreed to testify in exchange for immunity from prosecution. He declined UNMIK's offer of protection; on 14 April 2002 he was ambushed in western Kosovo and shot dead.

Police and prosecutors recognised that witnesses in war crimes and organised crime cases could never be expected to testify without an effective witness protection programme. UNMIK police were able to offer bodyguards to witnesses but admitted they couldn't offer effective protection to former members of organised groups, whether criminal or paramilitary. The problem was simply that Kosovo was too small and communities too intimate to hide witnesses. As the examples above show, men with guns could kill those who would testify against them if they could find them. The obvious solution was to move witnesses to foreign countries. Countries with major Albanian populations — Germany, Switzerland, the UK and the US — were out. Not surprisingly, it was difficult to persuade other countries to offer asylum to men who admitted to being on intimate terms with Kosovo's underworld.

More promisingly, the passage of time and relative calm were working their magic on a number of tycoons who had never before been overly concerned about the law. Moguls who built fortunes through audacious trading in the 1990s now wanted the law to protect their riches.[19] In the spring of 2003 a representative of Lluka, a major trader and alleged cigarette smuggler, approached an UNMIK official with a request to convey a peculiar message to the customs service. Without acknowledging that he was, as widely believed, the biggest cigarette smuggler in Kosovo, Lluka said he wanted to run an entirely legal business. But in order to be able to do so without being undercut by tax-evading competitors, Lluka said, UNMIK's Customs service would have to implement more effective measures for interdicting smugglers. He explained his proposed reforms in detail, including one to move Customs posts along the Kosovo-Montenegro boundary to eliminate a no-man's land exploited by illicit traders.[20] The aging and mellowing of businessmen who once operated outside the law may do more to end organised crime in Kosovo than years of UNMIK's law enforcement efforts.

KFOR. Even as international prosecutors in Kosovo and the ICTY in The Hague handed down indictments against high-profile Albanian war crimes suspects, KFOR was shrinking. The attacks of 9/11, which caused the US to re-focus its attention and to declare a zero-tolerance policy towards terrorism, had enormous reverberations in Kosovo.

Kosovo was one of the US's biggest overseas troop commitments when George Bush became President. With wars in Afghanistan and Iraq it came to seem an unaffordable luxury. Media reportage on Kosovo declined, taking with it international public support for keeping substantial forces in the territory. Ambassador Reno Harnish, Head of the US Office in Pristina during most of Steiner's tenure, sent many cables to Washington strenuously arguing against the troop reductions, but his warnings were ignored.

NATO had military arguments for drawing down troop numbers in Kosovo. Reducing soldiers' visibility was seen as part of the transition from conflict to normal life. Furthermore, it was not clear what they should actually be doing. Successfully disengaged from the non-military tasks passed on to them by UNMIK when the civilians lacked the capacity to deal with them, many KFOR soldiers felt under-employed. One former British officer said of KFOR Main, the central command of the operation near Pristina: 'Lots of the time people just sit around up there. The planners don't know what they're meant to be planning any more.'[21] NATO headquarters in Brussels set a force reduction schedule and subsequently stuck to it, irrespective of conditions on the ground.[22]

Because it is easier to move out frontline troops than their support system, the reduction of KFOR had a disproportionate effect on its operational capacity.[23] Of course, extra troops could be flown from Europe and the US in a few days if needed, but it meant that the troops in Kosovo would become even more risk-averse. KFOR tried to cover the gaps by changing the way it used its troops. Instead of static guard posts, it put more soldiers on patrol, to cover a wider area more lightly. Responsibility for law and order shifted to the promising but immature Kosovo Police Service.

The level of coordination, command, control and communication between the military and civilian sides of the international administration depended on the personal dynamics between the KFOR commander and the SRSG. When Marcel Valentin commanded KFOR, he and Steiner got on well and worked effectively together. When Fabio Mini replaced Valentin, this relationship collapsed. Mini made clear his intention to run the military operation as he saw fit, without regard for the UNMIK-led process of political reconstruction that it was ostensibly meant to support.[24]

Malcontents of various stripes continued to probe UNMIK's and KFOR's resolve. Most often they found it wanting. In the spring of 2003, French KFOR soldiers looking for illegal weapons staked out the compound of the family of KLA martyr Adem Jashari in Donji Prekaze (it was reckoned that there were some 30,000 unaccounted for small arms in Kosovo at this time[25]). When the soldiers got too close to the gate, several men burst into the street and beat several of them up. Just as Serbian forces had steered clear of the Jasharis after a gun battle in the mid-90s, KFOR now also gave the clan a wide berth.

An even more dramatic case in point ran through the summer of 2003: a dispute over the erection of a monument to KLA fighters in the centre of Kosovo's second city, Prizren. The group behind the statue was the Kosovo Veterans' Association. Given that Prizren remained a multi-ethnic town with populations of Turks, Bosniaks, Serbs and others, UNMIK informed the veterans' group that the mono-ethnic monument was unacceptable. The Veterans' Association said it would erect the statue regardless. UNMIK asked KFOR to enforce its decision. The German contingent of KFOR responsible for Prizren claimed its rules of engagement wouldn't allow it to interfere with construction of the statue. UNMIK asked the Kosovo-wide commander for another national contingent to be sent to uphold their decision in the Germans' stead, but Mini refused. In the face of UNMIK's strenuous and very public opposition, the Veterans' Association thumbed its nose, constructed its monument and got away with it. UNMIK's loss of credibility was humiliating, and had catastrophic consequences the following March.

The KPC. Enforcing the rule of law within the Kosovo Protection Corps (KPC) proved especially difficult and almost resulted in a dangerous showdown in the summer of 2003.

One observer had already noted that 'professionalism within the KPC is lacking; criminals and extremists remain within its ranks; and firm civilian control, eventually by Kosovo's elected authorities, is needed.'[26] In the two years leading up to early 2003, some 27 former KLA commanders and senior officers serving in the KPC had been detained on charges of violent crimes. Eleven of these were released for lack of evidence. But on 24 March 2003, the pace changed when a very prominent member of the KPC, Sali Veseli, was sentenced to ten years in prison for having 'encouraged, planned and paid for' the murder of another former KLA commander in a drive-by shooting in Prizren in May 2000.[27] The sentence against Veseli spread deep unease within the KPC, and its general staff responded with a robust statement: 'We do not oppose any investigations into our members because we respect the rule of law. But we have spoken out against our people being accused of war crimes because that is unacceptable. We consider such accusations make a wrongful comparison between the crimes carried out by the Serbian police and army in Kosovo and the just war waged by the KLA.'[28] The KPC was effectively claiming immunity from war crime prosecutions.

By May 2003, UNMIK was talking openly about links between the KPC and the Albanian National Army (ANA), a new terrorist group bent on ethnically cleansing Kosovo of non-Albanians. On 18 June 2003, CivPol arrested two men driving a KPC vehicle and wearing KPC uniforms on suspicion of kidnapping and assaulting an Albanian man the day before. Relations between KFOR and the KPC had reached a crisis point.

General Mini, the KFOR commander, asserted that 'all members of the KPC were criminals', and called for the whole institution to be purged. The KPC's KFOR adviser, British Major-General Andrew Cumming, opposed Mini's stance on principle and also feared its consequences; the KPC was immensely popular with Albanians, and an ill-considered move against it could be sure to provoke a massive backlash.

When Cumming asked Mini how he would explain this purge, Mini said he didn't need to, because all the evidence against the KPC members was based on 'intelligence that must remain confidential'.

The disagreement illustrates the difficulty of trying to root out dangerous elements after allowing them to become entrenched. KFOR should have imposed much stricter standards on the KPC from the beginning, when its moral authority was at its peak; but having failed to do so, purging the KPC four years into the mission, on the sole basis of secret intelligence and bypassing the courts, would have been counterproductive. As well as antagonising those with the greatest capacity for violence, it would have destroyed the credibility of the judiciary in the minds of conscientious Albanians. Cumming dug in his heels and the mass purge did not happen. Future actions against various malefactors would proceed on an individual basis, subject to judicial procedures.[29]

Inter-ethnic relations

As with every election before and since, the question of whether Serbs would participate in the municipal polls of October 2002 occupied much of UNMIK's energies. The stakes were high for the Serbs and for the future of multi-ethnicity in Kosovo. They had boycotted the first municipal polls in 2000 and remained reluctant to enhance the credibility of elections by participating this time. But the alternative, as UNMIK struggled to explain, was to spend the next four years in the political wilderness while critical decisions were being made.

Steiner's main initiative to encourage Serb participation was a seven-point plan for Mitrovica that he unveiled on 1 October. It was also, obviously, an effort to resolve perhaps UNMIK's most glaring failure to fulfil its mandate. 'I have a plan: to make Mitrovica a normal European town,' Steiner told an invited audience of local Serbs at the studios of the Serbian TV channel, which broadcast it live. 'A secure town. A town with a functioning administration. And with economic prospects. My plan is to replace fear with trust and confidence.' The plan included: a guarantee against incursions from the south; regular policing by Serb KPS officers; an arrangement to prevent a tyranny of the Albanian majority over the municipal assembly; decentralisation to municipal subunits, effectively minimising the issues that would require extensive cooperation between Serbs and Albanians; a quick economic boost delivered by relocating UN bodies to northern Mitrovica; and a donor conference for the city. The seventh element, on which most of the others hinged, was extensive Serb participation in the elections.

Steiner did manage to wring a call for Serb participation from the Belgrade leadership but just three days before the elections. Kosovo Serb leader Rada Trajkovic also called on Serbs to participate, while segregationists in northern Mitrovica still called for a boycott. The debate over whether to participate and the tug-of-war between Belgrade and local Serb leaders drowned out normal campaigning. 'It was pandemonium,' said Gyorgy Kakuk, UNMIK spokesman in Mitrovica. 'Politicians were openly contradicting each other on the airwaves and you could hardly keep up with who was saying what.' When Belgrade finally got around to calling on Kosovo's Serbs to vote, local politicians were either forced to make an unconvincing about-face from previous anti-voting stances or to flout Belgrade's instruction entirely — hardly confidence-building measures so close to election day.[30]

Serb voters boycotted the four polling stations in northern Mitrovica very effectively — fewer than 100 people cast votes there. This was despite a last-minute drive by UNMIK to encourage turnout by giving all voters a consultation sheet, asking them to rank their priorities for the town. Once they had marked whether they, for example, thought rubbish collection was more important than road improvements, they were to take the bright orange forms to the polling station where, hopefully, they might also vote. From a local Serb population of approximately 10,000, only 36 forms were returned.[31] The boycott meant that all 41 seats on Mitrovica's municipal Assembly went to Albanians in the south, 'leaving the north an unrepresented fortress of fear and parallel structures'.[32] Steiner had to postpone his decentralisation initiative and much of the rest of his seven-point plan.

Serbs were generally less hostile elsewhere in Kosovo but faced other problems. After running as a unified bloc in parliamentary elections the previous November, the Serbs had fractured into six major entities and 25 other citizens' initiatives and independent candidates. While voters waited for a more coherent signal from their political leaders, two weeks before Election Day *Vecernje Novosti*, a leading Belgrade paper, published a menu of three pessimistic options for Serbs: a total boycott of the elections; participation only in the five municipalities where Serbs are the majority; or organising parallel elections. Kosovo Minister of Agriculture Goran Bogdanovic, the only Serb in the Provisional Government, summed up the essence of the five-municipality plan: 'We do not want Albanian mayors in municipalities where Serbs were in a majority.'[33] This logic moved a number of Serb voters in the enclaves, who felt more vulnerable. They had no choice but to use their vote to seek a sustainable working relationship with the international administration and the Albanian majority. Many had a positive impression of Steiner, though scepticism still ran deep.

Those Serbs who voted seemed to be motivated by at least one of three sentiments: 'hope for the future and a wish for change, a desire to stay in Kosovo and some measure of trust in government.'[34] The municipalities of Strpce, Novo Brdo and Zubin Potok — all of which had Serb majorities but also significant Albanian populations — were among the four municipalities with the highest Serb turn out. Of the 82 municipal assembly seats won by Serbs throughout Kosovo, 68 were in these three and two other Serb-majority municipalities. In most of Kosovo, Serbs had only token representation if any. In Lipljan, which had a sizeable Serb minority, stiff competition between four parties and two independent candidates prevented any of the six from reaching the threshold for a seat, so no Serbs were elected at all.

Across Kosovo, a total of 27,970 votes were cast for Serb political entities — only about 20 per cent of all eligible Serb voters. The low turnout made it hard for UNMIK to include Serbs in the decision-making process. 'Kosovo Serbs, like members of other communities, need to defend their legitimate interests through political competition,' wrote UNMIK's Director of Public Information, Simon Haselock. 'But that can only happen effectively within Kosovo's institutions, in which, unfortunately, many Kosovo Serbs will not be represented. Competition means participation; non-participation means self-marginalisation.'[35]

One step forward, two back. On 30 July 2002, Michael Steiner delivered an upbeat report to the UN Security Council. 'I'm therefore delighted to inform you about the publishing of an open appeal in Pristina yesterday, signed in the Albanian, Serbian and English languages by all the non-Serb leaders of Kosovo. The appeal urges the refugees and displaced people in Serbia, Montenegro and Macedonia to return to Kosovo. I quote. "It is time for you to come home... We do not 'invite' you to come back to your home because Kosovo is already your home and you have the right to live here in peace... It is truly time to put the past behind us and move on...".' Steiner enthused: 'That is exactly the sort of concrete commitment by leaders that we've worked for to reassure displaced people. Kosovo doesn't belong to Albanians or to Serbs or to any other ethnic group — Kosovo belongs to all its people. Internalising this fact is the key to Kosovo's future.'[36]

Just hours after Steiner's Security Council address, a series of explosions ripped through five Serb houses in the village of Klokot. Two American soldiers investigating the first explosion were badly injured — just a day after the US contingent of KFOR had decided that the security situation had improved enough for its troops no longer to need flak jackets. The SRSG had also recently announced a new 4.5 million euro initiative to encourage displaced people from Peje/Pec and Klina to return. It was hoped that the project would result in the return of a few hundred people per month, leading to bigger numbers in the future. Serb leaders criticised the plan, saying that at this rate it would take 100 years for all the displaced Serbs to return.

As the number of inter-ethnic murders and attacks decreased — there was just one in the first six months of 2003 — some Kosovo Serbs began to feel less anxious about their physical security. A few brave Serbs walked in the streets of Pristina during the day. Usually these were staff employed by UNMIK (there were few other Serbs in the city), acutely aware of their vulnerability, and generally accompanied by internationals. But it was progress. When a youthful TV crew from Belgrade was persuaded to visit Pristina's most popular terrace bar, 'Katya's', they were pleasantly surprised: they passed a very enjoyable evening drinking and chatting with young Albanians in Serbian. The segregation was slowly beginning to thaw.

Among other benefits, the lowered tension meant that when an atrocity was committed, the police and KFOR had resources to devote to solving the crime. There were two such incidents in the summer of 2003. In the first, three members of the Serb Stolic family were murdered in their Obilic home — apparently after having been tortured. Later, two teenage Serbs were killed by automatic gunfire while swimming in a river in Gorazdevac, in northern Kosovo. UNMIK, desperate to establish credibility within the Serb community, and with strong circumstantial evidence that these murders were not carried out by Albanian extremists, offered rewards for information.[37] But no information came, and the cases remained unsolved.

Returns. At this stage UNMIK still measured its own success in fostering multi-ethnicity by the number of displaced Serbs and people of other ethnic minorities who had returned to Kosovo. The return of displaced people had been one of the three declared Allied war aims in 1999. A few Kosovo Albanians were still unable to return to their homes in the Serb-dominated municipalities of northern Kosovo and in Strpce. But their numbers were small compared to the much larger number of Serbs and other non-Albanians who left Kosovo in 1999 when the war ended. UNHCR reckoned some 230,000 non-Albanians were displaced, of whom just a few thousand had returned in the first three years since the war.[38] Most of the rest were in Serbia proper, Montenegro, or other areas neighbouring Kosovo, often languishing in bleak camps. Their return was seen as vital if Kosovo was to remain meaningfully multi-ethnic.

Belgrade wanted to implant sizeable communities in Kosovo, which it saw as the best way of maintaining a Serb population that would substantiate Serbia's continuing claims on the territory. It was an approach rooted in the forced migrations of a bygone era, of Milosevic and of the mammoth population exchanges between Greece and the Ottoman Empire after World War I. It was no longer an acceptable way to resolve ethnic disputes, particularly after an unprecedented intervention to prevent one ethnic group from violently imposing its will on another. 'Returns are not a politically driven process,' read a concept paper prepared by UNMIK's Officer of Returns and Communities ahead of a major donor conference in May 2002, 'but primarily dependent upon the choice of the individual to come back.'[39]

UNMIK's ethos of returns was clear: all should be voluntary, and priority should be given to support returns to people's places of origin. The international community had enshrined the 'right to return' as a sacred personal entitlement throughout the Balkans, especially Bosnia, where two million of people had been displaced by the war. UNMIK recognised that politically driven settlements would provoke extreme hostility by the Albanian majority and expose the returnees to a dangerous backlash. 'The concept of relocation, including proposals for clusters of new settlements, is not conducive to the long-term goal of promoting a multi-ethnic society in Kosovo, and will not be endorsed by UNMIK.'[40]

Supporting individual returns to places of origin entailed a two-pronged approach. The first prong consisted of outreach efforts to ensure that displaced people had adequate information on conditions in Kosovo. The second was 'working to ensure that the conditions on the ground for returnees are sustainable, including by promoting their integration into Kosovo society.'[41] This was code for getting local Albanian leaders on side.

Though most powers relating to minorities remained in the hands of the SRSG, the Kosovo government had important roles to play. Ministries were meant to 'promote the proportional participation of all communities in all levels of the executive branch of the Government' and in the civil service.[42] Most important of all, the government was encouraged to use its moral authority to back minority rights and returns.

SRSG Steiner established a revamped Office of Returns and Communities (ORC) empowered to cut through bureaucracy and get things done. Under the direction of Bosnian veteran Peggy Hicks, the ORC cajoled the newly elected Kosovo Albanian leaders into supporting the effort. Prime Minister Rexhepi was persuaded to take a leading role, visiting a range of return sites to show his support. This was especially vital after an atrocity had been committed, when the response of the Kosovo-Albanian leadership could define the violence as nationalist norm or odious aberration. A conference for international donors in November 2002 rated money for the returns process as the single most vital priority for international donor funds.

However, the whole returns process was held back by several obstacles. Though money for the returns process moved up the priority list, less than half the 37 million euros UNMIK sought was delivered. Even more serious were local political dynamics: hardliners in Belgrade claimed that if local hostility subsided all the displaced people would return at once, conjuring an image of more than 100,000 Serbs flooding back into Kosovo to reclaim land and property. Although there was no realistic prospect of such an influx, some Albanians, playing to nationalist sentiments, gave credence to the remarks. They also claimed that among the large numbers of returnees, many would be former war criminals. Earlier in 2002, grisly posters had been put up around

Pristina picturing a young Albanian child being killed. The slogan read 'Don't let the criminals return'. Some Albanian leaders, particularly at the municipal level, asked to be allowed to vet all potential returnees to ensure that those who had committed atrocities and war crimes were not among their number.[43] The whole issue of returns became politicised and polarised — exactly the opposite of the quiet, calm conditions required for them to flourish.

To try to quell fears among returnees, elaborate security mechanisms were established. KFOR set up sentry posts outside many return sites and patrolled others frequently. Most Serbs welcomed these. As KFOR shrank, many of these sentry posts were removed and the number of patrols reduced. As one KFOR adviser acknowledged, if clever Albanian extremists executed a well-planned hit-and-run attack against a returns site, they would probably get away with it.[44]

The Serbs' fears were, like all fears, ultimately a state of mind, which became entrenched through a cruel, circular logic. Serbs in the enclave of Gracanica just a few kilometres outside Pristina, for instance, would state with conviction that it would be suicidal for them to visit the city. This they knew because they hadn't been able to go to Pristina since 1999, because it was too dangerous. Their own fears became the proof of danger.

Distrustful of efforts by UNMIK and the Albanians to assimilate them into Kosovo, most Serbs were still oriented towards Belgrade. A large proportion of Kosovo Serbs participated in Serbian elections in October 2002 (many more than voted in Kosovo's poll). The majority spurned the two democratically-oriented candidates, Vojislav Kostunica and Miroljub Labus, and instead supported the extreme nationalist, Vojislav Seselj. Father Sava, the articulate Orthodox cleric known as 'the cyber monk' for his prolific internet output, argued that the result was a cry of protest. 'It more accurately reflects a mood of deep disillusionment with the policies that the international community, Belgrade and the ethnic Albanians are implementing in Kosovo. The votes that went to Seselj are first and foremost an expression of bitterness and disappointment in the UNMIK administration, which in three years has not managed to create even the minimum conditions for the free and dignified life of the non-Albanian, primarily Serb, population.'[45]

UNMIK tried hard to change this perception, but incorrigible hostility by much of the Albanian majority made this difficult. Just days after Sava's plea, a mob attacked a group of elderly Serbs who had been bused into Pec/Peje to collect their pensions. An Argentine KFOR soldier was injured in the melee. Steiner condemned the attack as 'deplorable, disgraceful and disgusting.' UNMIK's Director of Public Information, Simon Haselock, wrote a response to Sava in which he described the attack as an aberration and listed a number of positive developments. 'There are already 397 Serb officers in the Kosovo Police Service, the KPS. Another 87 will finish their training in December,' wrote Haselock. 'In July, UNMIK and the Ministry of Justice in Belgrade signed a joint declaration paving the way for the hiring of more Serb jurists... Last year's general elections put 22 Serbs in the Kosovo Assembly. And a Serbian university should soon be legalised under a pending law... UNMIK has offered Serbs free Kosovo license plates and an agreement with Belgrade is pending on [their] recognition... Most checkpoints around Serbian enclaves have been replaced by mobile patrols with no rise in incidents.'[46] As Haselock's letter listed UNMIK's achievements, it underscored the gulf between statistics and lived experience for most Serbs living in Kosovo at the time.

Serbs felt excluded from a range of Kosovo institutions. Even though ministers were meant to 'promote the proportional representation of all communities at all levels... of the Government'[47], the reality was that very few Serbs were employed, and those that were often felt isolated or maltreated. Almost half of the Kosovo Serbs hired to work for the new Provisional Institutions as civil servants resigned within six months, many reporting intimidation or discrimination from their Albanian counterparts. 'We found their computers broke down more often than the Albanians' — it could be small things, like finding there was never any paper in the photocopier for them,' explained the UN official trying to tackle the problem.[48] 'But some faced serious threats and violence; many feared the small things would lead to big things.'

The situation was particularly bad in the judiciary where, out of 320 local judges and prosecutors in Kosovo in July 2002, only four were Serbs. Serb jurists had been deterred from taking up posts in Kosovo by a combination of fear, local hostility and political directives from Belgrade including threats to their pensions. UNMIK finally won agreement from Belgrade to give its blessing to Serbs who wanted to work in the Kosovo judicial system.[49] Commentators in Pristina greeted this achievement with a barrage of paranoid rumours: one newspaper said that Milosevic's judges would be returning; others said that UNMIK had bribed the judges and prosecutors with promises that they would be given free housing and that all their relatives would be given jobs in the civil service. The reality, as UNMIK took pains to explain, was that all applications would be reviewed by a body with five international members, three Kosovo Albanians and one Serb. No one with a criminal record or who had engaged in discriminatory practices would be hired. For those with property in Kosovo, UNMIK promised to try to resolve any claims on the property as quickly as possible or to provide temporary housing, as it did for other displaced persons. Relatives would compete for jobs on the same basis as other Kosovo Serbs. Their only advantage was that Kosovo Serbs were dramatically underrepresented in the civil service, a situation UNMIK was mandated to rectify.

Political development

Steiner spent his first several months as SRSG mediating among the Albanian political parties, cajoling them into a coalition and persuading Serbs to participate. Finally, in early June, the deal was done and, on 12 June 2002, exactly three years after the UN Mission in Kosovo had begun, the new government was sworn into office. Amid much pomp and press excitement, the members of the new government recited an oath on the UN flag.[50] There were now two governments in Kosovo: one international, one local. Rivalry was inevitable. The hope for transfer of power in half-steps proved unexpectedly difficult.

It took three-and-a-half months after the election to bring the Kosovo Albanian parties together into a governing coalition, and a further three-and-a-half months to persuade Serbs to join. The Constitutional Framework guaranteed that one of the ten ministries would be led by a Serb, but debates about which post he should get stretched out interminably. Several Kosovo Serb leaders, including Rada Trajkovic, lobbied hard to become the Minister for Energy, not realising that energy policy would remain in UNMIK's hands and the post of Minister for Energy did not exist. The Serb caucus, Coalition Return, finally agreed to participate after securing two new senior positions, both dealing with the return of displaced people — one an inter-ministerial coordinator inside the new locally-led institutions, the other a senior adviser inside UNMIK.

Kosovo Albanians were now in control of the executive and legislature — up to a point. The government controlled ten portfolios, covering virtually all domestic issues. UNMIK departments were converted into ministries of: Finance and Economy, Education, Science and Technology, Culture, Youth and Sports, Transport and Communications; Trade and Industry, Public Services, Environmental and Spatial Planning, Labour and Social Welfare, Health, and Agriculture, Forestry and Rural Development. The Constitutional Framework explicitly reserved defence, security, policing, external affairs, much economic policy and minority issues for the SRSG. This was not, then, the holy grail of independence; but it was well along the road towards the substantial self-government and autonomy from Belgrade called for in 1244.

From the beginning, the Kosovo Assembly showed more interest in issues over which it had no authority than in the many important portfolios for which it was responsible. Steiner addressed the second session of the Assembly, which it had devoted to debating a number of external issues for which it lacked competence. He strove to express his respect for the Assembly members as democratically elected representatives while at the same time urging them to focus on their actual responsibilities. 'It's the simple truth that the better you handle the authority you already have, the more authority will come and that's my program and that's what we all want to achieve,' said Steiner. 'I fully understand that the Assembly wants to discuss important issues for Kosovo — and the issues you have discussed here are important for Kosovo, even if they are not your responsibility.... But I would also urge you not to be sidetracked from the urgent tasks which are in your competence. And please, even if you don't see it in this room, don't forget that there's also an international community out there. Don't antagonise the international community whose support I'm fighting for daily and whose support is not easy to win and keep.'[51] Steiner went on to urge the Assembly to focus on health care and education; he asked pointedly why there was not a single woman in the government; and he reminded them that resources were being pulled away from Kosovo, repeating the refrain: 'There is no time to waste.'

Six months after it was elected, the Assembly had yet to pass, or even debate, any piece of legislation within its competence. On 25 May, it debated a resolution which demanded the 'protection of Kosovo's territorial integrity' — an issue well beyond its authority and highly provocative to Serbs. The resolution also rejected the agreement between Haekkerup and Covic the previous November. The UN Security Council and the EU sent letters to the Assembly urging it not to adopt the resolution, but it was passed nonetheless, with 85 (out of 120) Assembly members voting in favour.

Within half an hour of the vote Steiner had declared it invalid and said the Assembly had exceeded its authority. (Contrary to the prevailing image of Steiner as arrogantly dismissive of Kosovo leaders, he was painfully conscious of the irony of an appointed democracy-builder like himself overruling democratically elected representatives.) The chairman of the UN Security Council followed up with a statement that: 'The members of the Council rejected the resolution adopted by the Kosovo Assembly...[52] The members of the Council express their full support for SRSG Steiner's decision to declare the resolution null and void.'[53]

Despite the international condemnation, Kosovo leaders were unrepentant. 'This is a success for this Parliament,' said Sabri Hamiti, head of the LDK Parliamentary Group. 'This is the level of responsibilities we have taken from Kosovo voters. We are convinced that our Assembly is exercising its competencies to protect the rights of Kosovo citizens. At the same time we do not believe that this resolution has anything to do with confronting the international administration in Kosovo.'[54] Fatmir Limaj, the PDK parliamentary group leader (and future ICTY indictee), explained, 'The PDK Parliamentary Group believes that this resolution has to be ratified.'[55] Assembly President Nexhat Daci said, 'I believe that the Kosovo Assembly has taken a politically mature decision and it was done at the right time.'[56]

Local media quoted Steiner as saying, 'The Resolution clearly violates the Constitutional Framework. I have explained the situation to the leaders yesterday and today... I had no other choice except to declare the resolution null and void.'[57] In a press conference that afternoon Simon Haselock questioned the utility of the resolution. 'The question arises, is the Kosovo Assembly working for the interests of the people? What is important is that the Kosovo Assembly should be dealing with issues that belong to them according to the Constitutional Framework, with substantial issues, and not act as if they were in a political theatre.'[58]

This clash opened a new phase in relations between UNMIK and local leaders characterised by increasing confrontation. Politicians continued to devote most of their energies to making declarations and denouncing

UNMIK rather than working on their own portfolios. Instead of trumpeting its achievements, the new government positioned itself against UNMIK. For example, during the electricity crisis that erupted in July 2002, when lightning caused a fire which destroyed most of Kosovo's electricity generating capacity, the government turned down the key role of persuading the public to conserve. If they could not control the whole issue, Kosovo leaders would barely pay it lip service.[59] Daci said UNMIK hindered Kosovo's development and that international officials clung to their posts because they'd become addicted to Kosovo's beautiful women and great restaurants. (In refuting this absurd accusation in background briefings with local reporters, UNMIK press officers pointedly focused only on the relatively modest quality of local eateries.) The most common complaint was that Kosovo leaders could do nothing of substance because all the key powers remained in UNMIK's hands. This claim contained a kernel of validity but also underestimated the powers already transferred to local institutions and the significance of local leaders' moral authority. While Kosovans didn't have authority over policing, for instance, it was nevertheless a fact that crime would virtually disappear if all the major political parties persuaded their supporters not to commit any.

Some observers of UNMIK have questioned why no SRSG, not even Steiner, ever dismissed a local official. Steiner insists that if he had tried, he would have been shot down by the Security Council, which was determined not to repeat the mistakes it felt had been made in Bosnia. Bosnia's international presence was established as a system of light oversight rather than full-blown administration, as in Kosovo. Over time, Bosnia's Office of the High Representative — the equivalent of Kosovo's SRSG — gradually acquired more and more powers until, in 2002, it was accused of resembling the Viceroy in British India.[60] In Kosovo, the Security Council intended to begin with a strong mandate and then to scale back quickly, creating democratic structures that would be accountable to the electorate. Steiner believed that removing any official would have been contrary to this whole approach. Once the precedent had been set, UNMIK would have been expected to go on sacking obstructive politicians. UNMIK hoped that the electorate, opposition, civil society and the media would hold Kosovo politicians to account, and believed they could do so far more effectively than internationals ever could.

Political culture. The history of Kosovo's political class fated it to disappoint. With the exception of Mahmut Bakalli of the AAK, none of the 120 members of the new Assembly had any experience with governance. Those who had political experience only knew the politics of opposition, which is about blaming the authorities rather than taking responsibility— a world of declarations, gestures and in-fighting, rather than policy initiatives, legislation and management. Learning to govern would require a profound shift in political culture. Change didn't come quickly, partly because it seemed to be only foreigners who were calling for it.

Starting a government from scratch would have been challenging enough even for experienced administrators. Inevitably there were teething problems. For example, in an effort to regulate lotteries within Kosovo, the government enacted legislation that would require lottery firms to seek a license and deposit a large amount of money as a guarantee of any payouts. However, it failed to specify how the money should be deposited. In the days and hours running up to the deadline, several lottery providers, some with large quantities of cash ready to be lodged, desperately sought advice. But the deadline passed, and no information was given. Hence, Kosovo had no licensed lottery operators and lost a valuable source of tax revenue.

In an established democracy, government incompetence like this would be eagerly exposed by the opposition and the media. By holding the government to account, they would normally either spur the government to improve its performance, or encourage the electorate to vote it out of office when the time came. Kosovo, however, lacked both these checks on government. The media reported on UNMIK and the international community and sometimes on the government in Belgrade, but they hardly reported at all on the Kosovo government. The all-party coalition meant there was no opposition either. Although the Serbs frequently tilted against the government, they rarely attacked particular policies. More often, they just responded to what they saw as frequent provocations in the Albanian-led Assembly. For their part, Albanian leaders blamed UNMIK and the Serbs for all their troubles.

Some of the government frustration was understandable. The issues people cared most about — electricity, unemployment, crime and status (whether Kosovo would become independent) — seemed beyond their power.[61] They had some peripheral influence on them — for example, through the Ministry of Trade and Industry, they could have made the conditions for business people in Kosovo less bureaucratic; through their power to persuade, they could have helped to make crime, in particular inter-ethnic crime, less accepted. But they chose not to use these powers.

All these factors added up to a Kosovo government that had little authority, little experience in how to use it, little sense of overall direction and little political incentive to improve. In this vacuum, all responsibilities rebounded to UNMIK. Although after the formation of democratically-elected institutions the mission had hoped to become an arbiter of last resort, on almost all issues it still had to take the initiative and face the consequences.

With the internationals continuing to stress pragmatism and local leaders voicing their existential fears and a culture of opposition, UNMIK and the provisional institutions of self-government soon grew exasperated with one another.

Initiatives. Steiner used two means to try to keep Kosovo on track. One was propaganda in the broad non-pejorative sense, to sway opinion; the other was a series of dramatic initiatives meant to resolve high-profile problems. Steiner was tireless and driven, pushing Kosovo with more initiatives than any SRSG before or since.

He tried to crack the problems of Mitrovica through a new political settlement, conceding to some Serb demands in return for Serbs accepting at least notional UNMIK authority over the north. He tried to initiate the first talks between Pristina and Belgrade since the war and came close to succeeding. Steiner also tried to decentralise power in Kosovo, to energise local government and give Serbs more control over the public services they depended on in daily life. He tried to invigorate civil society with a series of dinners and visits. He tried to reform UNMIK, and offered a more significant role to the OSCE. Perhaps most significant of all, he introduced the Standards — a set of eight objectives against which Kosovo's political and social development could be measured. Steiner's frenetic activity generated a momentum of its own, and partly succeeded in masking the mutual frustration increasingly poisoning relations between internationals and locals.

Each of Steiner's drives succeeded for some time in giving the impression of progress, but few were able to generate a long lasting consensus between Albanians and Serbs, or within the international community. The people and structures in UNMIK through which he tried to achieve results, moreover, were not geared to drive change; despite Steiner's own dynamism, most staff retained a view of their roles that was firmly rooted in the status quo. The entire UN bureaucracy was action-averse. In management terms, the incentive structure rewarded most people for avoiding blame for a glaring mistake rather than for actually accomplishing anything constructive.[62]

Transferring power. The international community expected UNMIK to empower local institutions yet held the UN mission accountable for everything that happened in Kosovo — from trafficking of persons to economic problems and even inter-ethnic tension. With both the international community and the new Kosovo government looking to

UNMIK for action, it was not surprising that UNMIK found it difficult to pass power to the new institutions.

In 2002, Steiner sent his chief planner, Minna Järvenpää, to visit every municipality and gauge the mood. 'Even before Michael took up his position as SRSG, we had discussed the need to hand over responsibilities to the Kosovo institutions, swiftly and across the board,' said Järvenpää.[63] 'My impression from the field visits was that most regional and municipal administrators (who all worked for UNMIK) still thought of themselves as the real executive authority across Kosovo, despite the fact that a second round of municipal elections was due in October 2002. I reported back to Michael that I felt the mentality in the mission needed to be changed. UNMIK staff needed to learn to understand the importance of developing local capacity; they needed to let go.' Steiner concurred and sent an email entitled 'The Art of Letting Go' to all UNMIK staff. It read in part: 'As we transfer power, the measure of our success is not what we accomplish but the degree to which we are ready to hand over, to allow for trial and error — to let go, so that the new institutions succeed. We need to see our role differently, in line with a development approach. It's about ownership. We should not plan roads and run schools anymore. The Kosovo institutions must get the credit or the blame for the delivery of services to the public. In the transferred areas our job is to train and to build capacity.... There is no space for paternalism or imperial attitudes. There are no more Habsburgs or Ottomans, and this region will not be ruled by outside powers.'[64]

Many UN staff who had been working in municipalities since the start of the mission found the new approach hard to adopt. Many had become accustomed to their neo-colonial roles. One reported that 'local people come to me when they need things — like to get a road re-built — how can I not do it?'[65]

Steiner tried to address this issue by establishing a 'Transfer Council' to oversee a carefully managed transfer of roles to the new government. But this high-profile exercise had no room for manoeuvre. The government complained about its general lack of authority but seemed unaware of most of the powers it already had. Steiner, meanwhile, was not able to win permission from the UN to extend the powers of the government beyond those set out in the Constitutional Framework. Consequently, the 'transfer' of powers discussed in the Transfer Council amounted to nothing more than encouraging the government to use powers it already had.

Its impotence did not prevent the Transfer Council from becoming highly politicised. Albanians, not realising that the Council could deliver little new power, became highly supportive of the initiative, while some in Belgrade saw it as a precursor to full independence. It also fell victim to a wider problem caused by friction in the international community over the US invasion of Iraq and concern about Serbia's stability after the assassination of Serb Prime Minister Zoran Djindjic. UNMIK worried that even the appearance of expanding the Kosovo government's power could supply political ammunition to nationalist figures in Serbia.

Mitrovica. Steiner tried to crack the problems of Mitrovica through a new political settlement. Following a secret agreement with Belgrade's point-man on Kosovo, the wily Deputy Prime Minister Nebojsa Covic, Steiner presented Serbs with a package of attractive reforms: more economic aid and more jobs — secured by relocating several parts of the UNMIK bureaucracy to the north — and more autonomy from the Albanian-dominated authorities in Pristina. The aim was to get Serbs to vote in the municipal elections of October 2002. As explained earlier, very few did. In the absence of elected representatives, Steiner established an UNMIK 'administrative office' in northern Mitrovica to rule that half of the town by fiat. UNMIK heralded it as a major breakthrough. In reality, the mission merely managed to establish a presence and still did not challenge the band of thugs known as 'the bridge watchers' who really ruled northern Mitrovica. To do so would have required robust action by KFOR and international police, which the contributing nations would not accept. 'The bridge watchers were only strong because we were so weak,' concluded Steiner.[66] Given this risk aversion on the part of the international community, the division of Mitrovica could only have been resolved in the first days of the international administration. Instead, the French had divided the town to protect Serbs in the north from rampaging Albanians. The *cordon sanitaire* had become a *frontière permanente*.

Dialogue. Kosovo Albanians had been pretending Belgrade didn't exist since they created parallel public services in the early 1990s. This attitude only deepened under UNMIK. But Pristina leaders had to learn to deal with their counterparts in Belgrade in order to make advances on a series of 'practical issues' (that is, not directly relevant to the status question): missing persons, returns, transport, communications and energy. Belgrade would also have to be brought on board to smooth the way for eventual talks on Kosovo's status. In the early spring of 2003, therefore, Steiner began trying to initiate the first talks between Pristina and Belgrade since the war. He came close to succeeding. The key problem was the rivalry between the two largest Albanian parties. Rugova, who talked to Belgrade during the 1999 war and lost a lot of credibility as a result, refused to talk to Belgrade again unless he was accompanied by the PDK. The PDK would not go with him. Steiner was working on breaking this deadlock when the reforming Serbian Prime Minister Zoran Djindjic was assassinated, in April 2003.[67] Worried about political fragmentationin Serbia, the international community and Belgrade agreed that dialogue be temporarily shelved.

It was the prospect of Kosovan participation in the EU's Thessaloniki summit in June 2003 that finally enabled Steiner to shift Kosovo Albanian sentiment. Using this powerful carrot, Steiner persuaded Kosovo's leaders that the EU would never accept their inclusion in the UNMIK delegation unless they embraced the spirit of the Union, which meant an openended commitment to dialogue. After the predictable round of negotiations the government eventually agreed to declare itself open to talking with anyone at the conference, which implicitly included Serbia. As their reward, Ibrahim Rugova and PM Bajram Rexhepi, along with the Inter-ministerial Coordinator for Returns, Milorad Todorovic, attended the summit along with Steiner. The European Commission President, Romano Prodi, declared: 'The process [of moving Kosovo towards the European Union] is irreversible.'

Steiner left Kosovo on 10 July 2003 and the momentum generated in Thessaloniki flagged during the interregnum before Holkeri arrived as his successor on 13 August. Under pressure from the Quint diplomatic offices (US, UK, Germany, France and Italy), Rugova and Daci agreed to attend talks with Belgrade on behalf of Kosovo, but crucially, not representing the government. With no Albanian members of the government on the delegation, UNMIK decided to also exclude the Serb and the other non-Albanian representative who had planned to participate. The Serbian government responded by saying that the delegation had been 'ethnically cleansed' and refused to participate. Only last minute telephone diplomacy persuaded the Belgrade authorities to turn up.

Dialogue was conspicuous by its absence from the 'launch' of the dialogue process in the Austrian Federal Chancellery's ornate Congress Hall — the very room where in 1815 the Congress of Vienna had redrawn the map of southeast Europe. Its main impact was to remind European leaders of Kosovo's political immaturity and Kosovo leaders that Europe had not forgotten them. President Rugova 'described Kosovo as entering a state of normality and of having a nationality policy valid for all the people of Kosovo.'[68] Serbian Prime Minister Zoran Zivkovic and Deputy PM Covic criticised UNMIK and Kosovo's Provisional Government for failing to build a multi-ethnic society or to provide for the large-scale return of Kosovo Serbs. EU High Representative Javier Solana criticised Pristina's 'great hesitation' and continued self-isolation from any contact with Belgrade. European Commissioner Chris Patten said the launch of the Dialogue was not a triumph for one side or the other. He warned that 'strident declarations are pointless and won't affect the final outcome', and called on the two sides to demonstrate the 'political will, determination and responsibility to make the Dialogue succeed.'[69]

There were many reasons Kosovo Albanian leaders resisted talking with Belgrade. Despite the vicious in fighting among Albanian political factions, Kosovo's political culture lays great stress on solidarity when facing outsiders. Albanian leaders are hobbled by fear of being perceived as having sold out their people. The definition of selling out is, moreover, an extraordinarily strict one. As one Albanian who attended the Rambouillet conference put it, 'Dialogue implies negotiation; negotiation implies compromise; compromise implies betrayal.' For all their protestations to the contrary, Albanian leaders also suffered from an inferiority complex. They knew that their opposite numbers in the Serbian government had much more experience with high level diplomacy and they worried about being outwitted. The US Institute for Peace tried to bolster their confidence by conducting simulated negotiating sessions. The sessions mostly served to reveal how few cards Kosovo Albanians held. They needed Belgrade's cooperation but couldn't offer or threaten much in return.

Belgrade. The fruits of political cooperation between Belgrade and Pristina were usually rotten. Only rarely did talking deliver some tangible benefits. On 26 March 2002, Serbia fulfilled part of the Common Document by transferring 146 Albanian prisoners to Kosovo — the last of some 2,000 prisoners who had been incarcerated in Serbia three years before; most were released the next day on the grounds that they had been wrongfully convicted or had served their terms. In May, Steiner attended a High Level Working Group meeting in Belgrade and returned to Pristina with a 6,000-year-old terracotta goddess figure from Kosovo that had been held by a museum in the Serbian capital. 'The statue was given over as a gesture, and she is proof that talking works!' Steiner declared triumphantly after touching down at

Pristina's airport. The meeting also produced an agreement allowing Belgrade-to-Skopje trains to run again through Kosovo, and another on police cooperation.

Such productive meetings were all too rare. In Belgrade, Kosovo was widely seen as a political liability; when Djindjic gave the portfolio to Covic, it was regarded as a poisoned chalice designed to discredit a political rival. Covic could only squeeze political capital from the Kosovo issue by outmanoeuvring or stonewalling the SRSG. After Belgrade misrepresented the Common Document as a package of concessions by Haekkerup, UNMIK also became wary of raising the ire of the Albanian majority by dealing with Belgrade. Hence, whenever they met, obstruction and grandstanding was the safest strategy for both parties.

Kosovo Compass. For its first three years, UNMIK had largely ignored the third part of its mandate — to create conditions that would lead to the resolution of Kosovo's final political status. But Steiner came to recognise that unless the Albanian majority saw some light at the end of the tunnel, relations between the mission and the local population would become increasingly sour. In March 2003, he gathered a small group of staffers to draft a bold demarche to put the status issue explicitly on the table for the first time. The 'Kosovo Compass' was a one-page proposal that Steiner presented to the members of the Contact Group in Berlin. It suggested that Kosovo's progress towards fulfilling the Standards should be formally assessed at an international meeting in the summer of 2004 — a 'review' date for Kosovo's status. Sending the proposal to New York was carefully timed so that it would be too late for the Secretariat to prevent him from passing it to the Contact Group.[70] Secretary-General Kofi Annan sent him an official reprimand for taking such a step without consulting with New York but also for the approach he advocated. Steiner's 'review date' idea was revitalised only after he left Kosovo. The US Undersecretary of State, Marc Grossman, announced the review date exactly as Steiner had suggested in January 2004,[71] embracing Steiner's logic of giving Albanian leaders a concrete incentive to try to rein in the militants and to dramatically improve their own performance.

Decentralisation. Some Serbs hoped that reformed local government in Kosovo could offer them more autonomy, protecting them from Albanian domination. Steiner tried to accommodate them with a plan for devolving many functions to municipal subunits, which would have allowed Serbs in mixed municipalities to manage their own affairs in most areas. The subunits would have a 'right to manage issues such as primary and secondary education, primary health care, urban and rural planning, and the development of services and facilities, in accordance with municipal policy.'[72] The plan was premised on strong Serb participation in municipal elections, which did not materialise. UNMIK had to cancel the original plan to draft a decentralisation scheme at a conference attended by elected municipal representatives.

Instead, Steiner brought in a team from the Council of Europe to examine whether another model of local government — perhaps from the Czech Republic, Italy, or the Swedish-speaking region of Finland — could be imported into Kosovo. Inevitably, the mission was torn between the political need to balance acceptability and feasibility. Rather than engage Kosovans in a meaningful discussion, the three-person Council of Europe team arrived with a pre-determined plan in mind, which rendered their consultations with local leaders transparently perfunctory. The team also failed to engage local media to help retain local momentum for the project and prevent it from being captured by Covic. Faced with Serb boycotts and Albanian suspicions that decentralisation would amount to division by another name, decentralisation stalled until the 2005 when it re-emerged as a top priority for UNMIK and, after it was linked to status, the Provisional Government as well.

Standards before Status. Steiner's best known initiative was 'the Standards'. This list of eight policy areas made explicit the areas in which Kosovo had to change in order to become a functional society in harmony with contemporary European values.

To formulate the Standards, Steiner organised a retreat for senior staff in Dubrovnik. 'Steiner wanted to ensure buy-in by Pillar Heads and other key players for his policies and priorities,' explained Minna Järvenpää.[73] The retreat discussed draft policy papers written by Järvenpää on Steiner's priorities as SRSG — the economy, rule of law and returns — but 'the most important outcome of the retreat was the finalisation of the eight Standards that we had worked on developing the week before, and giving the full mission leadership a sense of ownership over them.' Steiner first announced the Standards publicly in an address to the UN Security Council on 24 April 2002.

First and foremost, the Standards were intended to provide a sense of direction to locals and internationals alike who often felt they were wandering around in a dispiriting fog. As Steiner explained: 'From a completely unstructured situation in the beginning, now we have a work-oriented situation, be it when we talk about the government or about foreign relations.'[74] This was something of a landmark in UN peacekeeping: though Kosovo was the first mission without any predetermined destination, it was also the first to have a map of the way forward. At last there seemed to be a set of aims for Kosovo that the international community could unite around.

As an instrument for setting a course, the Standards could be compared to a rudder on a boat: without an engine, the Standards alone weren't going to take Kosovo anywhere. For over ninety per cent of Kosovo's population that was Albanian, the only engine that would be effective was the lure of independence. But this was precisely the driving force that UNSCR 1244 forbade any SRSG from using. In an attempt to square this circle, Steiner coined the phrase 'Standards before Status', implying (without actually saying) the former was somehow the key to the latter. Optimists hoped 'Standards before Status' might even reconcile Kosovo Serbs, who sought improved standards, with Albanians who sought status (i.e., independence). Steiner came to believe that it was a major mistake not to have addressed the status question more explicitly from the start: conditional independence was a realistic incentive that could have been used to achieve progress from 1999 onwards.[75]

Given the enormous handicaps imposed by UNSCR 1244, the eventual embrace of the Standards by the international community and all mainstream leaders in Kosovo was rather impressive. It might have been more successful still if Kosovo leaders had been brought into the process of drafting the Standards earlier on. There were other problems with the Standards: if a key standard fell within UNMIK's competence rather than the Kosovo government's, could the Kosovans really be denied status if it wasn't met? Also, could progress be measured objectively? Should any pass marks be set? The international community's enthusiasm for the Standards did not extend to ironing out these wrinkles until 2004. Like so much in Kosovo, the Standards and the 'Standards before status' formula proved to be more fluid than they appeared.

As putative emperor in Kosovo, Steiner may have had no clothes; but he moved so fast that no one could be sure. After his departure in the summer of 2003, UNMIK's lack of power to affect change became obvious, creating an environment that combusted in March 2004.

Hearts and minds

Michael Steiner tried to maintain public confidence and a sense of forward momentum with a continuous barrage of messages pitched at different levels — from speeches in international forums to sophisticated TV and radio spots, visits to local communities and sometimes dramatic interventions through the local media. Division of Public Information Director, Simon Haselock, became Steiner's most trusted adviser and the two men shared a view of DPI's role as engaging on all levels in a fiercely contested competition of ideas. While some local journalists felt antagonised by UNMIK's continuous challenges, Haselock emerged as one of the most respected international officials among local journalists and political leaders.[76] DPI's success under his leadership can be measured by the near universal acceptance of the Standards as representing Kosovo's priorities.

The most important theme in the Kosovo media throughout this period was, of course, tensions over the division of power between UNMIK and the provisional institutions. The newspapers, which continued to give more space to columnists than to reporters, would lambast the international administration for alleged acts of arrogance or insincerity. Such rhetoric was echoed and amplified by Albanian leaders. 'It was useful, crucial, in the early stage, but now UNMIK is an obstacle to Kosovo's development,' the Prime Minister, Bajram Rexhepi, said. 'They've given us control of education, health, social affairs, culture, the environment — but these are small-budget affairs. How can we do good for the people of Kosovo if we do not have an executive role in justice, the economy and foreign affairs?'[77]

The President of Kosovo's Assembly, Nexhat Daci, was even harsher. 'They'd like to stay for 200 years because they earn more than US senators,' he said. 'An UNMIK cleaner earns five times the 130 euros a month we can pay our teachers; a security guard earns as much as a minister! These two governments cannot live together. If UNMIK doesn't scale down soon, the frustrations will rise so much that all that has been achieved so far will be destroyed!'[78]

Daci's view was widely shared. Many Kosovans believed the Provisional Institutions of Self-Government could do little to remedy the territory's ills. This complaint was sometimes taken to absurd extremes: the director of an art gallery, for example, who complained that he couldn't deal with his counterparts abroad because of Kosovo's unresolved political status. But many Albanians were serious in believing themselves powerless. Here are two explanations.

First, most Kosovans were incapable of distinguishing between formal authority and actual power. This is unsurprising given that in their historical experience, formal authority and actual power had always been fused and 'civil society' hardly existed. The inability to distinguish between authority and power became dramatically apparent when Kosovans talked about crime. Because the formal authority for security, police and justice belonged to UNMIK, Kosovans claimed there was nothing they could do to defeat crime or nurture the rule of law. This obviously ignored the fact that it was the Kosovans themselves, not internationals, who committed virtually all the crime in Kosovo and that the greatest weakness in policing was the public's reluctance to provide information on crimes. Public reticence, in turn, reflected their leaders' reluctance to condemn violence convincingly.

Second, Albanians tended to see the portfolios that had been transferred to the government, most of which had to do with human and environmental welfare rather than coercive powers, as 'women's work'. Prime Minister Rexhepi described their competencies as 'peanuts'.[79]

UNMIK responded to jibes from Albanian leaders by urging the institutions to focus less on polemics and more on practical actions. Early in 2003 Steiner directed his staff to draft a TV address that became known internally as the 'sick and tired speech'. Officially dubbed 'Taking Responsibility for 2003', Steiner's speech was broadcast over all three TV stations on 20 January. He began by describing the territory's big challenges. 'In the economy — where far too many people have no jobs. With crime — where there is still mafia-style organised crime. On multi-ethnicity — where there is still no real multi-ethnic society. Where there are still enclaves and people from minorities are harassed all too often. And in this situation we have institutions, who have not yet grasped their responsibilities. You know the Kosovo blame game "We haven't got the competence — we can't do anything — it's the international community's fault." But this is a fake debate. What is the reality? The reality is that your leaders are not in opposition anymore. They are in power and they have real power. Your government controls 350 million euros. That's 700 million DM in old money! It has ten ministries.

It is responsible for essentials like schools, hospitals and transport. That means your children's education. It means your health. It means your roads. These are vital responsibilities in any government. These are the issues on which elections in Europe are won and lost. Are they not worth your leaders' attention?'[80] Steiner struggled to reach over the heads of Kosovo's leaders to appeal directly to the people. Feedback suggested that he failed to connect. Even those Albanians who actually shared Steiner's criticisms of the government resented hearing them expressed by a foreign proconsul.

While the public grew more resentful of Steiner's disciplinary interventions, DPI implemented a multifaceted strategy that had been planned during a weekend retreat at Brezovica in May 2002. The DPI staff was divided into four working groups covering UNMIK's top priority policy areas: security and the rule of law, minorities and returns, the economy and the Standards as a whole. The working group on security and the rule of law developed a very successful monthly television programme, *Dosja e Krimit* (Crime Files), modelled on the BBC production *Crimewatch*. Its tag line said: 'Watch the programme. Make the call. Fight back against crime.' Broadcast in Albanian on RTK, and hosted by three KPS officers, *Dosja* featured dramatic recreations of unsolved crimes filmed on location and based on actual police files. These were followed by requests for information. Callers, averaging thirty per show, were connected directly to police operators in the studio. In its first year, *Dosja* led to four suspects being arrested in Kosovo, two turning themselves in and one being extradited from Switzerland. The working group promoting returns and minority issues produced a series of radio spots by international champions of intervention in Kosovo, including former US President Bill Clinton, and organised a televised public forum on minority issue moderated by Jamie Shea, who had won fame and admiration in Kosovo as NATO's spokesman during the air war. The working group on the economy developed an ambitious marketing programme, but was undermined by the incorrigibly miserable state of the product it was trying to sell.

The Standards working group produced a series of slick TV commercials, radio spots, and billboards. It also organised a series of ten 'town hall meetings' — one in Albanian and one in Serbian in each of Kosovo's five regions. The meetings began by airing an emotive video followed by a powerpoint presentation. The majority of each meeting was devoted to questions from the audience to an international panel including representatives from the Office of the SRSG, UNMIK Police, the OSCE, UNMIK regional offices and, in most cases, the US Office in Pristina. In terms of participation, questions and atmosphere, the discussions varied dramatically. The discussion in Serbian in the northern part of Mitrovica was undoubtedly the angriest. The one in the Albanian part of the city south of the Ibar, though emotionally cooler, was a mirror image, with participants blaming all their woes on the ethnic community across town. The meetings in Pristina and Peja were the most constructive, largely thanks to the participation of the Head of the US Office, Reno Harnish, and his public information officer. Prizren had the distinction of hosting the meetings whose Albanian and Serb participants were most like-minded.

The good news that emerged from these meetings was that the Standards themselves now enjoyed broad acceptance among the informed public. The bad news was that most people devoted more time to describing obstacles than to devising solutions. Excuses for not contributing towards progress corresponded to unrealistic expectations that political and economic salvation would come from one of three sources: the resolution of Kosovo's final status, a paternalistic state or the subordination of one's ethnic rivals.

According to the first view, progress was impossible until Kosovo's status was resolved. For virtually all Kosovo Albanians, this meant independence. For almost all Serbs, it meant power being returned to or at least shared with Belgrade. Panellists in the discussions pointed out that many dysfunctional societies were politically sovereign while some societies whose political status was unresolved — most notably Taiwan — were thriving.

According to another common canard, ordinary people were powerless to shape their own destinies and could only hope for the intercession of powerful state authorities. Panellists struggled to explain that in the sort of democratic, free market society that Kosovo was becoming, the government's role was far more limited than it had been in the socialist and Milosevic eras. Private citizens had to take responsibility; they could not wait for salvation from the state (even once Kosovo became one).

The third perceived obstacle was the ethnic Other: an extraordinary number of people, both Albanians and Serbs, remained convinced that they could make no progress in the face of their ethnic rivals' supposed efforts to undermine them. For all communities, this view was rooted in genuine fear. In addition to fearing for their physical security, many Kosovo Serbs feared that their continuing travails were being misrepresented to the outside world. Panellists repeatedly insisted that far from painting a rosy picture of minorities' conditions in Kosovo, UNMIK and other international organisations consistently depicted limitations on freedom of movement and other problems afflicting minority communities as categorically unacceptable.

Some editors and columnists continued to stoke Albanian anxieties and suspicions with spurious innuendo and 'vigilante journalism' masquerading as factual reporting. In June and July 2002 the newspaper *24 Ore* published a series of articles accusing Tahir Zemaj of murdering dozens of Albanians. The first of these articles began: 'The history of Tahir Zemaj is long, dark and bloody.'[81] It went on to accuse him of belonging to a Serbian group called Death Arrow that liquidated some fifty opponents of the Yugoslav regime during the 1980s. It also accused him of being linked to Arkan (a notorious Serbian paramilitary commander) and collaborating with him in killing Albanian 'martyrs'.

Soon after publication of these articles Zemaj survived an assassination attempt and lodged a complaint against *24 Orë* with the Temporary Media Commisioner (TMC). In testifying before the Media Hearing Board, Zemaj told the representative of the newspaper: 'With these articles you have liquidated me.' In January 2003, Zemaj was shot dead along with his son and nephew. Following the Zemaj murders, *24 Orë* suspended publication, citing threats against its staff .

The most regular offender was the newspaper *Bota Sot*. In the summer of 2002, the paper was fined twice by the TMC — first a 12,500 euro fine for defaming the current and former editors of two leading newspapers, *Koha Ditore* and *Zeri*; then a 17,500 euro fine for accusing Xhavit Haliti, a member of the presidency of the PDK, and Salo Lajci, an officer in the Kosovo Protection Corps, of having been involved in the murders of pro-LDK activists during the Kosovo conflict. *Bota Sot* refused to pay either fine. Responding to the second judgement, *Bota Sot* editor Barhyl Ajeti told IWPR that his paper 'does not recognise the decision of the TMC and will therefore not pay a single cent'.[82]

In the face of this refusal, Temporary Media Commissioner Anna Di Lellio sought UNMIK's help in enforcing the sanction. UNMIK's Office of the Legal Adviser told the TMC that although the office had a right to impose monetary penalties, further regulations would have to be enacted to give her the authority to actually collect the fines. *Bota Sot* had thumbed its nose at the TMC and got away with it, fatefully undermining the credibility of the media regulatory structure. There is reason to question whether the TMC tried as hard as possible to enforce her own fine. After finishing her tenure as TMC, Anna Di Lellio, declared that her proudest achievement in the job was having successfully blocked efforts to financially penalise errant media.[83]

To compensate for the TMC's emasculation, UNMIK tried writing letters to the editor to rebut unprofessional reporting. A representative example of these attempts at moral suasion was a commentary by Simon Haselock entitled 'Respect Readers' Reason'.[84] It quoted the

American statesman Thomas Jefferson: '"No experiment can be more interesting than that we are now trying, and which we trust will end in establishing... that man may be governed by reason and truth. Our first object should therefore be, to leave open to him all the avenues to truth. The most effectual hitherto found, is the freedom of the press" (but) ... freedom of the press was never absolute in the United States... In societies where the rule of law is thoroughly institutionalised and the judicial system is fully developed, media organisations are deterred from libelling people by the threat of being sued. Because Kosovo's judicial system is not yet capable of preventing libel through laws against defamation alone, the Temporary Media Commissioner was created to exercise a similar restraining influence by acting as a watchdog... newspapers may not impugn with impunity anymore than a man can get away with yelling "Fire!" in a crowded theatre. The reason for proscribing both these examples of free speech is the same: words, deployed in certain reckless and malicious ways, can pose an immediate threat. This is especially true in a post-conflict environment like Kosovo, where accusations of past misdeeds could lead directly to vigilante murder.' The letter concluded by condemning 'terms designed to play on Kosovans' deepest anxieties. Not only does such language seek to stir fears from the past rather than inspiring hopes for the future, it appeals to readers' emotions rather than their intellects... Kosovans deserve media that honours their need for the unbiased and accurate information required for active and intelligent engagement in public life — particularly during this politically delicate election season.'

It is hard to judge the effectiveness of such arguments. *Koha Ditore* published a comment by Reno Harnish, Head of the US Office, that strongly endorsed UNMIK policy in several controversial areas; informal polling found that Albanian critics of UNMIK believed the American diplomat had been obliged to back the mission but didn't really mean it. Some journalists said that UNMIK's polemics merely antagonised the local media that UNMIK should instead have been wooing.

But in light of the mission's mandate to create democratic institutions, which obviously include vibrant and responsible media, it would have been hard to justify *not* challenging unprofessional coverage by local journalists. Indeed, the rebuttals indicated respect (an all too rare and only erratically validated) for the local media's ability to engage in rational debate.

The mission also sought ways to influence public opinion without relying on the media. In particular, Michael Steiner made frequent visits to the regions and held dinners with representatives of that nebulous caste. Outside Pristina, a visit from the SRSG was a major event. Steiner would arrive with a retinue of local politicians, assistants and media. By holding talks with select groups of intellectuals and community leaders, Steiner sought their help in forging a vision of Kosovo's future that might escape the 'all or nothing' logic of the elected politicians. His charisma and presence often surpassed expectations while the contributions of local civil society figures generally fell short of internationals' hopes. International officials were dismayed by the lack of constructive suggestions and the repetition, instead, of boilerplate rhetoric. Even if they had expressed fresh ideas, the civil society leaders admitted that they had little influence on public attitudes or the political process.

These disappointments illustrated the difficulty of changing Kosovo's political culture. UNMIK officials often talked about Kosovo's civil society as a bridge between UNMIK and that public whose opinion they hoped to win over. But that quest was as doomed as that of big game hunters going after a unicorn: their quarry, the Kosovo public, proved so elusive because it didn't exist. A 'public' in the sense of a community of persons who do not know one another directly yet feel bound together by some sense of common obligation does not arise spontaneously among people who happen to live near one another. Kosovo society was Balkanised. It was a waste of time for UNMIK to regard public opinion as a single box requiring a single key to open it; Kosovan views were held in many small boxes requiring many keys.[85]

The economy

By the summer of 2002, the flow of donor money into the economy had peaked, and humanitarian and infrastructure investments were starting to decline. With UNMIK and KFOR scaling back their operations, the amount of money that they spent on local staff and their international staff spent on local goods and services was also falling. The Kosovo diaspora, most of whom were working in Europe or the US, still sent back considerable sums of money, but it could not make up for the reduction in international largesse.[86]

'The key question for policy makers and donors,' read a report to the fourth donor coordination meeting, in November 2002, 'is to what extent the decline of these various inflows will be smooth and manageable, or to which it will be abrupt, potentially causing an unmanageable shock to the economy... not to mention the broader economic and political stability of Kosovo and therefore the region.'[87]

Kosovo was poorly prepared to withstand any reversal. The externally funded boom had created unrealistic expectations of continued growth. Although it was the poorest region of Europe outside the former USSR, some Kosovans had managed to get rich quickly under the international administration. There was something of a property boom, with many thousands of new homes being built, especially around Pristina.

But the new wealth was not widely spread. Unemployment remained high — the most credible estimates put it between 25 and 30 per cent, although some official figures suggested more than half the workforce was without a proper job.[88] Many of those with work were under-employed and miserably paid.

Economic powers were generally reserved to the international community and still coordinated by the EU Pillar of UNMIK. Now with an administrative budget more than three times the size of its funding for 1999, the Pillar had the means to tackle the tasks expected of it. But it still faced enormous political and legal obstacles.

Property rights were the most fraught issue. Ottoman despots, Communist commissars and Milosevic's cronies had continually messed about with the ownership of land, buildings and large firms. No large-scale investors would risk their money in the new Kosovo until they could be sure that the title to assets they bought would be secure. UN-MIK was unable to unravel the situation by referring to old property records, many of which had been stolen or destroyed by the Serb militia in 1999; and it was unwilling to impose a solution, worried that any formula would be unfair and leave them open to legal claims from those who lost out.

UNMIK's paralysis on this issue was most obvious with regard to Kosovo's socially owned enterprises (SOEs), conglomerates that included virtually all of Kosovo's industry and much of its arable land. They were beset by creditor claims and uncertain ownership that prevented their transformation into 'normal' firms. Many of the SOEs foundered and were stripped of their assets. UNMIK even had trouble assessing how many SOEs it had legal authority over — a figure of 370 non-agricultural SOEs seemed plausible, but even this took more than three years to reach. With only 11 international staff and 10 locals assigned to dealing with the issue in 2002, there was no way UNMIK had the administrative capacity to oversee each one.[89] The KLA appropriated most of them and, not wanting to rock the boat, KFOR and the police never kicked it out. In one court case, a defendant explained that his source of income was a shop in central Pristina that had been 'assigned' to him by the KLA for services rendered during the conflict.[90]

A number of commercial lawyers with expertise in privatisation from elsewhere in the former Eastern bloc were brought in. Supplied mainly by the US Agency for International Development (USAID) and the German government, the lawyers disagreed over strategy. Some favoured a 'quick and dirty' sell-off; others favoured a more measured approach, aiming to assuage the major stakeholders on the issue, including old creditors, workers, municipal authorities and new investors. Even when the American and German lawyers reached a common position, they still had to convince the UN, whose lawyers regarded any form of privatisation as overstepping Resolution 1244. In an effort to push the UN on the issue, Steiner declared in a speech to the UN (which the UN then endorsed) that he would privatise the SOEs. But UN lawyers could not agree on exactly what that meant, and Kosovo's privatisation programme nose-dived into a legal swamp.

Faced with the almost impossible requirements that privatisation had to be legal and yet there could be no new privatisation law, the USAID and German lawyers were forced to innovate. Some SOEs were 'commercialised', which meant they were leased for a specified number of years, with no implications for ownership; others were left untouched. Some were administered directly by EU employees — a recipe which, perhaps unsurprisingly, tended to provoke industrial unrest. One particularly inventive attempt relied on a re-interpretation of hardline communist commercial laws (the so-called 'Markovic laws' of the late 1980s) — firms were privatised out of their legal limbo by giving power to revamped workers' councils.

The result was simply confusion. 'Privatisation' was started and re-started in different forms. It was a classic case of high-level politicians and lawyers refusing to reconcile contradictory policies, leaving those working on the ground to cope as best they could. As long as the UN denied legal immunity to the individuals administering the process, these officials could be sued by creditors from the Milosevic era if they sold anything off. Several privatisation contracts went unsigned for fear that whoever wrote his name at the bottom could be liable for millions of dollars in lawsuits by Belgrade. With no viable framework for privatisation, or property rights and commercial law more generally, Kosovo's private sector was doomed to remain devoid of large-scale investment.

There were other ways to help the economy. Ever since the old communist days, Kosovans had been used to filling in many forms and returning them to various offices for the most simple of tasks. Cutting back this bureaucracy would help liberate the private sector to produce wealth. But the new institutions, from the Ministry of Trade and Industry to the new municipal structures, saw regulation as their job. Taking the lead from UNMIK, which had also become accustomed to solving problems by generating paperwork, most Albanian administrators were still enjoying the fact that instructions they issued were now legally binding. Nor did they confine their oversight to the most pressing cases, such as certifying which foodstuffs were safe to eat, or preventing fuel vendors from bulking out petrol with water. The burgeoning offices of central and municipal government created reams of forms, licenses and other demands, smothering the fledgling private sector before it had got off the ground. Any law-abiding firm, including most foreign entrepreneurs trying to start businesses in Kosovo, could lose thousands of euros, countless hours and, in several cases, emotional stability while trying to comply with the often infuriating requirements of Kosovo's new regime.

Steiner tried to reduce bureaucracy for businesses trading abroad. He cajoled the Stability Pact to allow Kosovo to sign free-trade agreements with its neighbours and signed EU-style memorandums with Albania and Macedonia. Motorists, previously deterred from travelling into neighbouring Albania and Macedonia by exorbitant vehicle insurance rates they were forced to pay when they crossed the border, benefited from an agreement that recognised Kosovan insurance abroad. In banking, Kosovo finally won access to the SWIFT code system — a move which required banks in Kosovo to work with the National Bank of Yugoslavia, since the SWIFT code system only recognised nation states.

Steiner's whole economic drive was almost shattered by a scandal which erupted in April 2002. The former head of the public utilities department, Jo Trutschler, was found to have siphoned off more than 4 million euros of donor funds into his own private bank account. (With evidence provided by UNMIK, Trutschler was subsequently arrested, tried, convicted and sentenced to three-and-a-half years in prison by a German court.) Trutschler's malfeasance emerged after a long-running whispering campaign that something was awry at the top of the Kosovo electricity company, KEK. Steiner tried to turn the crisis into an opportunity by declaring that UNMIK had 'zero tolerance' for corruption. With great fanfare, he announced that he was bringing in a team from the celebrated Italian anti-corruption police, the Guardia di Finanzia. But again, brio was deflated by bureaucracy. Their arrival was delayed by months. When the Italians finally began work, they found very little evidence of corruption. The Trutschler case was apparently unique. Steiner had hoped the inspectors would help to clean-up Kosovo's socialist dinosaurs, but discovered the mess was entirely legal.

THE RECKONING
MARCH 2004–MAY 2006

Twenty-one dead. Mayhem all over Kosovo. Dozens of Orthodox churches destroyed. Hundreds of houses burned and looted. Thousands of Kosovo Serbs finally convinced to leave their homes. Mobs attacking international staffers. The riots of March 2004 were the explosion that UNMIK and KFOR had always dreaded.[1]

They differed from any previous outbursts of violence in Kosovo since the intervention. Unlike the disturbances of February 2000 in Mitrovica, they did not inspire the international community to deploy more staff to where the troubles had begun. Unlike the attacks on KFOR and UNMIK in Mitrovica in February 2001, UNMIK HQ could not ignore them. Unlike the protests over various KLA arrests in 2002, UNMIK could not declare that the rule of law was gaining the upper hand in Kosovo. The riots of March 2004 were an unmitigated disaster: there was no silver lining and no obvious policy response. They produced a paradigm shift that some might describe as accepting reality and others as giving up. What everyone could agree on was that the scale and ferocity of the violence meant that Kosovo could not continue to be governed as it had been up until then.

A paper produced by the OSCE's Office of Political Affairs immediately after the riots[2] listed ten underlying factors that had created the conditions for the violence: organised nationalism; the feeling that Belgrade and the international community were blocking Kosovo's progress towards independence; frustration among poorly educated

and idle youth; the worsening economic crisis; populist and inflamma-
tory media; the unpopularity of UNMIK, which many blamed for all
Kosovo's troubles; the remoteness of political authorities from their
constituents; extremists' feeling of impunity; the perception of unconditional support from the US, despite American diplomats' best efforts
to correct this delusion; and the fear of being returned to Serbian control. In other words, just about everything.

The immediate fallout from the riots was predictable. Within hours,
condemnation hailed down on Kosovo from various foreign capitals,
reminding Kosovans, in the words of Mark Dickinson, Head of the UK
Office in Pristina, that 'this was not why the war had been fought.'[3] The
UN Security Council met in emergency session to discuss the situation and within weeks the international community, feeling the need
for allies in Kosovo, was making concessions to Kosovo's Provisional
Government. The government, for its part, made a commitment to
help clean up the mess, both physical and political. Within ten weeks
the SRSG, the phlegmatic Harri Holkeri of Finland, whose health had
worsened markedly following the violence, had resigned.

The reaction of local Albanians and Serbs was also predictable. They
interpreted the March riots as they interpreted most developments in
Kosovo — in terms of their impact on Kosovo's prospects for independence. Belgrade said the riots exposed Kosovo's unsuitability for
statehood. Veteran Albanian student activist Alban Kurti argued that,
'Much is made of the outbreak of violence in March as an example of
Kosova's (sic) unpreparedness for self-determination; in reality, it is the
economic crisis precipitated by Kosova's unresolved status that is the
root cause of the inter-communal tensions and resultant instability.'[4]

The riots also created an acute crisis of morale among international
staffers. Consultations of UNMIK's staff psychologist shot up. Some,
particularly those who had been working in Kosovo for several years,
began to question why they were there. 'It made me wonder whether
all our efforts were for nothing,' said Italian development worker Mas-

simo Gambi.[5] Others felt personally offended. One Dutch old-timer, Gilles Everts, remarked, 'We worked really hard for them — *really hard* — especially in the early days. And this is what they do!'[6]

Kofi Annan commissioned a 'comprehensive review' of what was happening in Kosovo. The report, prepared by a team under the direction of Norwegian ambassador and retired general Kai Eide, was issued at the end of July 2004. This first Eide Report (he wrote a second report in 2005), which was written in unusually blunt language for a diplomatic document, noted that 'Kosovo is characterised by growing dissatisfaction and frustration' and that 'our current policies are seen as static and unable to respond to the real problems facing [Kosovo].' Eide then went on to recommend what amounted to a manifesto for a radically new approach — moving as quickly as possible towards resolving Kosovo's status.

The man given primary responsibility for implementing these changes was the new SRSG, Holkeri's replacement, a suave and dynamic Dane who was a former professional football player and career UNDP official, Soeren Jessen-Petersen. Petersen acknowledged Eide's most radical recommendation — that Kosovo's status had to be tackled sooner rather than later. 'There is a limit to how long you can keep a place in limbo,' he said on his arrival in Pristina in August 2004. 'We may be moving towards the endgame — talks on final status.'[7] Violence had once again advanced the independence agenda as nothing else in the previous five years had.

The endgame was bound to be difficult. 'The more we near the talks on the status of the Province, the greater the risk from the eruption of violence,' Petersen warned the OSCE's Permanent Council in February 2005. 'This society is very fragile and very little is needed to set it on fire.'[8] Nevertheless, moving towards a discussion on Kosovo's status was seen, 'on balance', to be the least dangerous policy. Petersen and the whole international community in Kosovo faced problems whatever they did. UNMIK's withdrawal was not destined to be a comfortable retirement. Instead, it was to be a reckoning, a time when it was forced either to exorcise the demons it had managed to avoid until then, or else find a way to live with them.

At the same time, other dynamics shifted in UNMIK's favour. Local leaders were sobered by the March events and the international reaction to them. Particularly in the light of the review of Kosovo's progress scheduled for the summer of 2005, some felt that they urgently needed to lift their game. At the same time, UNMIK was lowering the bar with an abridged version of the Standards which many cynics dubbed 'Standards Light'. Some UNMIK officials argued that the change in the Standards was just a matter of 'sequencing', first demanding progress in areas that were prerequisite to progress on the rest. In the words of UNMIK Standards Coordinator Sarah Macintosh, 'All the other Standards are still out there.' Out there, that is, beyond Kosovo's independence; all but the first, easy tranche of the Standards were effectively decoupled from the status issue. The hope was that the Standards process would be woven seamlessly into the European partnership programme, leading eventually to membership of the European Union.

UNMIK insisted that the government launch a reconstruction programme to repair the almost one thousand buildings, both public and private, that the rioters had partially or completely wrecked. An 'Inter-Ministerial Reconstruction Commission' was duly established, mandated to reconstruct and repair buildings. After the March 2004 rioting, looting continued through to May — even of properties that were being reconstructed by the Kosovo government. By the end of June, about half of the material damage that had been registered with the Commission was being tackled in one way or another.

The political damage of March was harder to remedy. Kosovo Albanian relationships with both the international community and the Serb minority deteriorated dramatically from an already low base. The Kosovo institutions failed to investigate and sanction central and municipal authorities which contributed to the violence. With the international community unwilling or unable to investigate or prosecute the riot masters themselves, nationalist figures who had orchestrated a pogrom enjoyed effective impunity. Here was a manifest demonstration of the impotence of the international administration in Kosovo.

Unable to repair the rot in Kosovo's foundations, Petersen was determined at least to prop them up. An energetic and experienced international civil servant, Petersen had been in Kosovo before to deal with the refugee crisis at the end of the war. Yet when his appointment as SRSG was announced in July 2004, Veton Surroi, publisher of the respected newspaper *Koha Ditore*, chided him: 'You'll have god-like status in Kosovo, but no real power: no army, central bank, prosecutor, no constitution and no friends. Once you accept your job as Kosovo's chief administrator, ask for a definition of your mandate. The fact that you are omnipotent with a UN mandate does not add up to much. The bureaucrats will give you a list of things you should not do. Western capitals will talk about Standards. And some diplomats will warn you that you do not have much time, as the Kosovars' impatience is growing.'[9]

At the end of 2004 and even early in 2005, many UNMIK officials were dismayed if anyone dared to forecast how the international administration might conclude. A few months later, even the most pious believers in UNMIK's bible, UN Security Council Resolution 1244, and its injunction against prejudging Kosovo's final status, understood that the mission's end was drawing near. Barring a catastrophic derailment, Kosovo would receive the green light to begin status talks in the autumn of 2005. The international community hoped that the combination of lowered expectations and incrementally improved performance would allow it to declare a modest victory, grant Kosovo some qualified form of independence and dramatically downscale the international presence.

Security and the rule of law

Punishments for the events of March became a key test for Kosovo's institutions — and a politically-charged one. Six months after the riots, while visiting NATO's headquarters in Brussels, Petersen defended UNMIK's record to journalists: '270 persons have been arrested who were involved in the violence. Among those, 54 of the so-called ringleaders have been arrested. Indictments have been taken out already on 17 of those. So the judicial process is taking its course, and it will continue... Justice is being done.'[10] To UNMIK's credit, by the end of October 2004, more than 100 cases had been completed, leading to 85 convictions. Although many more than 85 Kosovans deserved criminal punishments, the rule of law was being applied.

As in earlier instances of inter-ethnic violence, however, investigations were hampered by the lack of witnesses willing to testify. A well known individual was allegedly at the head of a 1,500-strong crowd when the Peje/Pec rioters destroyed the Serb village of Bela Polje. Yet when police began investigating his role in the violence, they found no one willing to testify against him. On the contrary, potential witnesses attributed a serenity to his behaviour that day that would have been 'worthy of Gandhi'.[11]

As the mission entered its fifth year, the powerful still had a range of means for remaining above the law. Major figures in Kosovo rarely indulged in crime themselves — according to one highly-placed source, they had bodyguards do their dirty work for them.[12] Even when they were prosecuted, powerful figures were still being undercharged. Their cases were sent to minor offences courts where international prosecutors did not catch wind of them and the maximum jail term was just 60 days. 'They'll get a municipal court to produce a note requesting that their case be transferred from an overworked district court that's under the control of the local heavies,' said a source in the Department of Justice.[13]

The well-connected have been known to avoid trial by feigning mental illness, with their claims supported by the Pristina University Hospital (which is controlled by the PDK). If their case ever did go to trial, they would manipulate its outcome by generating fake alibis and intimidating witnesses. Even when a big fish was convicted, he would generally stay out of jail while his conviction was under appeal. One local mob leader cited a urinary tract infection as an excuse to evade prison despite a major offence — and a local court accepted it.[14]

KFOR. The NATO regional command in Naples ordered KFOR to pursue the ringleaders aggressively. Three days after the riots, KFOR acted on intelligence gathered at great personal risk to the informants and detained several instigators of the violence. The culprits were then released, the official line being that the intelligence against them couldn't be used in court. 'We were acting on orders from Naples,' recalls one intelligence officer bitterly, 'and ComKFOR stabbed us in the back!'

It was for such cases that KFOR had developed the practice of 'ComKFOR hold', the extrajudicial detention that previous KFOR commanders had used very effectively against thugocrats. Holger Kammerhoff's predecessor, Fabio Mini, used the ComKFOR hold very reluctantly; the German abandoned it altogether.[15] This meant that as long as the thugocrats could intimidate potential witnesses, they could continue doing as they pleased.

The riots also revealed other shortcomings on KFOR's part. 'The international community was caught by surprise by the March violence,' said Eide's Report, '(it) failed to read the mood of the majority population, its frustrations and impatience. It also failed to understand the potential for extremists to mobilise support for ethnic violence and the vulnerability of minorities — in particular the Serb population.'[16]

Coordination between KFOR and UNMIK proved ineffective at the crucial moment. Holkeri initially advised decision-makers outside Kosovo that reinforcements did not need to be flown in. KFOR then came to a contrary conclusion. By the time reinforcements finally arrived — three days after the violence erupted — it was all over.

'The response was slow and confused on both the military and civilian sides,' pronounced the Eide Report, although Eide did commend some steps taken after the riots to improve 'liaison and coordination'.[17] KFOR dramatically improved its intelligence capability by replacing the command staff of the Multinational Brigade Centre (which had passed to Finnish command) with a British intelligence unit with a reputation for efficiency. Plans to reduce the force to a skeleton presence were shelved. By the end of November 2004, there were still well over 17,000 KFOR troops in Kosovo, about the same number there had been before the March riots.

The poor response to the riots, however, reflected a widespread lack of communication between the UN mission headquarters and its far flung staff, who were often closer to the local population. Just as in 2001, officials in Pristina had been warned of an incendiary incident in Mitrovica, but had failed to act. 'Between September and December, I wrote a number of memos and special reports on the deteriorating situation,' said the city's UN municipal administrator, Minna Järvenpää, whom Steiner had moved from her previous position as his chief planner to step up political progress in the city. Järvenpää's reports went 'to the SRSG and senior officials in Pristina seeking to focus attention, and [called] for an urgent policy discussion on Mitrovica. In meetings and in phone calls, I warned that Mitrovica was about to explode. All of these efforts were ignored.'[18] When the spark finally came, it took several crucial hours to steer UNMIK's decision-making machine towards the fast-brewing crisis. 'We were behind events, reacting not leading,' said one highly-placed insider.[19]

More than a year after the riots, the security situation remained uncertain. One Western diplomat, speaking in August 2004, said, 'They could very easily do it again — they're just biding their time. But if independence is delayed, or if it's denied them, expect something much worse. And again, we probably wouldn't be able to stop it.'[20] Another international official described the tacit threat of another outburst of violence, worse than that of March 2004, as 'the big Albanian veto' — to be used against any status options they don't like. In reality, this 'veto' had hung in the air from the beginning and continually deterred UNMIK and KFOR from imposing the international community's will.

Police reforms. UNMIK's most effective response to the March violence was to recruit Kai Vittrup to lead CivPol and the KPS. The former chief of police in Copenhagen, Vittrup was a legend in Denmark. UNMIK particularly valued him for his expertise in crowd control and his broad strategic vision.

From the moment he arrived, Vittrup understood that the police had lost all credibility in the March riots. The force under his command included 3,700 international police, and 6,500 Kosovo Police Service officers. After sizing up the two forces, Vittrup immediately began implementing a three-pronged reform programme. First was a system for responding quickly and effectively to any signs that the riots were about to repeat themselves. Second was community policing and improving the image of the police, particularly among minorities. Third was making local KPS officers, not foreign CivPol, the main face of authority.

While 'KFOR is building fortresses', he explained, the police should focus on improving communications and response time. Vittrup introduced crime prevention councils in all municipalities.[21] An exercise in the autumn of 2004 brought 600 officers to headquarters in just 75 minutes. To minimise confusion under stress, each officer was given just three responsibilities. Crucially, local 'KPS officers will be the frontline in any demonstration,' said Vittrup.

Just before Vittrup's arrival in August, a group demonstrated in Pristina, demanding information about loved ones missing since the conflict. International police made a number of arrests but, following complaints, released everyone — 'another terrible loss of credibility', noted Vittrup. When the Missing Persons Association held its next demonstration, this time on Vittrup's watch, he met with the organisers beforehand and assured them that there would be a minimal police presence. The police went further, issuing a press release expressing respect for the Association's members' concern about the missing and their right to demonstrate, while Special Police Units were ready 'over the horizon'. The demonstration proceeded without incident.

Critics of the United Nations have often conjured an image of trigger-happy African policemen, ignorant of human rights, enjoying their deployment to Kosovo on account of their access to sex and power. This image is as inaccurate as it is racist. In Kosovo, measures were in place to ensure the police stayed in line. In the first four years of the UNMIK mission, ten UN police officers were reprimanded or repatriated for involvement with prostitutes.[22] Under Vittrup, the inspection regime became even tougher, and the sanctions harder.

He also pushed to raise local officers' salaries. Both the KPS and CivPol became increasingly effective against many categories of crime. On Kosovo's southern borders, CivPol were intercepting more than one cross border smuggling operation each day. Across the territory, Kosovo's security situation was stabilising at a level just below the average for South-Eastern Europe. Perhaps most impressively, by early autumn 2005, all 32 police stations in Kosovo had been put under the authority of the local KPS force.

'I believe that whenever we leave here, there will be well equipped, well trained police,' said Vittrup in November 2004. 'But they will still be subject to the authority of their clans and other social pressures.' This sums up the inevitable gap between new institutions and unreformed attitudes in a short-term nation-building programme.

As UNMIK had long maintained, Kosovo's social structures could also be used to help maintain law and order. As the first anniversary of the March riots approached in 2005, the LDK's network of informants became aware of plans by several regional veterans' associations to demonstrate for the release of Ramush Haradinaj (the former AAK leader and Kosovo Prime Minister who had just been taken into custody for war crimes in The Hague). The government responded by spreading the word that Ramush himself had ordered people not to demonstrate, and it was ready to plaster posters overnight throughout Pristina telling people to remain calm. The informal pressure smothered the demonstrators' plans in the cradle. On 16 March, informants again reported to the party bosses about planned demonstrations, including a convoy of cars that was to pass through the Dukagjin region, passing menacingly close to a Serb village. The acting Prime Minister, Hajrettin Salihaj, briefed the Police Commissioner in a face-to-face meeting. Again, the combination of intelligence and messages disseminated through informal channels pre-empted any rioting.[23]

The anniversary did not pass completely peacefully, though: a grenade exploded outside UNMIK headquarters, injuring the teenager who had been handling it. A few minutes later, snipers shot out microwave dishes on the roof of the UN headquarters that were essential for UNMIK's communications with two of the regions. A senior CivPol officer interpreted the incident as a warning from the extremists: they had acquired high-accuracy rifles and had the skill to use them. With their riots stillborn, the hardliners could not let the anniversary pass completely unmarked.

Popular sympathy for people operating outside the law posed a continuing challenge to police. A respected American political risk analysis firm, StratFor, reported that according to German intelligence in April 2005, Islamist terrorist training camps in Kosovo had sent graduates to Bosnia to carry out attacks on a European embassy. StratFor also contends that US and Israeli reports claimed that 'al Qaeda had recruited more than 1,000 people to train at the Kosovo camps.'[24] Rumours about terrorist camps in Kosovo have circulated for years. Such claims should be treated with scepticism, not least because the link to terrorism would suit Serbian objectives so neatly. Devout Muslims (and still more militant Islamists) are a rarity in Kosovo. But intelligence officials have suspected several Middle Eastern charities of being fronts for less benign activities and Kosovo's poverty, disaffection and lack of order, on the threshold of western Europe, would certainly make it attractive to terrorists. Several armed groups have appeared throughout UNMIK's reign, most recently a group in black uniforms roaming in Kosovo's far west calling itself the Army for the Independence of Kosova. People in the area expressed sympathy for their actions; one motorist stopped by the armed men described their behaviour as 'serious and correct'. The group warned UNMIK officials to be wary of crossing the region at night and threatened members of Kosovo's parliament with 'capital punishment' if they failed to declare independence by 15 October. The Assembly did not issue such a proclamation and no parliamentarian was attacked.

Amid these challenges to the legal authorities, three international judges on Kosovo's Supreme Court threw out the biggest war crimes convictions of the UNMIK era. The Court ordered a retrial in the case of Latif Gashi, Rrustem Mustafa (Commander Rremi) and two other alleged accomplices on charges of illegally detaining and torturing Albanian civilians in 1998. The Court did not dispute the facts of the charges against the men; it reversed the convictions because of a legal technicality, arguing that the defendants' actions did not constitute a breach of international law, including, amazingly, the Geneva Convention. One can only imagine the blow this reversal dealt to public confidence in the judiciary — particularly among the witnesses who had mustered the courage to testify in the trial.

Inter-ethnic relations

Vittrup adopted special measures for raising the confidence of minorities. He put four hundred more UN CivPol officers on patrol in minority areas,[25] and, in twenty-five of these areas, introduced community-based police stations.[26] In Gracanica, local Serbs declared their intention to construct a chapel near a police checkpoint in honour of a Serb who was killed at this spot. Instead of fighting this, Vittrup told the Serbs they had to compensate the police with land somewhere else for their post or he would pull all his police from the enclave. Not surprisingly, the Serbs quickly supplied the site. Petersen noted that in the year after the riots, 'there has been virtually no inter-ethnic violence; incidents are mostly related to local criminality, whose rates are not higher than comparable rates in Western Europe.' The bridge-watchers, the paramilitary thugs who haunted Kouchner, Haekkerup and Steiner, had left their northern Mitrovica lair, although there was still the occasional incident, like the car bomb that had almost killed Serb politician Oliver Ivanovic in February 2005.

For most Kosovo Serbs, the innovative community policing efforts were overshadowed by the failure to charge anyone for several previous murders of Serbs, including the machine-gunning of teenagers in Gorazdevac and the torture and murder of the Stolic family in Obiliq/c in 2003.[27] As Kosovo moved inexorably toward independence, murders that will probably never be solved continued. On 29 August 2005, two Kosovo Serbs, Ivan Dejanovic and Aleksandar Stankovic, were shot dead as they drove into the enclave of Strpce, with two other Serbs wounded. Their car's old Yugoslav number plates made their ethnicity easily indefinable. A few days later, the KPS commander for Gjilan, Dejan Jankovic, was wounded in an ambush.[28]

As ever, such attacks combined with pressure from Belgrade to deepen Kosovo Serbs' isolation. Serbian PM Kostunica responded to the March riots by urging members of the Serbian caucus elected to Kosovo's Assembly not to participate in the parliament's work — a move condemned as obstructive by most in the international community. Belgrade viewed participation in Kosovo's institutions as legitimising them without giving Serbs any real chance to shape policy. This position was echoed by most Kosovo Serbs, who looked to decentralisation and partition to keep Albanians at arm's length. Their experience of the first three years of the Assembly had been poor: they could list many times when the Assembly had stepped beyond its constitutional remit and almost none when they had managed to advance Serb interests.

Thus when the Assembly came to be re-elected in October 2004, the Serbs kept the international community guessing, as they had in previous election years, trying to extract as many concessions as possible in exchange for participating. International diplomats offered to redouble the international scrutiny of the Serbs' treatment in the Assembly. But it was not enough. Despite protestations by the canny north Mitrovica Serb leader Oliver Ivanovic, who called on his fellow Serbs to participate, very few Serbs cast their ballots; and the new Assembly was elected with no Serbs at all.[29]

The Albanian majority, of course, reciprocated the Serbs' disdain. As the mission drew towards its end, one staff member working for UN-MIK admitted, 'We have created a multi-ethnic society — everybody is welcome here except Serbs!'[30] The communities of Bosniaks, Turks and Goranis, each of which formed only a small fraction of Kosovo's two million population, had integrated relatively well. Divisions remained, as did concerns about special issues such as language rights in official documents. But most members of these non-Serb minority communities could now travel virtually everywhere in Kosovo. For them, Kosovo really was reasonably safe if not actually an idyll of cultural pluralism.

In a few isolated parts of Kosovo, even Serbs and Albanians mixed. The Serb-majority village of Brezovica, high in the mountains on Kosovo's southern border, actively encouraged Albanians to come, mostly to bring their euros into the enclave's ski resort. Serbs and Albanians used the ski runs together, with no reported incidents of serious violence. There was, however, an undercurrent of fear among Serbs and triumphalism among Albanians, especially between groups of teenagers. When some boisterous Albanian youths pushed their way to the front of a queue to hire ski equipment and were rebuked by internationals, they replied: 'We won — they (the Serbs) lost!' Serbs could be heard cursing the Albanians in return.[31]

The frosty interaction between Serbs and Albanians in Brezovica was much better than relations elsewhere. Even in the eastern municipality of Gnjilane, where tensions had never been as high as elsewhere in Kosovo, Serbs were severely marginalised. Serbs and Albanians had separate outdoor markets, the Serbs' occupying a tiny space in an alleyway. When asked about the March riots, an elderly Serb manning a vegetable stand, 78-year-old Velibor Zivkovic, shook his head. 'I live here in town. I never touched anyone and nobody ever touched me until March (2004),' he said. Zivkovic was at the market when the rioting spread to Gnjilane. He was surrounded by a mob and pushed around before being rescued by his Albanian neighbour, Feti Xhemaili, who sheltered him in his house for a couple of days. As riots spread through the city, crowds broke the windows of Zivkovic's house and kicked in his door. The municipal authorities repaired his windows and got him a new door, and although he said he 'hadn't been bothered' since, he was clearly uncomfortable. Soon after the riots, Zivkovic's son left Kosovo and resettled in Serbia, boarding up his house. Children passing by on their way to school often pounded on the old man's door and yelled insults at him. 'I wish their teachers would tell them not to do this,' he said.' (In light of such harassment, one wonders what Zivkovic or the journalist understood as being 'bothered'.)[32]

For virtually all Serbs, and the smaller ethnic groups associated with them — Roma, Ashkalis and 'Egyptians' — security fears inhibited them from travelling through most of the territory. 'How can Pristina be our capital if we can't even go there?' asked one Mitrovica-based Serb.[33] Commenting on a recent incident in which a bus carrying Serb returnees was stoned, SRSG Petersen acknowledged that most Serbs 'try to avoid encounters or confrontation with members of the majority community.'[34]

UNMIK strongly condemned inter-ethnic intimidation but wasn't quite sure what to do about it. When the Assembly's Albanian majority commissioned nationalist murals to be painted in the foyer of their building, and the Serbs responded with a boycott, UNMIK insisted that the offending friezes be covered by a drop cloth. But on most other occasions, it let these symbols stand, even though the Serbs found them highly offensive. For example, an enormous portrait of Adem Jashari (whom Albanians regard as a hero and Serbs as a terrorist) was allowed to dominate the sports stadium in downtown Pristina. The Jashari compound in Skenderaj, where much of the family was slaughtered by Serbian forces in 1998, was transformed into a secular shrine, visited by schoolchildren to stoke their inherited antipathy. Despite the UN's periodically repeated insistence that all public signs be bilingual, this was hardly ever enforced. The result was that most of Kosovo's landscape looked as if only Albanians had ever lived there.

Nevertheless, some progress was being made in the battle between symbols of triumphalism and tokens of reconciliation. Following the March riots, UNMIK placed 47 cultural heritage sites under protection throughout Kosovo and all of these sites received regular patrols and security checks, while others were under full time CivPol and KFOR protection. 'As we gradually hand over responsibilities to local authorities,' noted Petersen, 'I am confident that the local authorities will demonstrate the same concern for and protection of all cultural heritage in Kosovo.'[35] After some initial reluctance, the Kosovo government agreed to allocate 4.2 million euros to reconstruct Orthodox churches and monasteries damaged in the rioting of March 2004. Serbs initially refused to accept the money unless it was handed to them in cash to spend as they saw fit, but in March 2005, UNMIK finally convinced Patriarch Pavle to sign a Memorandum of Understanding with Kosovo's Minister of Culture. It established an implementing committee comprising Kosovo and Serbian officials, church representatives and the Council of Europe.

On 13 May 2005, the UN cultural agency UNESCO hosted a meeting of Serb, Albanian and international officials to discuss the reconstruction programme. Astrit Haraqija, Kosovo's Minister of Culture, tried to deliver a speech that would have set a new standard for inclusive oratory by Kosovo leaders. In the event, Serbian officials at the meeting protested that Kosovo should be represented by UNMIK and neither of its government's ministers should be allowed to speak. As a compromise, the SRSG read Haraqija's speech in his stead. Though it was ironic on one level, pre-empting this speech was entirely consistent with Belgrade's strategy of preventing Kosovo Albanians from ever looking progressive in the eyes of the international community. The Kosovo delegation undermined its otherwise impressive performance by distributing a brochure — despite a ban by UNESCO on the dissemination of any written material — containing divisive historical claims.

According to the results of a contemporary poll by UNDP, about half of Albanians, including most older Kosovo Albanians, blamed poor inter-ethnic relations on Belgrade[36] while slightly fewer, including many younger people, blamed a general unwillingness to integrate by the Serbs themselves.[37] Incredibly, more than half of all Kosovo Albanians thought that the March riots had had no effect at all on relations in their local area. This finding probably reflects the complete absence of Serb communities from large areas of Kosovo. Of the majority of Kosovo Albanians who agreed that relations were tense, half saw some light at the end of the tunnel while the other half thought improvement was unlikely — older Albanians being generally more pessimistic.

Serbs placed their blame elsewhere. Almost three-quarters of Kosovo Serbs[38] blamed Kosovo Albanian leaders for ethnic tensions.[39] Even though two-thirds did not feel safe in their own homes, most said they 'wouldn't help the police because they didn't trust them'.[40] Eleven out of every twelve Serbs thought the events of March had damaged relations,[41] and an overwhelming 98 per cent of Kosovo Serbs were pessimistic about the future, describing Albanian-Serb relations as 'tense and likely to remain so'.[42]

Returns. Returns were probably fatally stalled by the March riots. 'KFOR are still reducing their capacity to protect. Lots of returnees changed their minds after March,' said one young, idealistic but now demoralised member of UNMIK's Returns Unit.[43] 'We had hoped for two returns cycles this year, but that's all been scuppered now.' Another member of the Returns Unit felt that they had let the returnees down. 'We promised them they'd be safe — we kept telling them "we'll look after you, we'll look after you" — but when the crunch came in March, we couldn't deliver. We couldn't protect them when it really mattered. No wonder many of them don't believe us any more.'

The UN Secretary-General's report of November 2004 confirmed that 'the rate of returns following the March events has been significantly reduced, and the safety and sustainability of these returns remains fragile.'[44] The SRSG's Serb adviser on returns, Nenad Radosavljevic, resigned in January 2005, saying there was no reason 'to, without a possibility to prevent it, watch the further cleansing of my people instead of their return'.[45]

Serbs and Albanians also disagreed about returns. Although the 'right to return' was still very popular with almost all Serbs, only a narrow majority of Albanians supported it. Three out of every eight Albanians did not agree with returns at all.[46]

Given the persistence of such attitudes, Peggy Hicks, who headed UNMIK's Returns Unit between 2002 and 2004, said a higher profile for Kosovo's provisional government on security for minority communities would have helped a great deal. Early in his tenure, Petersen recognised that some municipalities were still 'hampering' returns. After Ramush Haradinaj became Prime Minister, Petersen pushed him hard on the issue. Haradinaj, in turn, cajoled municipal leaders to support returns. Though it may seem counterintuitive that former guerrillas would be effective proponents of minority rights, Haradinaj and Thaci had, in fact, always been more helpful on minority issues than Rugova. The ex-KLA commanders had nothing to prove when it came to robustly defending what most Albanians perceive as the national interest, while Rugova was scarred by his close brush with political suicide after meeting with Milosevic during the NATO air war. Still, neither Thaci nor Haradinaj had ever taken the initiative to reach out to minorities without being asked.

Hicks believed that the clarity and credibility of the returns process was seriously undermined by unrealistic expectations and over- ambitious rhetoric on the part of the UN mission.[47] 'We've really just been looking for separate communities who could live side by side in security,' said Hicks. 'The words "multi-ethnic" and "integration" are too loaded. By using them, we just muddied the waters.'[48] She believed that only with a greater emphasis on transport linking Serb enclaves to one another and to vital public services could the returns effort succeed.

Eide agreed,[49] rating the danger of institutionalising segregation as less important than the need to stabilise Kosovo's precarious statistical diversity. Eide recommended creating 'a number of new municipalities where in particular the Kosovo Serbs would have a comfortable majority' and, controversially, giving these new jurisdictions 'enhanced competencies in areas such as police, justice, education, culture, media and the economy, including the appointment of key officials.' Just as controversially — in view of UNMIK's long-held opposition to territorial division along ethnic lines — Eide said decentralisation 'could allow for horizontal links between Kosovo Serb majority municipalities. Arrangements could also be considered for special ties to Belgrade, without giving Belgrade any authority in such communities.' In an even more direct challenge to UNMIK policy, Eide called for consideration to be given to allowing displaced Kosovo Serbs to settle in parts of Kosovo other than those where they had previously lived. This marked a major tactical victory for Belgrade.

Eide's proposal to grant local control over police and justice set alarm bells ringing — not just among Albanians but among international observers of the crippling division of authority in Bosnia. Rada Trajkovic, a Gracanica-based politician who was Vice-President of the (Kosovo) Serb National Council, said: 'Since there is so much distrust between the two communities, we want a strong municipal police that would be powerful enough to approve or bar the entry of police from the centre of Pristina to the enclaves.' Dardan Gashi, adviser to Local Government Minister Lutfi Haziri, said the decentralised police proposals could have disastrous consequences: 'It literally equips opposing ethnic groups with guns and lets them loose, taking away any central control that could provide checks and balances.' An unnamed Kosovo government official predicted, realistically: 'There will be conflict immediately. The Albanians would want to attack Serbs even more if they know they are armed, and we would also have armed Serbs blocking main roads through municipalities.'[50]

Segregation had been a two-way process, with Albanians excluded from Serb-dominated areas just as Serbs were excluded from Albanian areas. In northern Kosovo, the purging of Albanians had become a systematic state policy, driven by Serbia proper. Belgrade was clearly preparing the ground for a partition of Kosovo along the Ibar. Nebojsa Covic, the Serbian Deputy Prime Minister who covered Kosovo for the Belgrade government, had bought up Albanian houses in the north at prices well above market levels. 'Albanians just can't resist the money — and I'm sure that, if they did, there'd be, you know, the old knock on the door at night, or a grenade let off nearby, to make sure they moved out' said an international contractor living in northern Mitrovica.[51]

Covic had been trying to prepare the way for a partition of Kosovo in other ways, too. He paid to asphalt a dirt road linking the two otherwise isolated parts of northern Kosovo, allowing those people in Serb-majority Zubin Potok to travel to Zvecan, Mitrovica and Leposavic without going through Albanian areas. Initially seen as a measure to enhance security — Serbs understandably felt afraid when they travelled through the south — it soon became clear that the project formed part of a long-term agenda to make northern Kosovo completely separable from the south. Telephone networks had already been divided along the Ibar river. The water system, which once left northern Kosovo dependent on a water treatment plant in the Albanian village of Shipolje, was also being split.

From the Serbs' point of view, the flaw in Covic's plan to divide Kosovo along the Ibar was that more than half of Kosovo Serbs lived south of the river. Belgrade's success in persuading Eide to endorse virtual autonomy for Serb areas and the right of displaced Serbs to settle anywhere in Kosovo may make 'returning' to enclaves south of the Ibar more appealing, but it would also dangerously increase the resentment and hostility of the surrounding Albanian majority.

Political developments

Reactions to the March riots were contradictory and confusing. After American, Russian and European leaders all condemned the violence, Western diplomats asked Kosovo Albanian leaders to explain what had caused it. Naturally enough, they cited their own unfulfilled hopes: frustrations over restrictions on the provisional institutions; the delays and conditions attached to final status as set out by the 'Standards before Status' process; and the slow moving privatisation of socially owned enterprises. Keen to win back their local partners, the international community made a series of minor concessions. An international adviser to the Prime Minister who had become unpopular with some Albanians for insisting on adherence to the Constitutional Framework was sacked; and UNMIK promised to accelerate privatisation.

The mixed signals were accompanied by a downscaling of the international civilian presence in Kosovo. 'People here have got to accept it's time for us to go' said one adviser to the SRSG.[52] 'Too many people in the mission here can't see the overall picture — we've done as much as we can; staying here longer isn't going to do anyone any good.'

The once overwhelming international NGO community was all but gone; NATO's presence was still under pressure to be reduced; and the UN Mission had shrivelled as staff and budgets were depleted. Although Petersen sought to restore to UNMIK the suppleness it once had in its youth, the lines of age were firmly etched in the mission's structures and in its image among the local population. Petersen had succeeded in slowing the decline — the UN's budget was set to fall by only fifteen per cent in his first year as SRSG, much less than some New York planners had pushed for. In late 2004, UNMIK had fewer than 900 international staff — still more than under Kouchner, but far fewer than the 3,000 plus it had in its heyday under Steiner.

Many of the diplomatic offices had in fact lost patience with UN-MIK from the beginning of Holkeri's tenure. 'Nobody listens to them any more,' said one diplomat working for the Pristina representative office of a Contact Group country.[53] Eide himself wrote that the international community was 'fragmented and without leadership' prior to the March riots. Indeed, since Holkeri's arrival the main power-brokers — the US, EU, UK, Germany, France, Italy and Russia — had all been trying to form direct links with important Kosovo Albanians, bypassing the UN and undermining UNMIK in the process. The Contact Group brought in a British diplomat and a senior fellow from the US Institute for Peace into UNMIK to formulate a plan to implement the Standards. Just as NATO had gone around the UN when it undertook the war, now, albeit more subtly, the same great powers were bypassing the UN again.

Eide condemned 'Standards before Status'— the slogan which for the past two-and-a-half years had summed up the international approach to Kosovo — as 'untenable in its present form'. He said the policy had lost credibility — with the Albanians who thought the Standards were 'unrealistically ambitious and unachievable', with Serbs, and with the international community itself, which he said 'publicly repeats the mantra, but with little conviction'.[54] Six months after the riots, the Contact Group told Petersen to develop 'Standards Light', as Eide stipulated. About two-thirds of the tests were dropped. Now only the most 'urgent priorities' needed to be met for Kosovo to qualify for status talks. It was confirmation that the date when Kosovo's status would be reviewed was etched into the political calendar. If Kosovo had not reached the Standards when the review came, then the Standards would probably be diluted further: Kosovo could not be allowed to fail. Once again, the international community was bowing to bullies, reinforcing the Balkan view that violence works.

The whole mission was reorienting towards getting out. The new Primary Deputy to the SRSG, Kosovo veteran Larry Rossin, believed that powers should be transferred to local institutions much faster (by contrast, New York had told Steiner to slow down on transfer of powers). While the mission tried to maintain its insistence on transferring powers only to competent hands, the distinction between transferable and reserved powers was disappearing. Eide wrote of the need for UNMIK to 'make greater use of sanctions and interventions'. Together these trends amounted to a new balance of power between UNMIK and the PISG. UNMIK would now step in only if the Kosovo institutions failed disastrously.

The LDK-AAK coalition government. While the international community reoriented its approach to Kosovo, Kosovo's local political landscape became energised but also more volatile. In autumn 2004, Veton Surroi made a bid for office with a new party called ORA that even included non Albanians (though no Serbs). After winning about one-twelfth of the votes, Surroi positioned himself as a strenuous but reasonable opposition leader, collaborating with Thaci against the government but yielding to international pressure more readily than the PDK leader.

The general elections of autumn 2004 led — after much delay — to the formation of a government comprising the Democratic League of

Kosovo (LDK) and the Alliance for the Future of Kosovo (AAK), with Ramush Haradinaj as Prime Minister. For three months, Haradinaj supplied energetic leadership and spurred action on the central and local levels. He urged locally elected mayors to do whatever they could to promote multi-ethnicity in their areas, in particular to correct road signs written only in Albanian. In his personal interactions with local Serb leaders, the former guerrilla acted as if they had grown up together. Nationalist triumphalism was out. When his cabinet suggested using government money to fund a contentious commemoration at the family compound of Adem Jashari, the Albanian resistance hero, Haradinaj replied: 'Are you out of your minds?'[55]

Virtually all observers in the international community credited his government with accomplishing more in one hundred days than had been achieved in the previous three years. The democratically elected Provisional Government created structures for achieving progress on 'the Standards' for the first time. Haradinaj also helped to create a positive climate for returns with strong public statements. Working groups that included formerly displaced Serbs who had returned to Kosovo drafted a plan to bring government closer to people by devolving power to local municipalities. With generous help from France, Italy, Germany, the United Kingdom and the US, this decentralisation process began with pilot projects in five villages. Slavisha Petkovic, a Serb who had been an 'internally displaced person' before returning to Kosovo, became head of the government's Ministry for Returns and (Minority) Communities. The government allocated his ministry 14 million euros — the third biggest budget of any ministry. Among other accomplishments, it succeeded in returning eighteen displaced minority families to Pristina. As Petkovic pointed out, this was far more people than Serbia's coordinator for Kosovo had managed to return in over three years.

On 25 February 2005, Haradinaj wrote an open letter to the people of Kosovo. It said: 'All Kosovo citizens have a moral and civic obligation to understand the importance of the processes which we are passing through as a country and society, and to support the centre and local institutions to implement the Standards, by fostering the sense of tolerance, understanding and respecting each other. Most Albanians have a special obligation to members of the Serb community.'[56]

Just a couple of weeks after this letter was issued, news broke that Haradinaj had been indicted by the international tribunal in The Hague. Haradinaj resigned immediately as Prime Minister. In a consummately composed and responsible statement, Haradinaj prevailed on his ministers to continue the work his government had been doing. He urged them to keep pursuing the Standards, thereby positioning Kosovo to get a pass mark from the Review and begin the process leading to resolution of its final status. On 9 March 2005, Haradinaj flew to The Hague, along with his young wife, and turned himself in to the Tribunal.

Overnight, posters and t-shirts appeared all over Pristina sporting a stylised image of Haradinaj and the phrase 'Our Prime has a job to do here.' Along with other political leaders and journalists around Europe, Petersen praised Haradinaj's courageous and dignified response and said he was losing a valued 'friend and partner'. In an article for *The Guardian*, former British Foreign Secretary Robin Cook wrote: 'Haradinaj has done a greater service for Kosovo by encouraging his people to accept the rule of international law than any action he could have taken by staying in office. As a result, Kosovo may now be nearer to international acceptance of eventual independent status.'[57]

Haradinaj returned to Kosovo, five weeks after being indicted, when he was granted permission to attend the funeral of his 24-year-old brother, Enver, who had been shot dead in a drive-by shooting. (Enver's death matched a six-year-old pattern of tit-for-tat revenge killings between the Haradinaj and Musaj clans.) Eighty thousand mourners attended Enver's funeral under dreary skies. The former Prime Minister and war crimes indictee still urged inter-ethnic tolerance, telling the mourners that it was important to ensure the 'protection not only of the lives of KLA soldiers and KLA veterans but (the) lives of every citizen of Kosovo. This is the best way to support the state-building process that is going on in Kosovo now.'[58]

Despite its strong sympathy for Ramush Haradinaj, after his indictment the international community immediately began pressuring President Rugova and other LDK and AAK leaders to form a broad coalition that included the PDK. Only a broad-based coalition of all the main Albanian leaders, they thought, would be able to make the historic compromises necessary to settle Kosovo's status. Only with Thaci as Prime Minister, according to this point of view, could discipline be maintained over the various officials, particularly those outside Pristina. They feared that Thaci could cause trouble, possibly including violence, if he remained marginalised, and believed Kosovo needed to present as unified a position as possible before going into status negotiations.[59] But the offices of the Quint (the US, UK, France, Germany and Italy) and the SRSG could not agree on who should lobby Kosovo's leaders to bring about Thaci's elevation. The Quint expected Petersen to take the lead and thought he had agreed to do so, but the SRSG never gave a strong push. International pressure to create a broad Thaci-led coalition quickly unravelled in the face of the incumbent coalition's determination to carry on. Bajram Kosumi, a former student activist who had spent ten years in Serbian prisons but had not been involved in guerrilla fighting, became Haradinaj's hand-picked successor.

UNMIK sought ways to appease Thaci, who was deeply embittered about having been denied the premiership yet again. The consolation prize was a place on a new 'joint body on status'. Like the KPC in 1999, this institution was invented to create a controlled environment for those who might otherwise cause havoc. As proposals for the composition and remit of the body became more detailed, the starkness of the divide between the winners and losers of the election became irreconcilable. Thaci insisted that it be composed of party leaders, giving him, as a relatively experienced politician with little else to do, a chance to dominate. But the coalition partners rejected his demands, and the PDK was forced to accept whatever it could get. Yet again, Thaci found himself neither top dog nor with full freedom to criticise those who were.

Looking for the exit. Michael Steiner had first raised the idea of conducting a formal assessment to determine whether Kosovo was ready to enter the process of resolving its final status when he was SRSG. He made his suggestion in March 2003, and expected the review to occur in two years or so. Positive reports by the SRSG to the UN Security Council and by the Contact Group in May 2005 set the stage for the Secretary-General to appoint Kai Eide to review Kosovo's progress and assess whether the time was ripe to begin status negotiations. In October 2005, Eide concluded that 'there will not be any good time for addressing Kosovo's status... Nevertheless, an overall assessment leads us to the conclusion that the time has come to commence this process.'[60]

What had changed was how the international community weighed the costs and benefits of maintaining the status quo. Members of the Contact Group recognised that the pressures that led to the explosion in March 2004 had not abated and could soon lead to a new eruption if no progress towards resolving Kosovo's status was seen. Apart from Serb-majority areas, Kosovo was already separate from Belgrade; the next step was for Kosovo to become a sovereign European country recognised by other states and, eventually, integrated into Europe. The challenge for the international community was to find a formula for an amicable divorce: an independent Kosovo that did not inspire nationalist forces in Serbia — at minimal cost to diplomatic capital.

Diplomats had also recognised that Kosovo represented an ever-increasing burden on democratic forces attempting to reform Serbia, still the single most important country in the region. The EU also recognised that having an area in the western Balkans that remained outside the Union indefinitely would pose a threat to its security. Hence, it became anxious to ensure that Kosovo, Serbia and Montenegro, Albania, Croatia, Macedonia and Bosnia were all actively engaged in a constructive pre-accession reform process, lured on by the prospect of EU membership some ten years away; Kosovo's sovereignty would have to be settled before EU membership could be a real possibility.

Eide recommended the appointment of special envoys to tackle the issue. Instead of trying to reach an agreement through a big conference like Dayton or Rambouillet, the details of recognising Kosovo's independence would be worked out through shuttle diplomacy between Pristina, Belgrade, European capitals, Washington and the UN in New York.

The UN appointed former Finnish President and veteran statesman Martti Ahtisaari as its envoy in the negotiations. In anticipation of the status talks, Rugova had named a negotiating team including himself, Prime Minister Bajram Kosumi (AAK), parliamentary speaker Nexhat Daci (LDK), Veton Surroi (ORA) and Hashim Thaci (PDK). Many worried that rivalries among these leaders particularly would make it impossible for them to work together.

President Rugova died of lung cancer on 21 January 2006, age 61, prompting a broad reshuffle of Kosovo leaders. LDK general secretary Fatmir Sejdiu, like Rugova a softspoken academic, became head of the party and President. Rugova's place in the delegation — expanded to eight members — was taken by the youthful and pragmatic Lutfi Haziri, most internationals' favourite Kosovo politician.

On 1 March 2006, Kosumi was persuaded to step down as Prime Minister and the LDK removed Nexhat Daci, who refused to resign, from his post as Assembly President. Sejdiu then invited Agim Ceku, Commander of the KPC, to form a government. In some ways Ceku was a surprising choice: he was unaffiliated with any party and Serbs believed that his actions while fighting with the Croat forces in the Krajina in the early 90s made him a war criminal. But Ceku consistently ranks as the most popular public figure in Kosovo, and internationals and locals alike believe he commands the respect necessary to maintain political discipline during the volatile status negotiations process.

Seven years after UNSCR 1244 was passed at the end of the war, Kosovo is set to be internationally recognised as an independent entity. Instead of negotiating Kosovo's status within Serbia, the negotiations will focus on Serbs' status within Kosovo. The status talks began in Vienna with two days of discussions on devolving powers to municipalities. Powers still reserved to UNMIK and KFOR, including powers over police and taxes, will be transferred to the government of Kosovo, but the European Union will probably pick up the UN's powers to intervene to protect human rights and minorities' interests, on the grounds that these are essential prerequisites of progress towards EU membership. Serbs will win a significant decentralisation of power and further quotas to safeguard their presence in the civil service and government; Serbian monasteries will probably be granted some special extraterritorial status, perhaps under some international body such as UNESCO. But the UN will probably stay in Mitrovica, perhaps governing the north along the lines of the former UN administration in Eastern Slavonia.

Hearts and minds

The March riots also galvanised progress in the media sector. In his report on the March 2004 violence, the Temporary Media Commissioner concluded that 'RTK [Radio and Television of Kosovo — the public broadcaster set up and largely funded by international donors], was chiefly if not exclusively responsible among the three Kosovo-wide television broadcasters for transforming the deaths of the three boys from a tragic news story into dangerous political theatre.' His report also concluded that, 'There are clear indications that the RTK board of directors is unable to provide the kind of corporate guidance and supervision that the governing board of a public broadcaster should provide.'[61]

RTK and the TMC reached a negotiated settlement, in which the public broadcaster publicly accepted that:

'1. The assertions of RTK news bulletins on 16 March that a group of Serbs was responsible for the drowning of three children were made without checking facts or making a full inquiry to verify the accuracy of broadcast material, notwithstanding the potential consequences. RTK also failed to correct these assertions in a timely manner.

2. RTK allowed interviews in live newscasts containing proclamations which could be considered as 'hate speech,' without proper challenge by RTK, that implied a specific ethnic category of people was responsible for criminal activity.'[62]

To prevent such incidents happening again, RTK undertook a range of reforms including new training for reporters and producers in reporting on conflicts and conflict management. The broadcaster revised its code of ethics and its reporting guidelines, brought on international advisers and changed several members of its board of directors. By December 2004, these changes seemed to have improved RTK's political coverage. The TMC noted that, 'The result of RTK's efforts have already been proven in its performance during the coverage of the 2004 parliamentary election campaign in Kosovo, which has received the highest positive evaluation by Kosovar and international institutions including the TMC.'[63] RTK also increased its programming for minorities, including both a new news programme and *Sesame Street* in Serbian. However, RTK had failed to convince Serbs that it had changed: also in December 2004, a poll found that 77 per cent of Albanians were 'happy with RTK' while only 3.9 per cent of Serbs were.[64]

The Independent Media Commissioner. During the summer of 2005, the various stakeholders in the Kosovo media — journalists, the OSCE, the Kosovo institutions and the representative offices of the US and several European countries — had finally agreed on the terms of a new, local body to regulate the media. This 'Independent Media Commissioner' had been intended from the beginning to take over from the international TMC as media arbiter and regulator in the earliest days of the mission. Ironically, the six-year delay had not been caused by concerns over its independence, or a fear that it might not perform properly. Instead, there was a trans-Atlantic cultural rift over public broadcasting. At issue was how much advertising revenue RTK should be allowed to earn in addition to the subsidy paid through the electrical utility. Those who understood the principles of public broadcasting, mostly Europeans, argued that to be effective, a public broadcaster has to have some revenue that was entirely insulated from government and state pressure.[65]

The US, which has no tradition of public broadcasting in the European sense, disagreed. Americans had fought — sometimes quite viciously — to force the public broadcasters in Kosovo, Bosnia and elsewhere, to be wholly dependent on state funds while private channels, to which the US government provided generous seed money, had the advertising market to themselves. The American case was strengthened by the dominance of RTK: in 1999, it had moved into the premises of the old state broadcaster and began broadcasting over its frequency, giving it a massive head start and most of Kosovo's broadcast audience; it captured and held the lion's share of the market for five years. It took until 2004 for the private stations TV21 and KohaVision to establish themselves with viewers, and in 2005 their ratings suddenly shot up at RTK's expense. This reversal in fortunes paved the way for the Americans to agree to allow the public broadcaster, RTK, to sell a significant amount of advertising, all overseen by a local media regulator. As in other areas, it was not that local people had reached some magical threshold of readiness that qualified them for the transfer of power, but that a new and quite separate consensus had been reached within the international community.

While Kosovo media were gaining credibility, UNMIK's Department of Public Information was losing it. Many in Kosovo's political class — most importantly the local and international media — regarded the fifty-strong department as an expensive non-entity.[66] Some staff of the once influential DPI doubted it had the capacity to roll out even a basic public information strategy. DPI had marginalised itself, and at times the whole mission: after the departures of Steiner and Haselock, it stopped monitoring television news. This meant that for several months the mission knew nothing of the medium through which over 90 per cent of Kosovans followed current events. Nor did it effectively engage international media. In April 2005 the *Economist*'s correspondent complained of having to wait eight days to receive an answer to a simple question that a Kosovo government spokesman gave him in a matter of minutes.[67] Without meaning to, UNMIK's Department of Public Information had transferred to Kosovo institutions the power to persuade. It could be argued that UNMIK's laryngitis didn't matter: the mission was on its way out and the Petersen's own popularity ratings were as high as any SRSG's had ever been.

Public views. Almost six years into the mission, UNDP opinion surveys suggested some institutions had carried hearts and minds, while others clearly had not. Most popular among Kosovo Albanians were the KPC (96 per cent satisfied[68]), the Kosovo Police Service (88 per cent[69]) and KFOR (85 per cent[70]). SRSG Petersen also scored well — three-quarters of Kosovo Albanians approved of him, up from a dismal 32 per cent for Holkeri in March 2004. A majority of Kosovo Albanians were also positive about 'Kosovo's political direction'.[71] On the other side of the spectrum only two out of every five Kosovo Albanians were satisfied with UNMIK Police and the Kosovo courts; and UNMIK itself was popular with only 20 per cent of respondents.[72]

Most Kosovo Serbs gave very downbeat responses to the survey.[73] They were generally 'very dissatisfied' with Kosovo's political direction, and three-quarters disapproved of SRSG Petersen — a figure he must have found ungracious, given his efforts to accommodate them. They were even less impressed by UNMIK than the Albanians.[74] If UNMIK had been up for election, it would have needed to campaign hard to win votes from anybody in Kosovo other than its own staff.

Although few Kosovo Albanians had been persuaded of the need for reconciliation with Serbs, opinions were not homogeneous. Just walking into a small town café revealed how much views differed. 'We Albanians need to be more tolerant, we need to move on,' said one young man in Slatina. 'We used to play together before 1999. We had to flee after Serb [sic   Serbian] soldiers were here [in our village] for 21 days, but it was just the soldiers who were bad.' His views contrasted vividly with those of three men sitting elsewhere in the café. 'Serbs don't accept the reality that Kosovo is independent; they have changed the facts,' said a gruff middle-aged man. 'UNMIK treats them better than us: if we had blocked a road at Caglavica [a reference to the Serb roadblock that helped precipitate the March 2004 violence] we would have been ejected immediately. Only Serbs who haven't done anything should feel safe walking in Pristina. Albanians have a history of fighting fascism and we will continue to do so.'[75]

Youth. Kosovo had the largest proportion of young people in the region. Young people were not only, as the hackneyed phrase continually reminds us, 'the future'; they were also the present — an estimated 60 per cent of Kosovans were under twenty-five years old. Most of this upcoming generation were being fed propaganda at school: nationalist elements 'persevered in the curriculum'; political appointments were 'prevalent' in Kosovo's education system; and many teachers had urged their students to partake in the March 2004 pogrom. After this unenlightening basic education, fewer than a third of people between fifteen and nineteen enrolled in further education or training programmes — most young people were 'living without prospects for employment, worthwhile current activity, or faith in the future.'[76]

When it became apparent that no part of UNMIK was focusing on young people, some in the OSCE Pillar suggested trying to fill the gap. They proposed new resources for civic education and to 'encourage democratic processes in the management and operation of educational establishments'; improvements in the way of various educational activities were administered; and a public information campaign to raise awareness of education's importance. None of these measures addressed the poison at the heart of education in Kosovo — its domination by ideologically driven political forces. Nevertheless, even this modest approach encountered fierce resistance from the OSCE's Permanent Council in Vienna, which was wary of 'interfering too much in local culture'.[77] The OSCE's Mission in Kosovo had been mandated to build democratic institutions and foster respect for human rights, responsible media and the rule of law, but the OSCE's leaders were unwilling to confront the forces that undermined all these worthy goals.

The intelligentsia. On 30 September 2005, the first new film production from Kosovo in seventeen years, *Kukumi*, premiered at Pristina's slick ABC Cinema. Directed by Isa Qosja, *Kukumi*, which won awards at film festivals in Italy and Bosnia, told the story of three inmates in a lunatic asylum amid the euphoria and anarchy of post-war Kosovo. '*Kukumi* portrays Kosovo as a land of idyllic hills, beautiful woods, purple skies and pretty wooden cottages inhabited by harsh and backward peasants. The villages themselves have a character of their own which threaten(s) to crush any sign of individuality or original thought. The old men of the Albanian village in their *plis* — the traditional white hats — take on the appearance of a gang of mafia dons, eager to find someone to crucify instead of their more traditional roles as pillars of the local community,' wrote the reviewer, Jeta Xharra. Instead of focusing on Albanians' suffering at the hands of Serbs, as most would have predicted from Kosovo's first film since the conflict, Qosja focused instead on how Albanians reacted to anarchy, and, in particular, how some took brutal advantage of it. A village thug extorted money from returning refugees in the film, and men raped their brothers' wives, thinking they could get away with it. Xharra wrote: 'The casual brutality that emerged in post-war Kosovo stemmed from an older set of patriarchal laws which were used as an excuse to rob property from the weak and deny care to the vulnerable.' A real-life example of such bullying behaviour, *Kukumi* depicts a ten-year old boy who remained an orphan because his father was killed in a massacre by Serbs — Albanian tradition prohibited his mother's new husband from raising another man's child. Xharra concluded: 'It is particularly refreshing to see the film's main character mock old politicians' stereotypically stern speeches about "the intelligent people of Kosovo" while the camera focuses on a dull and ignorant crowd of men, clapping their hands without actually understanding the politician's words.'

'Although efforts were made to add glitz and glamour to Kosovo's first feature film premiere, reality intruded to make the end result far less appealing. The microphones used for the film's presentation did not work; the film's projection began with a black line down the middle of the screen and the lack of any seating plan ensured that many in the audience were left to stand.' Twenty minutes before the film's end, a bomb threat required the cinema to be evacuated. 'The film ending with a bomb scare only added to the feeling of a dysfunctional land waiting to explode.'[78]

Both *Kukumi* and Xharra's review of it were produced by members of a small cultural elite whose conversation, mainly in Pristina's handful of stylish bars and cafes, frequently sparkles with wry insights into Kosovo society. It is a well educated, international group in which women are disproportionately represented. Xharra herself, for instance, is a founding member of the Balkan Investigative Reporting Network, an ensemble of eleven journalists spread across the former Yugoslavia; all but two are from the former Yugoslavia and all but one are women. Among the most important factors shaping Kosovo's future will be whether this group can find an idiom through which to capture the imaginations of less cosmopolitan Kosovans and how much increasing opportunities for education and travel may transform the intelligentsia from an elite into a broader middle class.

The economy

By 2004, the economic bubble had disappeared. Unemployment was around 30 per cent, with many workers underemployed. The mainstays of the economy remained remittances from the diaspora and income generated by the international presence, both of which were declining.

Public perceptions of the economy lagged behind actual trends. In 2002 and 2003, when most donors had already reduced their aid, many Kosovans were still enjoying previously unknown wealth. It took until 2004 for the illusion of prosperity to evaporate. By the time Petersen arrived, nearly everyone had finally begun to realise that the economy was not steaming ahead as hoped. Many cited the economy as the international community's biggest failure; an even greater number recognised the problem but couldn't decide whom to blame for it.

If economic privation was a spur to the lethal violence of March of that year, it was no coincidence that the riots occurred when they did. 2004 was the year people woke up to their manifest poverty. Prosperity, like independence, seemed to have been postponed much longer than initially hoped; by 2004, many had concluded it would never arrive. Mid-March, at the end of a tough Balkan winter, was when people were most aware of the failings of the local power supply. Privatisation seemed to be foundering more than ever. And in March, the many Kosovans who were seasonally employed — especially in agriculture — would have been unpaid for many months. Poverty no more presents an excuse for the ethnic violence of March 2004 than a deprived upbringing should count as an excuse for other violent crime; but if there was a causal link, it is that the 'feel-good factor', fleetingly delivered by the reconstruction effort in the early days, had gone into reverse.

Petersen recognised the acuteness of the economic crisis and did his best to apply first aid. 'Quick impact projects at the municipal level will be implemented with donors and United Nations agencies in order to lay the groundwork for the recovery of the economy,' he wrote.[79]

These schemes are not long-term infrastructure projects. They amount to employing largely unskilled labour, often for only ten weeks or so — an approach first undertaken in Kouchner's time. UNMIK's capacity to generate long-term employment prospects had hardly improved since the mission started.

Such progress as there was laid bare deeper problems. Whereas early economic reports spoke of destroyed infrastructure, homeless refugees and emergency assistance, reports from 2004 treated Kosovo like a semi-developed country. They spoke of private sector investment, capital accumulation and government spending distortions. In other words, in the five years since the war, Kosovo's economy and infrastructure had graduated from the top of the catastrophe league without quite reaching the developing one.

Though graduation from catastrophe was progress, by 'normal' criteria Kosovo's economy looked even worse. In December 2001, the IMF had estimated Kosovo's GDP to be 1.85 million euros. By June 2003, this figure had dropped to 1.57 million, and by December 2003, to 1.34 million.[80] In effect, Kosovo's temporary emergency had masked its deeper impoverishment.

The IMF acknowledged 'modest growth in 2003', but said that by 2004, 'activity in most areas has stagnated, given flat or even declining incomes'.[81] The main reason for this was a 'sharp fall in foreign assistance', which was practically irreversible. The IMF also raised two other concerns. First, it sensed a 'lack of fiscal strategy'. This, it said, had emerged from Kosovo's emergency revenue and spending regime being continued longer than appropriate. In the early days, when there had been plenty of cash (thanks mainly to generous donors) but a cash-flow problem (caused by many donors delivering their aid slowly), the priority had been to make sure that budget officers didn't spend money that wasn't yet in the bank account. Consequently, spending requests had always been checked against cash reserves. To avoid large cash surpluses at year end, autumn had come to be marked by spending frenzies, as budget officers desperately tried to spend their allocations. This naturally led to some unnecessary projects being funded while serious needs that arose earlier in the year — and the private sector that had provided the tax revenue in the first place — went without.

By 2004, tax revenues were approaching 37 per cent of GDP — the same level as in Britain and much higher than in the US. According to World Bank estimates, the PISG's mandated fiscal prudence had resulted in a total government surplus worth a massive one quarter of annual GDP by 2003. The IMF recommended a more normal budgeting procedure, but acknowledged that such a change would be difficult. Kosovo's continuing inability to borrow money internationally meant that overspending would cause a fiscal crisis; budget planners still had to err on the side of caution.

KEK. The IMF's other major concern was the 'slow progress in restructuring public enterprises'. The largest of these was KEK, Kosovo's electricity dinosaur. Many commentators urged UNMIK to 'tackle the electricity problem' as if there were an obvious solution. Every SRSG had tilted at KEK, almost like a rite of passage: Kouchner had set up an 'Energy Task Force' and imported electricity from Serbia; Haekkerup had called for more donor support and tried to crack down on illegal connections; Steiner had set up an 'UNMIK-PISG Energy Committee' and brought in a top electricity manager from Germany; Holkeri had sought more local involvement by setting up an energy office working with the Prime Minister; and, under Petersen, the idea of a new power station being built in the territory was mooted and international 'turn-around management' was brought in. None of these brought about a radical change in KEK's performance, although the turnaround management did make a belated impact on bill payment rates. Whatever was tried, there was still not enough power to satisfy consumer demand, which had tripled since 1999, and KEK required repeated handouts to cover costs. With half a billion euros of donor aid but poor collection rates from consumers, the electricity sector still needed regular bailouts from the government budget to keep it going.

Though all remedies to date have been found wanting, three general conclusions can be deduced about the 'KEK problem' and the attempts to solve it. First, there is not just one problem at the firm but many: the decrepit infrastructure, the staff, the finances, the consumers who connect to the grid without paying, and the way the whole system fits together. Second, which of these has been the biggest problem has changed several times since the war. There used to be a problem with corruption, but this was tackled (hopefully) when the former director Jo Trutschler was convicted of embezzlement in 2003. There may have been a problem with workers sabotaging infrastructure because they got paid more to repair it than to run it, but this was solved when the financial incentive was removed. Hence, the various solutions have not all failed; most of them have succeeded in tackling part of the overall problem, perhaps continually staving off a complete collapse. And third, because of these other two conclusions, it is unfair to look at the endemic problems at KEK and conclude that UNMIK, the EU, or any other body in Kosovo ought to be blamed or reprimanded. It is not that UNMIK and the EU haven't tried; if anything, they tried too hard. Advice was taken from local experts, international governments, contractors and many others, and much of it was implemented. KEK had to cope with massive changes: a tripling of energy demand; a collapse in the payment system; and a massive influx of unskilled staff to replace the old technicians. If the rule of law prevailed in Kosovo, then illegal connections could have been properly punished, bill collection enforced and poor staff trained or replaced. But without the rule of law, KEK's performance probably could never have been improved in a sustainable way in the time available.

Privatisation. The other objects of the IMF's concern were the so-called socially owned enterprises (SOEs) inherited from the Yugoslav system — moribund bundles of assets at the centre of the stalled privatisation process. In addition to factories and mines, huge tracts of agricultural land were on the books of these companies. The practical challenge was to liberate various salvageable assets from the dead legal shell that surrounded them; the political wrangle was over who should be liable if any previous creditors to the companies brought legal action. The UN continued to argue that since it could not extend its immunity to cover the sell-offs because they were not explicitly sanctioned by UNSCR 1244, some very unfortunate official would be personally liable. By 2004, the legal manoeuvrings attempting to solve this dilemma had become too obscure for any but the most seasoned lawyer to puzzle through.[82]

The privatisation teams did all they could until the long-sought legal formula arrived, including making a detailed log of all the investors with claims to the old firms. Nikolaus Lambsdorff, who headed the EU Pillar at the time, publicly tried to justify the delay, telling the BBC, 'How would you like it if someone sold off your assets without bothering to check they got the details right?'[83] But privately he was anxious to progress with the issue, fully aware how urgent it was. Indeed, several firms had already been sold off in a bidding process, started during a lull in the legal wrangling, but these sell-offs had been frozen following legal challenges. Privatisation was deadlocked at the time of the March riots. In the political post-mortem that followed it was cited by the Provisional Government as a key reason for popular discontent.

Lambsdorff knew that if he tried to deal with competing legal claims to every property he had to privatise, the process would be doomed. He cabled the UN lawyers in New York with a proposal to assert the American legal concept of 'eminent domain', according to which the Kosovo Trust Agency, the privatisation agency working under the aegis of the EU Pillar, would have the right to appropriate property and only later pay cash compensation to anyone who could establish title to the seized asset.[84] The UN accepted.[85]

As in many other areas, the riots broke the privatisation logjam in a way no amount of legal wrangling had managed to previously. Finally, almost six years into the UNMIK mission, privatisation was underway. Under the new legal arrangement, UNMIK's latest privatisation czar, Josh Dick, put forward a plan to sell-off ninety per cent of all the SOEs by spring 2006, and it was accepted.[86]

But the long-delayed legal success did not solve all the problems of Kosovo's SOEs. Many potential investors were discouraged by the con tinuing security problems. Ramazan Hajdini planned to invest the small fortune he had made running a chain of restaurants in Chicago. When he bid for enterprises in Kosovo, he received threats over the phone to withdraw from the bidding. Another entrepreneur, Bekim Kuqi, owned a large department store in Ferizaj/Urosevac. When he showed interest in bidding in a privatisation in November 2004, a car bomb crashed into his store and destroyed it. Kuqi lost $5 million. Other investors complained about horrendous inefficiency on the part of local and international officials.

The hopes many Kosovans invested in the privatisation process were wildly exaggerated. The industrial assets at stake were derelict. Most had already been asset stripped, few could become profitable, and they didn't provide many jobs — far fewer than 20,000 across the territory,[87] although no-one was sure of the exact number. Privatisation didn't restart failing firms; it just allowed their assets to be re-used, usually in a completely different way.

The socially owned enterprises distracted from Kosovo's real economy. Despite its aspirations (and often delusions), fuelled in part by propaganda of the Tito era, Kosovo was never an industrial region. It remains what it has always been: an area of small businesses, mainly traders and farmers. A quarter of Kosovo's GDP is agricultural[88] — and this figure does not count the large portion of Kosovo's population which has ducked out of the system, trying to become self-sufficient with modest kitchen-gardens. Furthermore, whereas in the past Kosovans were able to emigrate, in particular to Germany and Switzerland, from where they could remit money, by 2005 this route had been largely closed. Gerald Knaus, Director of the European Stability Initiative, concluded: 'In sum, the post-war private sector that seemed to many foreign observers to be emerging with impressive speed in the first years after the war had proved to be shallow and short-lived. In many respects, it was a return to the private sector of the past, with roots in the pre-socialist times, which persisted to some extent throughout the Yugoslav era as "small business", and expanded in Kosovo during the 1990s. . . . There were now simply more importers, corner-shops, cafes, hairdressers, carpenters and taxi-drivers.' Hence, Knaus concluded, 'in the absence of a radical shift in policy, the next generation of young Kosovars (sic) has very little to look forward to except declining standards of living.'[89]

By 2005, the international community was unwilling to undertake such a radical shift. Knause's think-tank lobbied the European Commission to offer Kosovo the same generous breaks it had extended so successfully to other post-communist states in Eastern Europe. In particular, he called in vain for EU structural funds to be made available, whereby European money would be invested in Kosovo on the condition that Kosovo put forward matching funds of its own. According to the EU, while Kosovo was 'not yet ready' for structural funds, it was also 'too advanced' for the simple infrastructure aid of the early days.

The readiness of local institutions to take over from the EU Pillar was certainly questionable. The Ministry of Trade and Industry, for example, had very little to show for the first four years of its existence; one exception was the creation of a board to regulate the petroleum market, of which every single participant was a member of the minister's extended family.[90] The Ministry of Transport and Communications had done virtually nothing to break down the effective apartheid of service provision — one set of telephones, mobiles, roads and buses for Albanians, another for Serbs. But these failings tended to be overlooked by the international community, out of necessity rather than choice. When the imperative of passing responsibility to local institutions clashed with the ethos of holding those institutions to strict standards, the former invariably won out.

A final factor which precipitated the shift in power to the Kosovo government was the budget processes in New York, Vienna and Brussels, which determined the resources available for the international institutions. These had set the timetable for the downscaling of institutions like the EU Pillar long in advance. If local Kosovan politicians had wanted to know when they would be given power, they could have found out years beforehand by looking at the budget projections for the UN, OSCE and EU missions in Kosovo.

Economic Statistics

There have always been problems measuring Kosovo's economy. Before the war, the real picture was clouded by socialist subsidies, Milosevic's propaganda and a sizable grey economy. The chaos of 1999 defied economic measurement, and it took several years for Kosovo to develop a respectable statistical office after the intervention. Nevertheless, the World Bank and the International Monetary Fund are becoming reasonably confident of some basic measures of Kosovo's wealth and income (below).

Kosovo's economy was clearly in decline from the 1970s, fell further during the 1980s and crashed during the 1990s. There was a quick boom after the war, fuelled largely by donor money and other international cash. Some infrastructure was repaired or revamped, and the threat of inflation was largely avoided, but Kosovo has failed to establish a new industrial base. Consequently, Kosovo suffers from a huge trade deficit.

The post-war boom subsided three or four years after the war, leaving Kosovo with a rate of unemployment moving back towards the levels of the 1990s. The economy is still held back by problems with commercial law, a low skills base and infrastructure failings, notably in the electricity sector.

Gross Domestic Product (GDP), 2003:	€1.34 billion
Total Consumption, 2003:	€2.83 billion
GDP per capita 2003:	€700;
GDP per capita 1995:	$ 400 USD (roughly €400)
Average annual GDP growth 1989-1998:	− 12 percent
GDP growth rate 1999:	− 20 percent
GDP growth rate 2000:	+ 21.2 percent
GDP growth rate 2003:	+ 4.7 percent
Total imports 2003:	€971 million
Total exports 2003:	€37 million
Inflation rate 2000:	11 percent
Inflation rate 2003:	0 percent
Unemployment 2003, registered:	50-60 percent
Unemployment 2003, World Bank figure:	23 percent - 33 percent

PART II

WHY THE WORLD FAILED TO TRANSFORM KOSOVO

MEASURING SUCCESS

So, how does the international community's record in Kosovo measure up?

It is hard to assess whether the international community achieved its goals because it deliberately gave such vague instructions to both UNMIK and KFOR. UN Security Council Resolution (UNSCR) 1244 mandated KFOR to 'ensure public safety and order', but was silent on what level of crime or harassment should be considered acceptable. UNMIK was to 'organise and oversee the development of provisional institutions of democratic and autonomous self-government', which could mean anything from building structures devoid of content to creating a genuinely flourishing democratic system on a par with any in Western Europe.

Vague mandates did not just obscure the international community's performance; they also affected it. Indistinct objectives meant in the early days UNMIK and KFOR both erred towards a minimalist interpretation of their role. When KFOR first entered Kosovo, certain national units did little to protect some minorities from revenge attacks. UNMIK, understaffed, bowed to the American reluctance to pursue war crimes suspects for fear of provoking a backlash.

As the most pressing daily demands were tackled, and as resources increased, the international administration gradually became more ambitious. The Constitutional Framework included several elements resisted by local political leaders, such as reserved seats for women and ethnic minorities. By disconnecting electricity consumers who did not pay their bills and introducing laws against hate speech, UNMIK was trying to impose itself on local behaviour. Vague mandates had allowed 'mission creep'.

Once the first government was formed in 2002, the basic requirements of the UN resolution had been fulfilled. At this point, the international community had to redefine its role. Thus were born the columns of objectives and success indicators first known as 'the benchmarks' and soon redubbed 'the Standards'. The Standards comprised those elements of public life regarded as necessary for a sustainable and equitable peace, and for preparing Kosovo to eventually join the European Union. From 2003 on, the entire international community embraced the Standards as representing its goals in Kosovo and used them as the basis of all progress reports.

Because the Standards were agreed three years after the mission began, they only focused on the problems that still remained. The humanitarian successes of 1999, the administrative achievements of 2000 and the first steps towards constitutional democracy in 2001 were already taken for granted when the eight Standards were drawn up. Hence, although they have formed the basis of all post-2002 progress reports, it is unfair to assess the international community's performance in Kosovo solely on the basis of the Standards; Kosovo was starting from a much lower base in 1999. The Standards charted the way to the top of the mountain; they did not record the considerable distance to base-camp that had already been travelled.

Nevertheless, it was the Standards that the international community used to make its most momentous decision: whether Kosovo was ready to move towards resolving its political status — which could only be some form of independence. The person Kofi Annan appointed to make the assessment, the Norwegian General Kai Eide, judged that the status process should begin. But the picture he painted was extremely downbeat in most areas. In so doing, he also gave an implicit assessment of the whole international project in Kosovo — not just whether goals had been met, but whether the right goals had been set in the first place. Leaders of all Kosovo's major parties agreed with Serbian leaders that it was broadly fair and accurate.

This is where Kosovo stood with regard to each of the eight Standards at the moment when the UN recognised that its usefulness had come to an end (unless otherwise indicated, all quotations are from Eide's Review, October 2005):

Standard 1. Functioning Democratic Institutions: the Standards required democratic governance, revenue collection and the efficient delivery of public services, minority political participation and access to public services and public employment, PISG authority throughout Kosovo.

Eide notes that the establishment of a 'comprehensive set of new institutions' from a 'total institutional vacuum' constituted a 'tremendous achievement'. He praised the parliamentary elections of 2004 and said, 'The work of the Kosovo Assembly has steadily improved'.

But a closer look suggests that there was something superficial about these achievements: 'The development of new institutions is undermined by a strong tendency among politicians to see themselves as accountable to their political parties rather than to the public they serve. Political parties tend to consider new institutions and the civil service as "their" domains. Appointments are, therefore, regularly made on the basis of political or clan affiliation rather than competence.'

The Kosovo government, working in accordance with the Constitutional Framework, enabled Ramush Haradinaj to become Prime Minister just months before he was indicted for war crimes. Although the media were free, they often showed scant concern for factual reporting or responsible journalism.

Although the elections were free and fair, less than 1 per cent of the Serb population voted in October 2004. There were few Serbs or other minority members in the civil service, especially in senior management

positions. Serbs continued to use parallel health and educational structures financed mainly by Belgrade.

*Standard 2. Rule of Law: Organised crime networks should be disrupted, fi-
nancial crime checked, extremist violence ended, public respect for police and
judiciary, judges and the KPS impartial, all suspected criminals prosecuted, fair
trials guaranteed to everyone and minority representation sufficient.*

'Combating serious crime, including organised crime and corruption,
has proven to be difficult for the KPS and justice system. It is hindered
by family or clan solidarity, intimidation of witnesses as well as of law
enforcement and judicial officials… Far too few perpetrators of serious
crimes are ever brought to justice…'

The government's steps against corruption were 'slow and without a
convincing sense of commitment. Over the past six years, international
police, prosecutors and intelligence officials have tried — but failed
— to go much beyond the surface of the corruption problem. Clan
solidarity, codes of silence, language problems and inexperienced local
law enforcement institutions have all contributed to this failure.'

'Respect for rule of law is inadequately entrenched and the mechanisms to enforce it are not sufficiently developed… The Kosovo justice
system is generally regarded as the weakest of Kosovo's institutions.'

*Standard 3. Freedom of Movement: All communities should be able to circulate
freely throughout Kosovo, including city centres, and use their language.*

This Standard was particularly difficult to measure because 'freedom'
in this context is a state of mind. Most Serbs and other Serbian-speak-
ing minorities did not feel safe in most Albanian-inhabited areas. This
perception of risk was perpetuated by crimes and harassment that often went unreported, by the weak or non-existent condemnation of
atrocities against minorities by Albanian leaders and civil society, and by
the very low conviction rate. 'When perpetrators remain at large, the
sense of impunity prevails. Where there is freedom of movement for

the perpetrators, it is hard to convince the victim that he or she enjoys the same freedom.'

Standard 4. Returns and Reintegration: All Kosovo inhabitants should have their right to remain, right to property and right to return respected throughout Kosovo.

'Regrettably, little has been achieved to create a foundation for a multi-ethnic society....'

'The overall return process has virtually come to a halt. Kosovo Albanian leaders have committed themselves to the return process. However, this is the "Pristina reality". The reality on the ground is different. With very few exceptions, Albanian leaders pay lip service to multi-ethnicity but do little to translate their words into meaningful actions — or even to utter forceful words at sensitive moments or to local officials who are particularly hostile to minorities. The security situation, insufficient access to justice, lack of protection of property rights, and uncertain political and economic prospects discourage returns.'

Kosovo's return programme had gone into reverse, with more minorities leaving Kosovo than coming back to their homes. The main reason for this was the events of March 2004, which had instilled fear into minority communities. There were only 1,300 returns in the first eight months of 2004, compared with more than 3,000 the previous year. The number of returnees may pick up again, but this is not certain. It depends, in part, on UNMIK and KFOR being trusted again by the returnees. The international mission succeeded in reducing the death toll only by overseeing a process of segregation.

Standard 5. The Economy: There should be a sound institutional and legal basis for a market economy, a balanced budget, and socially owned assets should be privatised.

As with political institutions, in the economic sector Eide lauded the establishment of much-needed institutions, including regulators, the banking sector and 'a well-functioning Ministry of Finance and Economy'. He reported that the Kosovo Trust Agency expected that 90 per cent of the value of socially-owned enterprises would have been privatised by the spring of 2006. But 'high-level government officials are concerned that many of the investments will not lead to productive business activity. There is also the potential for using the privatisation process for money laundering purposes.'

More generally, Kosovo's economy remained 'precarious'. People were very poor by western European standards. Unemployment was very high, and Kosovo had very few exports, the result being a massive trade deficit. Government income was forecast to undershoot the revenue needed to cover its basic expenses.

Standard 6. Property Rights: All property, including residential property, land, enterprises and other socially owned assets, should have a clear and rightful owner.

'A great number of agricultural and commercial properties remain illegally occupied.' Though most residential property claims had been adjudicated (in itself an enormous achievement), 'less than half the decisions have been implemented'.

Standard 7. Dialogue with Belgrade: There should be normal relations with Belgrade and eventually with other neighbouring areas.

Dialogue was 'launched' with a purely symbolic meeting between Kosovo's President and Serbia's Prime Minister in Vienna in October 2003, but the process UNMIK had hoped this meeting would start was derailed by the violence the following March. Direct talks did not resume at a political level until October 2005, when the Kosovo Ministers of Culture and of Local Government and their Serbian counterparts met informally.

Standard 8. Kosovo Protection Corps: The KPC should comply with its mandate as a civilian organisation, scale down its troop numbers to its approved active strength and integrate Serbs and other minorities into its ranks.

Among Kosovo Albanians, the Kosovo Protection Corps was the most trusted institution within Kosovo. Eide credited its leaders with steady improvements in professionalism and adhering to its mandate.

Efforts to make the KPC multi-ethnic had been less successful — about 5 per cent of members were non-Albanian, compared with a target of 10 per cent. Many minority members of the KPC, especially Serbs, were leaving the Corps following intimidation from Belgrade and hardliners in their own local community.

The overall record. The record in Kosovo is mixed. The international community was very successful where there was a strong and unified international will to tackle a straightforward physical task: it tackled the humanitarian catastrophe of 1999, organised free and fair elections and refurbished Kosovo's infrastructure. Even in the category of physical challenges, the record is not all bright: the electric utility will not be able to satisfy demand in the foreseeable future, meaning that Kosovo will continue to experience the sorts of blackout characteristic of the Third World.

Where the international protectorate almost completely failed was in changing the way people thought and behaved. Unfortunately for would be nation-builders, it is this human factor that determines the character of a society, not its physical or institutional infrastructure. After six years of unprecedented international support, Kosovo remained a place where the strong bullied the weak, where might made right and where there remained an extraordinary lack of public spirit.

This is less than Western democracies hoped for when they intervened to stop barbarities in Kosovo in 1999, and much less than most of the thousands of foreigners and Kosovans of all communities believed they were working towards between 1999 and 2005.

EXPLAINING FAILURES

The international community's failures in Kosovo cannot be blamed on spectacularly incompetent individuals. Staff were hired from all over the world. The majority of them were experienced, most were dedicated and many were talented. They left families and loved ones to face uncertain risks in a difficult environment. A few died in Kosovo. Certainly there were individuals who performed less effectively than they might have, and a very small number have been prosecuted for malfeasance. But in few cases can a shortcoming of the mission as a whole be atrributed to a particular culprit within UNMIK. To blame the personnel of UNMIK and KFOR for everything that went wrong in Kosovo is to miss the point.

Similarly, most of the policy makers back in foreign capitals did their best to support the effort. The Western leaders who took NATO to war over Kosovo very much wanted the international administration to succeed. The international community put twenty-five times as much money and fifty times as many troops into Kosovo, on a per capita basis, as into Afghanistan. And yet despite this enormous commitment of resources and effort, by the mission's own standards it still largely failed. This is the tragedy that demands explanation.

Mission impossible? Perhaps UNMIK's ambitions were unrealistic. Some scholars have argued that after an ethnically-based conflict, a multi-ethnic society can never be reconstituted.[1] This view rests on the rigidity of roles in the conflict: partisans in ethnic conflicts cannot truly be won over. Unlike those driven by ideology, who might eventually be per-

240

suaded to change their views, soldiers fighting for an ethnicity know they will never be anything else — Serbs cannot become Albanian, just as Albanians cannot become Serb. This means leaders in one community have no incentive to reach out to the other. Certainly, in Kosovo, hardly any leaders felt that working with members of rival communities was worthwhile: it risked censure from their own community without any prospect of being rewarded by the other. However, this theory ignores the possibility that ethnic divisions can be transcended, for example through the generation of greater wealth or the creation of a supra-ethnic common identity, to create a society in which the old divisions are less important than new, common interests. It also ignores the strong international influence that could be brought to bear: diplomatic, financial and military pressure, and the prospect of eventual European integration, make strong persuaders. In Kosovo, these carrots eventually succeeded in turning most leaders, with varying degrees of enthusiasm, to embrace, at least rhetorically, the raft of policies required to make multi-ethnicity viable. The leader who was converted most dramatically in this way was Ramush Haradinaj.

Others argue that for democracy to emerge from conflict, a substantial civil society must already exist.[2] Whether such a civil society existed in Kosovo is debatable. There was certainly a structure capable of running a parallel education and healthcare system for nearly a decade, but it was geared more towards protest than implementing a positive political programme. Even this embryonic civil society was stunted by two ruthless rivals: the Serbian security apparatus and Albanian militants. Some Albanian moderates were killed by the Serb security forces just before the war (notably Fehmi Agani), while others adopted rigidly nationalist postures, afraid of being seen to grant concessions to the Serbs. The fear of being gunned down by internal opponents drove many moderate activists to keep a low profile — years after UNMIK had arrived, even President Rugova was sometimes afraid to leave his residence. Kosovo's civil society hardly offered firm bedrock on which democracy could be built.

Even so, the international community in Kosovo could have done more to foster a constructive civil society. A more robust security presence starting in June 1999 would have created space for moderates; carefully calibrated sticks and carrots could have more effectively rewarded progressive actions and punished retrogressive ones; and more decisive intervention in the marketplace of ideas, including both the media and education, would have helped progressive leaders to convince their constituents that moderation would produce positive results while militancy was doomed.

A third argument holds that the Albanians' struggle against their Serbian overlords artificially suppressed acute divisions within the Albanian community itself.[3] Certainly, many internationals who arrived in Kosovo expecting to reconcile Serbs and Albanians were shocked by the fierce animosity between the LDK and PDK, and other intra-Albanian feuds. According to this view, Kosovo had to go through a destructive phase of internal conflict before it would be sufficiently cohesive to become a viable state. It is a sobering fact that virtually all states that are generally stable today have gone through violent internal conflicts in the past (Australia, New Zealand and Canada, apart from their violence towards indigenous peoples, are exceptions). The challenge of modern post-conflict political construction is to replicate the positive aspects of successful nation building experiences without the violence that has nearly always accompanied them. Given the paucity of examples, peaceful nation-building may be an oxymoron.

UNMIK knew of the ferocious local rivalries and took some modest steps towards undercutting factionalism. In order to prevent the construction of regional power bases, it decided early on, for instance, that members of the Assembly would not represent geographically based constituencies. However, much more could have been done to create cross-cutting alliances. Employment schemes that encouraged young people to work in different parts of Kosovo, for example, might have inculcated a sense of broader civic identity by giving people a chance to develop relationships beyond their local areas. Boarding schools, a multiethnic national service programme and investment cooperatives for young people could have diluted the influence of KLA veterans while building a sense of community that extended beyond an individual's village, region or extended family. They might even have fostered relationships between people from different ethnic communities.

Six sources of failure

Most analyses of international administrations examine them sector by sector, much like the foregoing chronology chapters. While this approach can yield useful lessons, it invariably focuses on symptoms rather than sources of underperformance. Big issues can be lost in a welter of detail. The international administration in Kosovo was not blown off course by a series of technocratic failures; the course was set by the character of the so-called international community itself. In Kosovo, the international community was animated by the peculiar combination of ambitions and constraints, fears and blind spots that prevail at this juncture in history. This is where the explanations lie. More specifically, the various shortcomings of the international administration can all be attributed to six kinds of failure: failures of understanding, ideology, unity, structure, will and time.

Failures of understanding. The international community decided to intervene in Kosovo to stop massive human rights abuses, and it assumed this could be achieved by forcing out Serbian security forces. It failed to understand that the Kosovo conflict of the late nineties, however unequal when government security forces faced lightly armed guerrillas or even unarmed civilians, was only the latest chapter in a long-running competition between two peoples for control of territory. The international community realised too late that its alliance with Albanian militants was somewhat arbitrary. Both opposed Serb atrocities, but while the international community was against the atrocities, the guerrillas were primarily against the Serbs. Most Albanians who took up arms to challenge Serbian oppression did not object to one ethnic group bullying all the others; they simply wanted their group to be the one on top.

Having fundamentally misunderstood the nature of the conflict, the international actors involved in Kosovo naturally took the wrong approach to remedying it. As discussed in the first chronological chapter, KFOR was oriented towards protecting Kosovo's borders against aggression from Serbia. Much as in Iraq in 2003, there was little thought given to how to maintain order within Kosovo after the Yugoslav security forces withdrew. The violence against minorities — motivated by both 'revenge' and simple opportunism — established demographic facts on the ground that proved impossible to reverse. Some KLA fighters, and others claiming to be linked to them, profited from the chaos by capturing almost all the resources of Kosovo's tiny economy, thus entrenching themselves as a 'thugocracy'. The international community more than tolerated the so-called 'provisional government' declared by Hashim Thaci — a stance ostentatiously symbolised by US Secretary of State Madeleine Albright kissing Thaci on TV during her visit to Pristina in the summer of 1999.

The international administration also made a number of mistaken assumptions about the standing and capacity of local institutions. Kosovo's political parties were treated as if they resembled their Western counterparts — a group of civic minded people bound together by a shared commitment to certain ideological principles. In reality, they were personality driven patronage networks, some of them rooted in the KLA. The international community invested in local NGOs who did advocacy work, not realising that many had no commitment to 'democratic values'. In short, there was a failure to understand Kosovo's past and its contemporary society; it is not surprising that the international community could not mould Kosovo's future as it wished.

To understand where people in a society are coming from, officials in future missions will have to look beneath their usual radar. They must understand the features of the society that led to conflict and how these play out in daily life.

Failures of ideology. Fatefully reinforcing the misunderstandings of Kosovo's problems was a deep reluctance to tell Kosovans what they should do or how their society should change.

At a meeting in late 2003, senior UNMIK officials were discussing how to reformulate the mission's statement of purpose. Most people in the room were tinkering with some version of the formulation: 'To transform Kosovo into a society in which all its people could live in security and dignity'. The most senior UN official in the room pronounced: 'I'm not comfortable with the word "transform"; I'd prefer the word "support".'[4] Four years into the mission, this was a shocking display of not getting it.

Despite the ambiguity inherent in UNMIK's mandate, its general aim was clear enough: to stop the violence and prevent it from recurring. This would require Kosovo to become a kind of society it had never been before. It did not have to become a carbon copy of western Europe, but it did have to abandon aggressive nationalism and violence as a way of settling disputes and it had to embrace the rule of law. To be sustainable, these changes would have to be underpinned by an unprecedented respect for civic responsibility on the part of political leaders and ordinary citizens alike. Clearly, achieving these changes would entail a thoroughgoing transformation of Kosovo society.

Though Kosovo society had clearly failed, many internationals blamed the breakdown exclusively on Milosevic. This view could have been dispelled by the wave of killings during the summer of 1999 or a short glance at Kosovo's troubled history — it had been in crisis since at least 1981, eight years before Milosevic came to power. Kosovo had never had the institutions, political culture or economy that it would need to be part of Europe in the twenty-first century. Banishing Milo-sevic's forces was not enough to change this.

Many career UN officials, especially Europeans, felt it was wrong to interfere in the local way of doing things. 'Who are we to tell them how their society should be?' was a common refrain from post-imperial would-be progressives. It was a view often forged in opposition to the worst sorts of crusading zeal, or from a sense of guilt about historical colonial abuses, or from sympathy for downtrodden people who had been forced to conform to alien customs. It reflected a respect for cul-tural diversity that is often admirable and healthy. In Kosovo, it was reinforced by the Security Council's determination not to repeat the demonstrably unsuccessful heavy-handedness of the High Representa-tive in Bosnia. But the resulting desire to be unobtrusive was misplaced: tolerance of the intolerant is a dead-end strategy, particularly in a post-conflict environment with no tradition of pluralism. Where bullying is the norm, an unobtrusive approach to local culture favours the strong at the expense of the weak.

Americans tended to be less relativistic. Most had no doubt about what made a stable society: it should resemble the US as closely as pos-sible. But many of those who thought this way also seemed to imagine that that inside every apparently embittered militant was a tolerant, pluralist democrat waiting to emerge once favourable conditions had been created. Americans, perhaps more than Europeans, tended to view Albanians as passive victims: create a benign environment, went the myth, and divisive, dysfunctional attitudes wrought over genera-tions will correct themselves automatically. In policy terms, this meant creating appropriate structures and letting Kosovo society repair itself.

Though starting from nearly opposite premises, the American and European views shared the same fundamental flaw: neither wanted to assert control over the means by which public attitudes were shaped. Infused by wishful thinking, most parts of the mission did not even attempt to use the levers of soft power — educational reform, control of the media, propaganda — to transform public attitudes.[5] UNMIK never made any serious effort to depoliticise the education system. The media were allowed to incite revenge killings and to stoke ethnic tensions. Divisive nationalist symbols were allowed to dominate public spaces, while efforts to enforce dual language signs were erratic and ineffectual. KFOR and UNMIK meddled with propaganda, but often with little understanding of political communications, and even less of the cultural context in which they were operating. Still less did they use force. UNMIK neither compelled nor persuaded Kosovans to change their attitudes or behaviour. If such a transformation was to happen, it would have to happen spontaneously.

The belief that institutional shells would automatically give rise to democratic substance inspired the race to elect local leaders as soon as practically possible. The first elections to municipal assemblies were called in October 2000, and the general election a year later. All the main Albanian parties campaigned for independence, while the Serbs campaigned for the opposite, even though the issue of status was not at stake in any of the polls. The votes reinforced Kosovo's polarisation just when the international community was trying to bring people together. With the partial exception of Ramush Haradinaj, who became PM in a power-sharing deal in the autumn of 2004, not a single Kosovo politician at any level was elected on a platform of bringing Serbs and Albanians together. As they had in Bosnia (Bosnia suffered a far higher level of violence than Kosovo and consequently suffered from this problem more) elections institutionalised the status quo of inter-ethnic intolerance. At the same time, the elections created institutions that further undermined UNMIK's limited power to coax change. Who were these unelected foreigners to tell Kosovo's democratically elected leaders what to do? The elections created institutions in Kosovo that further undermined UNMIK's limited power to coax change.

Some academics have argued that democracy takes root more solidly if it is delayed in places like Kosovo. While established democracies tend to be peaceful, the process of democratising can exacerbate existing conflicts. 'By resisting calls for early elections, peacebuilders can allow passions to cool with the passage of time…' wrote Roland Paris recently.[6] 'Peacebuilders should proceed with elections only when there is evidence that "moderate" parties — or those that seem genuinely committed to resolving disputes through peaceful negotiation and to inter-communal reconciliation — have sufficient popular support to prevail over "immoderate" parties at the polls.'[7]

This is a controversial view. Democracy is a central tenet of the system that UNMIK and most other peace-building missions are mandated to nurture, and there is something deeply paradoxical about establishing democracy by delaying elections. Self-determination, too, has become established as a right (however imperfectly upheld). But both of these values are only parts of the model the international community was trying to establish. Self-determination was the main argument used by Milosevic to justify his regime's right to brutally repress internal dissent without outside interference. He could even cite democracy, on the grounds that a majority in the whole of the then Yugoslavia wanted Kosovo to remain firmly in the fold. Both democracy and self-determination need to be tempered by respect for minority rights. And it was to protect human rights — not to support Kosovo's right to self-determination — that NATO intervened against Yugoslavia. Of course, elections had to take place at some point, but UNMIK would have done more to create the essential preconditions for democracy if elections had been delayed. In Kosovo, the rush to democracy was self-defeating.

Failures of unity. The divergent attitudes towards Kosovo and Serbia under Milosevic first manifested themselves in the failure to secure a UN mandate for the NATO military campaign. When hostilities ended, the protectorate might have been administered by the leading country in NATO, the US, but America was unwilling to take on this enormous project alone. Also, Milosevic insisted that the mandate for the protectorate should come from the UN Security Council — a body where Serbia's historic (but perfidious) patron, Russia, had leverage.

Russia's veto on the Security Council meant that UNMIK's mandate included the crippling stipulation that nothing the mission did could prejudice Kosovo's future political status. The mission intended to lay the foundations of peace was thus prohibited from addressing the cause of the war. UNMIK was created without a clear purpose, a timetable or an exit strategy.

After the UN emerged as the lead organisation, the UN's Department of Peacekeeping Operations (DPKO), which lacked the capacity to take on the protectorate alone, brought in the UN High Commission for Refugees, the OSCE and the EU as partners. Deployment would have taken even longer without the extra contributions, but there was no consensus about which organisations should take on which responsibilities. Important objectives were not completed because of inter-agency rivalries. For example, a dispute between the UN led pillar responsible for civil administration and the OSCE-led pillar, responsible for democratisation and institution-building, delayed by more than two years the creation of a school for training civil servants. One reason that this enormous peace building mission never had a unit dedicated to conflict resolution was that none of the contributing institutions would be happy to see one of its partners controlling it.

With four institutions under one roof — the UN, UNHCR, OSCE and EU — UNMIK suffered from having too many masters. Senior policy makers within the mission were most obviously accountable to the UN Secretariat and Security Council, the body which had put them in Kosovo and could, in theory at least, withdraw them whenever it wanted to. But, in addition to the UN, there were the EU structures — the European Parliament, the Commission, the Directorates-General dealing with overseas development and external relations and the Office of Javier Solana, the EU's High Representative for Foreign and Security Policy. There was also the OSCE secretariat in Vienna, whose

Permanent Council took regular reports from the Mission in Kosovo. Largely because most staff were seconded by member states, the OSCE in Kosovo never fired any of its hundreds of staff for poor performance. Finally, there were the nation states — both individually and grouped together in the Contact Group, the Quint and other structures. SRSGs had to devote a large portion of their time to keeping these diverse masters on side. UNMIK's policies reflected a cumbersome compromise with all interested parties. Little wonder, then, that the mission suffered a degree of incoherence.

Failures of structure. The civil mission's lack of preparedness is most striking when compared with the military. NATO's tanks rolled into Kosovo according to a plan prepared months in advance. Soldiers already knew their roles — behind the front-line troops and their reserves there were planners, logisticians and intelligence officers, all ready to perform specialised tasks for which they had been trained. They were even ready for last-minute changes.

By contrast, the Department of Peacekeeping Operations couldn't begin planning for the mission before the Security Council passed Resolution 1244 without appearing to prejudge its outcome. Nor was it realistic to prepare the mission surreptitiously, it being impossible to keep anything secret in an organisation comprising virtually the entire world. The first SRSG, Sergio Vieira de Mello, had to prepare his core team — just a handful of people, three of whom later died with him in Baghdad — only a week before they arrived in Kosovo to 'take charge'. As General Bill Nash, an early Regional Administrator in Mitrovica, said, they were forced to 'assemble a civilian army on the battlefield'. Staff were recruited ad hoc, and often they were placed in positions for which they had little training. Long after the UN's Brahimi Report had highlighted the need to be able to deploy people quickly[8], UNMIK offices regularly waited several months to fill posts. Moreover, personnel officers in the UN's New York headquarters would often dictate who would go on the short list of candidates, regularly rejecting people who had been strongly recommended by the heads of the respective offices.

As Michael Steiner was dismayed to discover, the UN was not geared towards achieving concrete results. Although the mission employed engineers, businesspeople and other professionals who in ordinary circumstances would produce tangible products, the UN's organisational culture placed a premium not on completing tasks but on following procedures. After the first year or so, during which Kosovo was generally full of well-intentioned idealists, the incentive structure within the mission gradually created a culture of caution. Many people were being paid well for their work in Kosovo — extremely well compared to salaries in the developing world or former communist countries from which they hailed. They could expect little reward for doing especially well, but their contracts might not be renewed if they took a risk which went wrong, encouraging caution over initiative. This effect was compounded by creeping bureaucratic sclerosis. As UNMIK evolved from a sprawling mess into a tightly-ordered regime, people within the mission became inward-looking. Consequently, UNMIK became less able to project itself on to the society it existed to transform.

The mission was particularly bereft of control over security. KFOR comprised national contingents which answered to their respective capitals, each with its own rules of engagement. In Prizren, the Germans' rules prohibited them from interfering in civil disorder. In Mitrovica, France's political sympathies for the Serbs and general risk aversion meant its contingent was generally unwilling to confront militants. The UN's civilian police force, apart from being undermanned, was for the most part staffed by policemen with little experience of tackling serious crimes, much less a post-conflict environment. Virtually none of them spoke Albanian and so they were dependent on hastily recruited local interpreters. While the police at first had virtually no capacity to penetrate criminal networks, UNMIK's own structures were an open book to interested parties.[9] This imbalance in favour of criminal elements destroyed UNMIK's credibility from its inception in this vital sphere of intelligence.

The resources UNMIK did have were often deployed inefficiently. A vivid illustration of this can be seen by comparing the staffing of the Customs service with the elections department in 2003. The three international staff in the UNMIK Customs service oversaw the annual collection of approximately half a billion euros in revenue; the twenty-five international staff in the OSCE elections department ran no elections. This example is by no means unique. In general, the OSCE had some of the most talented, intelligent and highly-motivated staff, but bureaucratic Chinese walls made it impossible to give them more substantial roles. In 2003 UNMIK tried to get the OSCE's elections field staff to help promote the Standards; they refused and the OSCE's management was unable to compel them.

These problems were compounded by the SRSG's lack of authority over the entire mission. When the SRSG ordered one quarter of UNMIK to move to northern Mitrovica in 2002, to give the Serbs a greater stake in the mission and to help provide jobs to the city, his instructions were quietly but firmly rejected by the UN and OSCE. Only part of the EU agreed to relocate to the north[10] and even then EU staff postponed the move until it was finally abandoned. The SRSG could not fire staffers even for insubordination; it was the respective headquarters of the UN, EU and OSCE that controlled appointments and appropriations. The result was that many of the staff in Kosovo were unsuited to the jobs they ended up doing, and many of the jobs that ended up being done, in turn, were unsuited to Kosovo's needs. While many professional staff had expertise in the norms of stable societies, few had any understanding of how to heal and develop a brutalised and poor one.

UNMIK failed to use its economic power to advance the larger goals of the international administration. This failure began with the decision to locate most of the international mission in Pristina, thereby allowing the lion's share of international spending to flow into a mono-ethnic city — Albanians saw no economic incentive in working with Serbs, and Serbs saw little benefit in working with the international community. The problem was further compounded by the way donors spent their money — again, the massive investments in the energy and water sectors were made without any conditions on multi-ethnicity. A modest and belated effort was made to ensure that some Serb houses were rebuilt, but it proved difficult to implement. The main economic objectives were, first, to construct or reconstruct a basic infrastructure, and then general development, in the expectation that both would eventually contribute to the normalisation of Kosovo society. These objectives, and the way they were pursued, tended to bypass the central objective of the mission as a whole.

Although Kosovo enjoyed unprecedented largesse from the donor community, many donors adapted to the environment poorly. Most preferred to fund projects of a certain scale — often those costing between ten and fifty thousand euros. Projects costing very little, or much more, proved difficult to finance. Even when they received funds, lags in the system meant that a political decision to fund a project — perhaps as a reward for a welcome gesture of reconciliation — could take a year or more to result in a real improvement, long after the political payback was needed. Furthermore, most locals were smart enough to know why investments were being made — money tended to flow towards flashpoints, rarely as a reward for stability. Even when money did make a positive impact in a troublespot, the angry young men who committed most violent acts were unlikely to be its main beneficiaries. Economic power is a slow, blunt tool for transforming a place like Kosovo.

Failures of will. None of the weaknesses discussed so far would have been insurmountable had the leading countries, particularly the Contact Group (the US, UK, France, Germany, Italy and Russia), mustered enough political will to overcome them. But they did not. Instead of addressing the weaknesses with which UNMIK began, the international

community used these defects as excuses for failing to match brave
rhetoric with equally brave action. The result: the words and deeds of
Western statecraft drifted apart, like those of Yugoslav socialism and
Milosevic's authoritarianism beforehand, leading many Albanians to
become cynical about the international community.

These failures of will began in the early days, when hundreds of
Serbs and other minority people were murdered while KFOR was
meant to be in control; henceforth, Serbs never trusted KFOR. With
a few impressive exceptions, their scepticism was validated during the
rioting in March 2004.

Only a tiny fraction of war crimes charges were ever properly investigated and fewer still were brought to trial. Even after Regulation
2000/64 allowed International Prosecutors to choose cases, the mission never had enough of them to prosecute a serious number of war
crimes. The shortage of personnel was exacerbated by UNMIK direct-
ing International Prosecutors to focus on whatever cases happened to
be political priorities at the moment.

As the mission aged, UNMIK made more and more rules but then
took no action when they were broken. For example, it conducted
public information campaigns to promote water conservation and created fines for offenders, but they were virtually never imposed. On the
contrary, police would stroll without comment past shopkeepers who,
in the midst of severe water shortages, were spending twenty minutes
hosing the street to lay down the dust. The Temporary Media Commissioner imposed fines that, with only a couple of exceptions, were not
collected. Rules that all road signs had to be in both the Albanian and
Serb languages were flouted without any sort of sanction at all. UNMIK
told veterans in Prizren that under no circumstances would they be
allowed to erect a nationalist monument to 'war heroes' in the centre
of the multi-ethnic town, then did nothing when the veterans ignored
this injunction and erected the monument. This failure fuelled the sense
of impunity that set the stage for the March riots.

Even without using physical force, UNMIK had the authority to use other means to impose discipline on Kosovo's institutions, power it almost never used. No SRSG had support from the Security Council to sack recalcitrant officials — even when they operated well outside the Constitutional Framework or incited inter-ethnic intolerance. The worst that happened was that a couple of motions passed by the Assembly were ruled out of order by the SRSG, with no further sanction. While UNMIK officials cajoled the Assembly to act within its mandate, the legislators knew that passing motions outside their competence amounted to a cost-free form of protest.

Failure of time. An ambitious study of nation-building efforts by the American RAND Corporation has concluded that the length of an international administration is the single most important determinant of its success.[11] How long an international administration continues depends, in turn, on political will, which is hard to sustain as memory of a conflict fades. The political horizons of those who decide when international administrations begin and end, and the budgetary cycles of their bureaucracies, tend to be short; the process of transforming a conflict-ridden society into a peaceful one takes much longer. This lack of political stamina inspires many of the other problems seen in Kosovo — precipitate elections, the eagerness to draw down troop levels and the over-hasty declaration of success. It is the classic misfit of short-term solutions to long-term problems.

The misfit is exacerbated by a paradox. If a mission appears to be succeeding, it becomes very difficult for political leaders or bureaucrats to justify continuing to commit resources to it while newer, more acute crises clamour for attention. If, on the other hand, after several years an international administration still faces the threat of widespread instability, it is difficult to justify continuing to throw good money after bad. The political will to continue the international administration in Kosovo suffered from both these factors: when Kosovo was out of the headlines, politicians felt no pressure from voters to stay the course there, especially when they were diverted elsewhere by the terrorist attacks of 11 September 2001. After the March 2004 riots, politicians were afraid there might be an even bigger explosion and didn't want to be linked to a foreign policy failure, even one which began before their term in office.

There is no obvious solution to these dilemmas. If violent places like Kosovo are to be transformed into peaceful ones, voters in the most powerful countires must allow their elected leaders to take risks and to remain engaged long after the conflict has faded from the headlines. But democracies tend to be slow to recognize dangers and quick to tire.[12] Given that places requiring intervention are likely to remain obscure to most in the West, gaining public support will be difficult. The best hope is for the bodies involved in international administrations to improve their own institutional memories and to be frank with their political masters and the public.

DOING BETTER

Ten lessons from Kosovo

The lessons from Kosovo have already been learned many times and by many people, from philosophers to management gurus to the UN's own panel on peace operations. Unfortunately, though, these lessons are even more often ignored. Most international staff in Kosovo were unaware of lessons from other missions (much less from other analogous experiences). Similarly, many of the lessons from Kosovo were ignored in Iraq.

A host of immutable factors — not least human nature, the balance of power in the world and the chaotic circumstances that call forth an enterprise like the Kosovo mission — mean intervention can never be immaculate. Nevertheless, as long as the UN and other institutions are continuing to try to improve their performance, as they are, it is worth restating what experience in Kosovo has taught us.

1. Peace deals should be oriented less to ending wars than to establishing a just and sustainable peace.

Some form of independence should have been on the table from the beginning, conditional on the fulfilment of certain criteria, particularly the rule of law and rights of minorities. This would have encouraged progressive Albanians to help rein in their obstructive, reactionary countrymen and given the SRSGs the compelling inducements they lacked.

2. A mission must be prepared to assert its authority from day one.

The Kosovo international administration got off to a weak start because no international civilian organisation was properly prepared. Member states had not equipped the UN to do the right training and strategic planning before the mission began, or to deploy people and supplies quickly once it was underway. To perform better in the future, leading contributors to peace building missions should invest in creating a substantial standby capacity — preferably through the UN — analogous to that of a large military alliance like NATO.

3. All soldiers, civilians and institutions must answer to a single authority.

To speak with authority within the mission and the wider society, the international administrator must have ultimate control over all the tools through which he implements the mission's programme of change. The lack of such authority fatally undermined the credibility of SRSGs in Kosovo.

4. An overall vision is more important than detailed objectives.

Mission staff and the wider society must understand how the society is being changed, why these changes are essential to the overall objective of a just and lasting peace and how individual parts contribute to the whole. All members of the mission must understand that their role is first and foremost to advance this process of change, and only secondarily to perform their specific functions.

5. The truly important must take precedence over the merely urgent.

Objectives that are central to a mission, such as facilitating inter-ethnic cooperation, cannot be habitually set aside to expedite an immediate need, such as getting a utility working. Getting the priorities straight will be facilitated by everyone understanding the larger process of change.

6. *Plan for and achieve quick wins.*

Tangible achievements are essential for public confidence and staff morale. Most people in UNMIK were not action-oriented. Creating the capacity for quick wins will require cultural and structural changes in future missions.

7. *Enforce the law consistently.*

No police force, particularly one that observes high standards of human rights, can enforce law without broad public support. The police and courts must be consistent and professional. Nothing was more destructive to the transformational process attempted in Kosovo than the perceived impunity of large classes of criminals and militants — including those responsible for the atrocities of the late 1990s. To create credibility in a population with no experience of impartial justice, the independence of the judiciary must be respected.

8. *Learn as you go.*

Peace-building missions must expect the unexpected. This requires specialised staff tasked with continuously learning lessons, and the inclination and capacity throughout the rest of the mission to implement those lessons.

9. *Install democracy comprehensively but only after security and the rule of law are established.*

The first order of business for any peace-building mission must be to establish order. Holding an election before security is established is like asking a person to sign a contract while a gun is being held to his or her head. If elections are held in an insecure environment, the outcome will merely entrench thugocrats and ethnic divides.

10. *Building peace means changing bad habits — however 'traditional' they may be.*

The move towards peace is a struggle in which the mission must take sides. Building peace does not require a mission to create clones of Western society. But it does require working to change 'traditional' attitudes if they are holding a society back. Corruption and cronyism may be deeply ingrained, but they retard development and ought to be rooted out. Where the international community intervenes, moral consistency requires it to support fairness and opportunity. Peace-building missions should not hesitate, for example, to try to improve the opportunities for women.

Conclusion

UNMIK performed straightforward physical, administrative and institution-building functions quite effectively. Indeed, a list of all the improvements undertaken or institutions created by UNMIK — new roads and houses, a new legal code, parliament and courts, customs and tax authorities, a new currency — recalls the line uttered by an ancient Judean in Monty Python's *The Life of Brian*: 'What have the Romans ever done for us?'

There were exceptions, such as the administration of KEK, the perennially underpowered electrical utility, where the internationals had just enough control to be blamed for its breakdowns and just enough money to apply a short term fix, but not enough of either to apply a proper longterm solution. UNMIK also failed to assert its authority over northern Kosovo, despite repeated attempts.

But it was the efforts to turn Kosovo into a multi-ethnic democracy subject to the rule of law that failed so spectacularly. After six years as an international protectorate, Kosovo's political culture remained largely unchanged. The OSCE was charged with democratisation; as it contemplated its departure, parties were neither internally democratic nor distinguished by a political philosophy, the amount of grassroots activism was minute and political violence was commonplace. The EU was supposed to create the conditions for a modern liberal economy; six years on, two thirds of the population had no proper employment, most people still lived off remittances from relatives abroad and most food was imported, despite Kosovo's large agricultural potential. The UN mission was supposed to build up the rule of law, but most crimes went unprosecuted, local judicial capacity was woefully underdeveloped and organised crime remained endemic. Only a few thousand displaced people returned to their homes and they lived fearfully in isolated enclaves; rapprochement between the two main ethnic groups has been practically non-existent. Instead of turning Kosovo into a pluralist democracy subject to the rule of law, the international community merely presided over a reversal of positions between Serbs and Albanians.

UNMIK will hand over to a conditionally independent Kosovo having achieved only a small part of what it set out to achieve. This failure had several causes, but the most profound was the international community's misunderstanding of the nature of the conflict and, following from this misunderstanding, its addressing Kosovo's problems with the wrong kinds of power.

The international community did not recognise the depredations of the Milosevic regime as the latest stage in an old competition for territory between Serbs and Albanians. Instead, they imagined they were coming to rescue a population of victims — who by definition, it was thought, must be either politically inert or benign. Albanians were allowed to believe the internationals were their allies in a zero-sum struggle, rather than disinterested champions of universal principles. With a few conspicuous exceptions — the requirements for minority and female representation in the Assembly, for instance — the interveners believed they had neither the need nor the right to foist their notions of a good society on Kosovo. Instead, they set out to create an environment that would be conducive to democratic governance only in the narrowest sense of majoritarian rule.

The international administration neither compelled nor persuaded Kosovans to adhere to the rules and norms of a peaceful, pluralist society. In the realm of hard power, the international presence commanded an overwhelming physical force. But this unparalleled might was crippled by the emphasis on force protection: almost all national contingents placed a far higher premium on avoiding casualties than on asserting the will of the international community. The international police — undermined by their late arrival, poor knowledge of the local environment and minimal forensic skills and tools —lacked incentives to take risks in the performance of their duties. Little wonder that no international policeman died as a result of having confronted an avoidable danger.

In the realm of soft power, the mission barely dented the political culture underlying Kosovo's instability. Even when it saw the need to change attitudes, it was often reluctant to act. The tools for changing attitudes at the heart of transformational occupations in post-war Germany and Japan, and in British efforts to prepare colonies for statehood — educational reform, effective regulation of the media, propaganda and war crimes trials used as object lessons — played only bit parts in the drama of post-conflict Kosovo.

None of this means Kosovo is doomed to remain a dependent, crime-ridden political netherworld. Dynamics outside UNMIK's control will continue to drive progress. Many families who have built up fortunes illegally now prefer to enjoy their wealth with the security that only the rule of law makes possible. If Kosovo's institutions, with help from outside, prevent these groups from infiltrating the media and political life, many of its kingpins can probably be turned into law-abiding citizens, just like robber barons-turned-philanthropists such as Andrew Carnegie were in the US a century ago. If the EU wholeheartedly embraces the need to develop the western Balkans region, it will exert a strong and positive influence throughout Kosovo society. The revival of agriculture and mining, along with significantly improved trading relations with its neighbours, might yet inject new life into Kosovo's feeble economy.

Independence, which is coming in some conditional form, will not be the panacea that many Albanians imagine — or, if the international community remains sufficiently engaged, the cataclysm that Serbs fear. Its most important consequence will be to force Albanian leaders and their constituents to take responsibility for their own actions.

But Kosovo's demographics point towards poverty and mono-ethnicity. Over 60 per cent of Kosovo's population is under twenty-five.[1] Those in school are taught by miserably paid teachers, appointed on the basis of political connections rather than merit, overworked from teaching three or four shifts of children a day. Kosovo Albanians in their twenties were educated deficiently in the apartment classrooms of the parallel system maintained under Milosevic; few possess the skills required for success in today's Europe. Meanwhile, most young Serbs have left — gone north or elsewhere — turning many enclaves into sad retirement villages. When this generation dies, the ghost of multi-ethnicity will go with them.

The overriding lesson from Kosovo is this: stable societies don't just happen, they are built. An international administration must be prepared to confront and defeat the forces that preserve the unacceptable aspects of the status quo. It must establish its authority and then impose a programme of progressive change, ideally harnessing at least latent support in the society itself. Transforming a violent, dysfunctional society like Kosovo's into one in which all its people can live in security and dignity requires the political equivalent of combat engineers: people equipped to build bridges under fire.

'Out of the crooked timber of humanity, no straight thing was ever made,' said Immanuel Kant.[2] As long as they are carried out by human beings, interventions to put weak societies on a more stable footing will never be perfect. As in Kosovo, they will continue to suffer from our flawed understanding, ideological blinkers, maladapted structures, divisiveness, weak will and short-sightedness. But we are also capable, albeit inefficiently, of learning from our mistakes. For anyone who believes in applying reason to improving humanity's lot, the experience in Kosovo contains some the most valuable lessons in recent history. Applying these lessons ultimately depends on political will, and the lessons of Kosovo can also help to generate and sustain that will. As Michael Steiner said as SRSG, 'political will and our belief in our own abilities are closely connected: Where we know there's a way, we're more likely to find the will.' The UN's creation of a peace-building commission promises to provide a rich bank of collective wisdom. May it be drawn on regularly — and spent liberally — by men and women of vision and courage.

A CHRONOLOGY OF EVENTS
IN KOSOVO

4th Century BC: People whom the contemporary Kosovo Albanians regard as their ancestors, the Illyrians, are conquered by the Greeks.

28 BC: Modern day Kosovo becomes part of the Roman province of Dardania.

6th Century: As the Roman empire collapses, Slavs cross the Danube and move south into the Balkans.

1190: Kosovo becomes the administrative and cultural centre of a medieval Serbian state.

28 June 1389: Serbs and their allies, including Albanians, are defeated in the Battle of Kosovo Polje, just outside Pristina – one of several decisive battles leading to five centuries of Ottoman rule.

1443-68: Skanderbeg, the Albanian national hero, revolts against the Ottomans.

1690: The Patriarch of Pec leads 'the Great Exodus'; most Kosovo Serbs flee to Hungary.

1830-33: Under Milos Obrenovic, Serbia wins autonomy within the Ottoman Empire.

1876-78: Warfare between Serbs and Ottomans forces some 30,000 Serbs from Kosovo and an equal number of Albanians from southern Serbia.

1878: Treaties of San Stefano and Berlin redraw national boundaries in the Balkans, at the expense of the Ottoman Empire. Serbia's new boundary extends south to include northern Kosovo.

1889: Serbia celebrates the five hundredth anniversary of the Battle of Kosovo Polje, moulding national myths around the battle.

1912: In the first Balkan War, Serb forces take control of the rest of Kosovo and commit widespread atrocities against civilians.

1913: Treaty of London creates a new Albanian state — which leaves most Albanians outside it — and recognizes Serbian sovereignty in Kosovo.

1914-1918: Kosovo is invaded by Bulgaria and Austria-Hungary in the First World War.

1918: At war's end, the Central Powers collapse, delegates in Belgrade declare the 'Kingdom of the Serbs, Croats and Slovenes'.

6-17 April 1941: Nazi Germany invades and conquers Yugoslavia. Kosovo is partitioned between German, Bulgarian and Italian zones, with the latter two later administered from Albania.

1944: After leading successful guerrilla resistance to Nazi occupation, Communist Partisan leader Josip Tito emerges as Yugoslavia's new supremo.

1946: Yugoslavia's new communist constitution makes Kosovo an 'Autonomous Region' within the Republic of Serbia.

1961: A census reveals that two-thirds of the population of modern Kosovo is Albanian.

1963: Kosovo gains more autonomy, as it becomes an 'Autonomous Province' within Serbia but under federal authority.

1967: Tito visits Kosovo and makes concessions regarding Albanian language rights and education.

1974: A new Yugoslav constitution gives Kosovo yet more autonomy. The Province now enjoys virtually the same prerogatives as a republic except the right to secede from the Federation.

4 May 1980: Tito dies.

1981: Riots at Pristina University, protesting against poor conditions and political developments since Tito's death, are suppressed by Yugoslav troops.

11 April 1985: Albanian dictator Enver Hoxha dies.

1986: Kosovo Serbs protest against intimidation by Albanians.

1987: Slobodan Milosevic rallies a crowd of Kosovo Serbs, who are protesting against alleged harassment by Albanians. He becomes president of Serbia.

1989: Serbian President Slobodan Milosevic removes Kosovo's autonomy, restoring rule from Belgrade.

July 1990: Ethnic Albanian leaders declare independence from Serbia. Belgrade dissolves the Kosovo government.

September 1990: More than 100,000 ethnic Albanian workers, including government employees and media workers, are sacked, prompting a general strike.

1991: As Slovenia and Croatia declare independence from Yugoslavia, Kosovo Albanians hold an unofficial referendum which votes to secede from the Federation. Only Albania recognises the vote.

April 1992: Following a referendum on independence from Yugoslavia, war breaks out in Bosnia.

July 1992: In an unofficial vote across Kosovo, writer Ibrahim Rugova is elected president of the self-proclaimed republic. A provincial assembly and government are established.

December 1995: The Dayton agreement ends the Bosnian war. Kosovo's status is excluded from the discussions, disappointing many Kosovo Albanians.

1996: The Kosovo Liberation Army (KLA) emerges, claiming responsibility for a number of bombings and attacks against Serbian police, state officials, and Albanians loyal to Serbia.

Early 1997: Following the collapse of pyramid banking schemes, Albania descends into anarchy, arms depots are looted and weapons become available to Kosovo militants.

1997: Ethnic tension and armed unrest escalate; Milosevic deploys
    heavy weaponry to crack down on the KLA.

September 1997: Serb police crush Albanian student demonstra-
    tions.

1998

Open conflict erupts between Serb police and separatist Kosovo Lib-
    eration Army (KLA). Serb forces launch a brutal crackdown.
    Thousands of civilians are driven from their homes.

June: and with KLA commanders.

July: A UN Security Council resolution, initiated by France and the
    UK, attempts to bring about a ceasefire.

September: NATO presents President Milosevic with an ultimatum
    to halt the crackdown on Kosovo Albanians.

23 September: The UN Security Council approves (with China ab-
    staining) resolution 1199, which demands a cessation of hos-
    tilities and warns that, 'should the measures demanded in this
    resolution... not be taken... additional measures to maintain
    or restore peace and stability in the region' will be consid-
    ered.

24 September: NATO prepares for military intervention in Kosovo,
    approving plans for air strikes and for monitoring any cease-
    fire agreement.

29 September: The UN High Commissioner for Refugees announces
    that as many as 200,000 civilians have been displaced within
    Kosovo since fighting began escalating in February.

12 October: Just before NATO airstrikes are due to begin, Milosevic
    promises to comply fully with UN resolution 1199, and to
    allow for a verification regime.

November: The Kosovo Verification Mission, organised through the
    OSCE, begins deploying 1,800 monitors throughout Kosovo.

December: Hostilities continue, despite the ceasefire agreement and the presence of international monitors.

1999

16 January: The bodies of more than forty ethnic Albanians, shot at close range, are discovered in Racak, central Kosovo.

6 February: Peace talks open in Rambouillet, France, under the auspices of the Contact Group.

23 February: Rambouillet talks are halted; the Kosovo Albanian delegation consults opinion at home.

15 March: The ethnic Albanian delegation accepts the autonomy deal proposed at Rambouillet; Milosevic rejects it.

19 March: The peace talks adjourn in failure, following the refusal of the Serbs to sign up. International monitors prepare to leave Kosovo.

22 March: The outskirts of Pristina come under Serb artillery fire.

24 March: NATO begins air strikes on targets in Yugoslavia.

29 March: The tide of refugees fleeing Kosovo for Albania, Macedonia and Montenegro increases amid reports of Serbian atrocities.

12 April: UK Foreign Secretary Robin Cook declares the key objective of the war to be the return of displaced refugees 'under international military protection'.

27 May: Milosevic is indicted for war crimes by the United Nations' International Criminal Tribunal for the former Yugoslavia.

3 June: The Serbian parliament approves a peace plan drawn up by the G-8.

9 June: Yugoslav and NATO generals sign an agreement on the withdrawal of Serb troops from Kosovo, following marathon talks near the Yugoslav-Macedonian border.

10 June: The UN Security Council passes resolution 1244, establishing UNMIK. NATO suspends air strikes as Yugoslavia begins withdrawing its security forces from Kosovo.

12 June: Russian troops arrive in Pristina and seize the airport; NATO troops arrive hours later.

13 June: SRSG Sergio Vieira de Mello arrives in Kosovo to open UNMIK's new office.

28 June: UNMIK appoints seven local experts to help appoint a new judiciary in Kosovo. First judges and prosecutors are appointed on 30 June.

15 July: Dr Bernard Kouchner replaces Vieira de Mello to become Kosovo's second SRSG. UNMIK's four pillar structure is confirmed.

16 July: Kouchner establishes the Kosovo Transitional Council, allowing local leaders informal input into policy discussions.

24 July: Kouchner strongly condemns the murder of fourteen Serb farmers, one of many atrocities being conducted against minorities at this time.

25 July: Kouchner issues UNMIK's first regulation.

1 September: UNMIK launches a Customs Service, taxing imports entering Kosovo from Macedonia.

2 September: The deutschmark becomes a legally accepted currency in Kosovo.

21 September: The Kosovo Liberation Army (KLA) agrees to disband and disarm; the Kosovo Protection Corps is created.

6 October: New Kosovo Transitional Council condemns the abuse of freedom of speech in the media.

11 October: UN Secretary-General visits Kosovo; UNMIK staff member Valentin Krumov murdered in central Pristina.

15 October: Commercial flights from Pristina airport resume.

16 October: First Kosovo Police Service officers graduate from the OSCE police school.

8 November: Central Fiscal Authority created.

12 November: A UN World Food Programme plane crashes while cir-
cling Pristina, killing twenty-four international staff.

17 November: Banking and Payments authority and Housing and Property Directorate established.

15 December: UNMIK and Kosovo Albanian leaders agree to a Joint
Administrative Structure; Serbs boycott the agreement.

30 December: Kosovo's main railway line restarts under heavy security,
carrying passengers of several ethnicities.

2000

25 January: First private bank opens in Pristina.

1 February: A grenade attack on a bus in Mitrovica kills two Serbs and
sparks major riots in the city.

3 February: Rioting and paramilitary activity in Mitrovica leaves seven
Kosovo Albanians dead.

5 February: KFOR flood Mitrovica with troops, and a night-time curfew is imposed in the city.

11 February: Kouchner announces a multi-ethnic 'confidence zone' in
the centre of Mitrovica.

17 February: First international prosecutor appointed in Kosovo.

3 April: 2,767 houses rebuilt in reconstruction programme so far.

28-30 April: UN Security Council delegation visits Kosovo, overshadowed by riots in Mitrovica.

30 April: Kouchner launches a Joint Committee on Returns, with Serb
Archbishop Artemije.

16 May: UNMIK employee Petar Topoljski is killed after a Kosovo Albanian newspaper accuses him of being a war criminal. Kouchner
tries to shut down the newspaper.

9 August: UNMIK establishes an international Temporary Media Commissioner to regulate the media.

14 August: UNMIK takes control of the Trepca lead smelter in Zvecan.

24-5 September: Milosevic re-elected President of Yugoslavia; independent monitors condemn the poll as rigged.

5 October: Milosevic evicted from power after mass demonstrations in Belgrade.

28 October: Municipal elections throughout Kosovo.

15 November: A 'Council of Ministers' is created as a new unelected policy forum in Kosovo.

2001

12 January: Kouchner leaves Kosovo.

15 January: The new SRSG, Hans Haekkerup, arrives.

30 January: Riots in northern Kosovo leave one Albanian dead and one Serb seriously injured; the UNMIK regional HQ is cut off.

16 February: Nis Express bus is bombed, killing seven Serbs.

16 February: UNMIK announces it will establish tax collection offices on Kosovo's northern boundary, sparking fierce debate among both internationals and locals.

27 February: Ramush Haradinaj joins the Interim Administrative Council, alongside Rugova, Thaci and Serb representative Rada Trajkovic.

16 April: Tax collection offices established on Kosovo's northern boundary. Northern Kosovo is paralysed by street blockades for three weeks.

3 May: UNMIK clarifies that the northern tax points are 'tax' not 'Customs' points, defusing the tax collection crisis.

May: Florim Ejupi, the main suspect in the attack on the Nis Express in February, escapes from US custody at Camp Bondsteel.

15 May: SRSG signs the Constitutional Framework.

21 May: A new Pillar One is created within UNMIK, dealing with policing and justice.

25 May: Following an agreement between NATO and Belgrade, Yugoslav troops re-enter the buffer zone and the insurgency in the Presevo valley ends.

20 June: UNHCR announces 50,000 refugees have entered Kosovo as a result of increasing violence in northern Macedonia.

28 June: Milosevic transferred to the ICTY in The Hague.

24 July: US President Bush visits Kosovo.

2 October: Kosovo Transitional Council meets for the last time.

15 October: UNMIK issues its one millionth ID card in Kosovo.

5 November: SRSG Haekkerup and Deputy Prime Minister Covic sign the 'Common Document' in Belgrade, inviting Serbs to vote in the forthcoming Kosovo election.

11 November: UN Security Council urges Kosovo Serbs to vote.

17 November: General election throughout Kosovo; some Serbs vote, but turnout is lower than among Kosovo Albanians.

10 December: The newly elected Assembly meets for the first time. Thaci walks out during Haekkerup's opening statement in protest at the arrangements made.

28 December: Haekkerup resigns as SRSG.

2002

1 January: Kosovo begins introducing the euro as its main currency, to replace the deutschmark. The Yugoslav dinar remains Kosovo's official currency, but it is used in only a small fraction of transactions.

17 January: LDK Assembly member Ismael Hajdaraj is murdered.

14 February: New SRSG Michael Steiner arrives in Kosovo.

28 February: Under international pressure, Kosovo Albanian leaders agree to a coalition government. Ibrahim Rugova is elected as President, and Dr Bajram Rexhepi becomes Prime Minister.

28 February: UNMIK introduces income tax into Kosovo.

27 March: 146 Kosovo Albanian prisoners held in Serbian jails since 1999 are returned to Kosovo. 80 are released the next day.

April: The 'Standards before Status' idea emerges.

24 April: Earthquake measuring 5.6 on the Richter scale destroys buildings in eastern Kosovo, killing one.

30 April: A formal investigation into the finances of KEK, Kosovo's electricity corporation, is made public. German citizen Jo Trutschler is later convicted of embezzling 4.5 million dollars.

17 May: SRSG Steiner vetoes an attempt by the Assembly to discuss Kosovo's border with Macedonia.

30 May: Steiner signs the Overseas Private Investment Corporation agreement to encourage international investment.

12 June: With Serb ministers agreeing to take up posts, Kosovo's new Provisional Government is formally sworn into office, three years after KFOR's arrival into Kosovo.

19 July: Lightning strikes Kosovo's main electricity generator, exacerbating Kosovo's power crisis. Steiner forms a joint energy committee with the Provisional Government.

30 July: The Provisional Government tries unsuccessfully to regulate lotteries in Kosovo.

19 August: Rrustem 'Rremi' Mustafa and others are arrested. The Provisional Government condemns the move as 'politically motivated'.

20 September: As part of a campaign to crack down on the non-payment of electricity bills, the SRSG signs new laws making it easier for KEK to cut off non-payers.

1 October: Steiner unveils 'seven point plan' for Mitrovica.

20 October: Second municipal elections throughout Kosovo; turnout among Serbs is low.

25 November: New office opened in northern Mitrovica to assert UNMIK control over the area.

2003

24 January: After a long boycott, Serb members vote to return to the Kosovo Assembly.

10 February: Council of Europe delegation begins work in Kosovo to establish a system of decentralisation.

19 February: Fatmir Limaj is arrested in Slovenia and flown to The Hague under an indictment from the International Criminal Tribunal for the Former Yugoslavia.

12 March: Serbian Prime Minister Zoran Djindjic is assassinated, halting efforts to establish the first direct talks between Pristina and Belgrade.

8 April: A joint Transfer Council, co-chaired by the Prime Minister and the SRSG, meets for the first time to discuss passing more responsibility from UNMIK to the Provisional Institutions.

24 April: SRSG vetoes Assembly's attempt to rewrite election law.

10 July: Steiner leaves Kosovo.

13 August: New SRSG Harri Holkeri arrives in Kosovo.

15 October: First direct talks between Belgrade and Kosovo Albanian leaders since the NATO intervention are held in Vienna.

10 December: The Standards are 'relaunched' along with a detailed roadmap on implementation.

2004

10 January: Following widespread press allegations that UNMIK is harbouring corrupt international officials, the SRSG reiterates the 'zero-tolerance' policy on corruption, while confirming that no action will be taken without evidence.

16 February: Several KPC members are arrested and charged with serious criminal activity.

24 February: Bomb injures Environment Minister Ceku.

12 March: Grenade explodes outside the house of President Rugova.

16 March: Local broadcasters report three Albanian children chased to
    their death in the river Ibar by Serbs with dogs, sparking wide-
    spread rioting.

17-18 March: 19 people are killed in the worst clashes between Serbs
    and ethnic Albanians since 1999; two more die later from their
    injuries.

10 April: SRSG Holkeri sacks the international director of the privatisa-
    tion agency in what is widely seen as a concession to the Provi-
    sional Institutions.

25 May: SRSG Holkeri resigns from his post on grounds of ill health.

25 July: Kai Eide delivers his critical strategic review of policy in Kos-
    ovo.

15 August: Soren Jessen-Petersen arrives in Kosovo as the sixth SRSG.

22 October: SRSG Petersen announces a major spending programme for
    Mitrovica on the eve of elections and encourages Serbs to par-
    ticipate.

23 October: Municipal and general election in Kosovo. Little change in
    voting between main Albanian parties; most Serbs boycott the
    poll.

10 November: SRSG Petersen urges NATO to 'stay the course' and not
    reduce its troop contingent in Kosovo prematurely.

3 December: New Kosovo Assembly meets for the first time. Rugova is
    re-elected as President, and former rebel commander Ramush
    Haradinaj eventually becomes Prime Minister at the head of a
    coalition government. Thaci's PDK leads an opposition block in
    the Assembly.

17 December: The SRSG and Haradinaj launch a new 'Standards' process,
    with prioritised targets that are easier to meet.

2005

January: Preparations begin for Kosovo's first proper census since 1981
    (Milosevic's census of 1991 was widely boycotted by Albani-

ans). It will probably to be conducted in early 2007, when its efforts to calculate Kosovo's new ethnic make-up may well prove controversial.

13 January: A CivPol officer from Nigeria is killed in a bomb explosion in Prizren.

8 March: Prime Minister Ramush Haradinaj is indicted to face UN war crimes. He resigns and travels to The Hague the next day, urging the population to remain calm.

15 March: A grenade attack damages the vehicle in which President Rugova is travelling.

23 March: Ramush Haradinaj's deputy, Bajram Kosumi, becomes Prime Minister in his place.

24 March: The International Civilian Police pass control of a whole region – Gnjilane region, probably the calmest area of Kosovo – to the control of the Kosovo Police Service for the first time.

22 April: The new privatisation law is signed, finally allowing the process to move forward.

27 May: The UN Security Council discusses Kosovo's recent progress and considers whether the time is ripe for status talks.

3 June: UN Secretary-General Kofi Annan appoints Kai Eide to conduct a new assessment of Kosovo's readiness for status talks.

7 June: The Kosovo Forum meets a new body created to include political figures outside government in decisions concerning possible status talks for the first time.

19 July: A report on mines and unexploded ordinance in Kosovo reveals that 44 areas are still considered 'dangerous'. Responsibility for mine clearance is transferred from KFOR to the Kosovo Protection Corps.

12 August: Five decentralisation pilot projects finally go ahead.

28 August: Two Serbs are killed and two wounded in a drive-by shooting near Strpce.

5 September: President Rugova announces he has lung cancer but refuses to stand down.

19 September: Rugova announces he will represent Kosovo in future talks on status, leading a delegation comprising himself, Assembly Speaker Nexhat Daci, PDK leader Hasim Thaci, former Prime Minister Bajram Rexhepi, and opposition party leader and newspaper magnate Veton Surroi.

7 October: Eide completes his assessment of Kosovo's progress, and concludes that, although progress has been poor, status talks should begin nonetheless.

13 October: Former Prime Minister Ramush Haradinaj is allowed to travel to Kosovo and re-engage in politics while on provisional release from The Hague.

24 October: On the UN's 60th anniversary the Security Council endorses Eide's assessment and calls for talks which will resolve Kosovo's status to begin.

2006

21 January: President Rugova dies of cancer, aged 61.

20 February: Negotiations on Kosovo's final status begin in Vienna

1 March: PM Bajram Kosumi steps down and Assembly President Nexhat Daci is removed by his party, the LDK.

2 March: President Fatmir Sejdiu asks the KPC commander, Agim Ceku, to form a government.

11 March: Former President Milosevic found dead in his prison cell in The Hague.

NOTES

PREFACE AND ACKOWLEDGEMENTS

1   Details can be found in the note on the authors on the front flap of the jacket.
2   RAND, 'Post-War Nationbuilding from Germany to Iraq', 2003, p. 125.

INTRODUCTION

1   UK Ministry of Defence.
2   *The Kosovo Report*, by the Independent International Commission on Kosovo, p. 306, which sets out an excellent summary of the disputed number of deaths during this time, and the difficulties in arriving at a consensus on the statistics.
3   Savezni Zavod Statistiki, 1961-1988, Demografska.
4   Tim Judah, *Kosovo: War and Revenge,* (New Haven, 2000), pp.1-32.
5   Two people died of their injuries several days later, taking the death toll to 21; 19 is the official figure, of which 11 were Albanian and 8 Serb.
6   The website of the UN Mission in Kosovo, www.unmikonline.org — see the report to the UN Security Council dated 30 April, for more on this.
7   This account is drawn from several international officials who witnessed these events.
8   Tim Cooper, 'Could we have Seen it Coming?' in *Focus Kosovo*, March/May 2004. Past copies are available online, at www.unmikonline.org.
9   Ibid.
10   This information was provided by a KFOR Intelligence Officer.
11   This was relayed to us in confidence by a senior UN employee whom we regard as credible, and was backed up by information from a local diplomat; nobody has been prepared to make this claim publicly.
12   Information from a KFOR Intelligence Officer.

13   *Secretary-General's Report to the Security Council*, 30 April 2004.
14   Ibid.
15   Blerim Shala, editor of the popular Kosovo-Albanian daily newspaper, *Zeri*.
16   Miklos Heratzi, 'The Role of Media in the March 2004 Events in Kosovo' OSCE Representative on Freedom of the Media, Vienna, 2004.
17   Ibid.
18   Ibid.
19   KFOR intelligence based on monitoring phone traffic.
20   *OSCE Report*.
21   Terence Bellingham, a British contractor working in north Mitrovica at the time who had extensive contacts with the local Serb community.
22   *OSCE Report*.
23   A Kosovo-Albanian employee of the European Union in Mitrovica, interviewed Aug. 2004.
24   *OSCE Report*.
25   UNMIK-EU employee Siobian Smith, interviewed Aug. 2004. Siobian created an ad hoc coordination centre for the EU Pillar during the crisis, which helped to track fast-moving events and provided advice to endangered employees.
26   UN employee, interviewed Aug. 2004.
27   Ibid.
28   Ibid.
29   Ibid.
30   This information was provided by a KFOR Intelligence Officer.
31   Ibid.
32   George Huber, interviewed June 2005.
33   *Secretary-General's Report to the Security Council*, 30 April 2004.
34   These militants were described as 'Islamic extremists' by a senior UN employee, interviewed Aug. 2004.
35   Senior UN employee, interviewed Aug. 2004.
36   Ibid.
37   Ibid.
38   Senior employee of the Kosovo Department of Justice, July 2004.
39   UN employee, interviewed Aug. 2004.
40   *Secretary General's Report to the UN*, 30 April, 2004.
41   Scandinavian Army colonel, interviewed Aug. 2004.
42   Senior EU employee, interviewed Aug. 2004.
43   Senior UN employee, interviewed Aug. 2004.
44   Ibid.

45   Interviews in Mitrovica, Aug. 2004.
46   The IMF, the World Bank and the local Central Fiscal Authority and Kosovo
      Statistical Office have produced a range of statistics on Kosovo's economy
      and society. Although Kosovo became much richer, and less poverty-stricken,
      after the international intervention in 1999, an economic downturn was
      apparent by the time of the March 2004 crisis.
47   International Crisis Group and Andreas Wittkowksy.
48   Terence Bellingham.
49   International diplomat, interviewed Aug. 2004.
50   Senior EU official, interviewed Aug. 2004.
51   Kosovo Ministry of Culture.
52   A Kosovo Albanian employed by UNMIK-EU in Mitrovica, interviewed in
      Aug. 2004.
53   Press statements issued by the US State Department.
54   This view was held by almost all senior UNMIK officials throughout this
      period, and was the consensus reached without dissent whenever the matter
      was raised in UNMIK's executive committee.
55   Employee of the UNMIK Returns Unit, interviewed Aug. 2004.
56   Senior UNMIK official.
57   Senior employee of the UNMIK Returns Unit, interviewed Aug. 2004.

KOSOVO AND HUMANITARIAN INTERVENTION

1   Noel Malcolm, *Kosovo: A Short History* (London, 1998), p. 40.
2   Olga Zirojevic, 'Kosovo in the Collective Memory', *The Road to War in
      Serbia* (Budapest, 2000), p. 195.
3   Miranda Vickers, *The Albanians* (London, 1995), p. 17.
4   John R. Lampe, *Yugoslavia in History: Twice there was a Country* (Cambridge,
      1996), p. 55.
5   Malcolm, p. xlvi.
6   Vickers, p. 33.
7   Vickers, p. 46.
8   Lampe, p. 92.
9   Lampe, p. 95.
10   Now in the part of southern Serbia that witnessed an Albanian insurgency in
      2001.
11   Vickers, p. 69.
12   Lampe, p. 97.

[13] Ivo, Banac, *The National Question in Yugoslavia* (Ithaca, NY, 1984), p. 143.

[14] Vickers, p. 96.

[15] Lampe, p. 228.

[16] Vickers, p. 161.

[17] Ibid., p. 161.

[18] Vickers, p. 165.

[19] Julie A. Mertus, *Kosovo: How Myths and Truths Started a War* (London, 1999), p. 23.

[20] Mertus, p. 29.

[21] Malcolm, p. 334.

[22] Mertus, p. 31.

[23] Ibid., p. 97.

[24] Ibid., p. 109.

[25] Ibid., pp. 109-110.

[26] Judah, p. 53.

[27] Ibid., p. 53

[28] Ibid., p. 54.

[29] Ibid., p. 55.

[30] Ibid., p. 56.

[31] Malcolm, p. 182.

[32] Zirojevic, p. 207.

[33] Sabrina Ramet, *Balkan Babel: The Disintegration of Yugoslavia from the Death of Tito to the War for Kosovo* (Boulder, CO, 1999).

[34] 76.44 per cent.

[35] *Independent International Commission on Kosovo, The Kosovo Report* (Oxford, 2000), pp. 44-5.

[36] Mertus, p. 202. Under UN administration after 1999, the international community would work for years to get Albanian leaders to produce as progressive a commitment to multi-ethnicity.

[37] Judah, p. 115.

[38] *The Kosovo Report*, p. 59.

[39] Ibid., p. 67.

[40] Ibid., p. 74.

[41] Ibid., p. 75.

[42] Ibid., p. 75.

[43] Ibid., p. 79.

[44] Ibid., p. 79.

[45] Ibid., p. 81.

[46] Ibid., p. 81.

47   Arnold and Ruland, *Peaceful Persuasion: the Geopolitics of Nonviolent Rhetoric*
        2004, p. 22.
48   Paul Lewis, 'A Short History of United Nations Peacekeeping' in Barbara
        Benton (ed.), *Soldiers for Peace* (New York, 1996), p. 38.

PART I. THE FOUR PHASES OF INTERNATIONAL
ADMINISTRATION IN KOSOVO

EMERGENCY

1   On 5 Oct. 1999, OSCE, 'As Seen As Told', p. 102.
2   web.amnesty.org/library/Index/ENGEURR701061999?open&of=ENG-
        2U5.
3   www.nato.int/doc/facts/2000/Kosovo-ff.htm.
4   Interview with a senior figure within Kosovo's Department of Justice,
        2004.
5   M. Ignatieff, 'The Reluctant Imperialist', *New York Times*, 6 Aug. 2000.
6   Kosovo/Kosova, quoted in Eileen Simpson's unpublished MA thesis, Cam-
        bridge University, June 2003.
7   Ibid.
8   Contemporary comments from KFOR spokesperson, Major Jan Joosten,
        NATO/KFOR website.
9   Interview with former Dutch military adviser, Aug. 2004.
10   Interview with former Swedish military adviser, Jonas Alboroth, July 2002.
11   Remarks from senior EU official Roy Dickinson, 2001.
12   The Independent International Commission on Kosovo.
13   Witnessed by Whit Mason in Feb. 2000.
14   ICG, *The Policing Gap*, Aug. 1999, available at www.crisisgroup.org
15   ICG, *What Happened to the KLA?*, March 2000, available at www.crisisgroup.
        org
16   Ibid.
17   From a British major-general (2002).
18   ICG, *What Happened to the KLA?,* March 2000.
19   Susan Manuel.
20   Terence Bellingham, UNMIK KPC coordinator in the Mitrovica region in
        2000.
21   Confidential NATO Report, 2000, quoted in Jeffrey Smith, 'Rule of Law is
        Elusive in Kosovo', *Washington Post*, 29 July 2001.

22   Senior official in UNMIK's Department of Justice.

23   Ibid.

24   Interview with Christer Karphammar, March 2005.

25   Interview with senior figure in UNMIK's Department of Justice, 2003.

26   Only on 27 June 2001, six months after the last elections in Serbia-proper,
     and after Lushtaku was put on an Executive Order list of those 'who threat-
     en international stabilization efforts in the Western Balkans' by US President
     Bush, was Hartmann informed that if he wanted to arrest and prosecute he
     could do so. By that time the international witness had left Kosovo.

27   Interview with senior figure in UNMIK's Department of Justice, 2004.

28   Interview with Christer Karphammar, March 2005.

29   Witnessed by Iain King, 2000.

30   Ibid.

31   Richard Caplan, *International Governance of War-Torn Territories*, (Oxford,
     2005), p. 61.

32   Ibid., p. 66.

33   Interview with a senior figure in UNMIK's Department of Justice.

34   Ibid.

35   Interview with Michael Hartmann, UNMIK Department of Justice, 2005.

36   Ibid.

37   Ibid.

38   Ibid.

39   Regulation 2000/34.

40   An American soldier later contradicted Zeqiri's alibi.

41   Interview with Michael Hartmann, UNMIK Department of Justice, 2005.

42   Ibid.

43   Jeffrey Smith, *Washington Post*, 18 Dec. 2000.

44   Independent International Commission on Kosovo.

45   Bernard Kouchner, *Los Angeles Times*, 27 Oct.1999.

46   Kosovo Albanians would argue that the Serbs hadn't deserved the positions
     they occupied; but the communist system had never been based on meri-
     tocracy, even between 1974 and 1989 when most positions in Kosovo were
     occupied by Albanians.

47   Interview with Karin von Hippel, 2005.

48   The exact number of Serbs who left Kosovo is disputed. According to the
     UNHCR registration of IDPs in 2000 and UNHCR statistics from Jan. 2002,
     the following left Kosovo for Serbia and Montenegro: 147, 879 Serbs; 17,
     606 Montenegrins; 8,339 Bosniaks; 26,168 Roma; 1,496 Albanians; 1,588
     Egyptians; 4,071 Others. The Belgrade-based Coordinating Committee

for Kosovo, in a 2002 report, says the following left Kosovo for Serbia and Montenegro: 226, 000 Serbs (this probably includes Montenegrins as well); 37,000 Roma; 15,000 Bosniaks; 9,000 Others. The CCK figure is certainly too high; the UNHCR figure has also been criticised for a certain amount of double counting. The authors believe that 'at least 100,000' is a reasonable estimate.

49   Witnessed by Iain King, after much interaction with many Serbs in north Mitrovica during 2000.

50   UNMIK daily security reports, 2000.

51   Witnessed by Iain King, 2000.

52   Comments like this were commonplace during 2000, and were no doubt fuelled by the burn-out and frustration felt by many internationals at this time.

53   These negotiations were led by the regional administrator, General Bill Nash, in Oct. 2000, with Iain King.

54   Funded by USAID and the EU's European Agency for Reconstruction, it was probably the most intensive aid effort in all of Kosovo.

55   Tim Judah, *Kosovo*, p. 277.

56   Council of Europe/OSCE report.

57   ICG Report, *Waiting for UNMIK*, Oct. 1999.

58   Interview with Susan Manual, who worked in the UNMIK Press Office from 1999 to 2002.

59   ICG Report, *Waiting for UNMIK*, Oct. 1999.

60   Independent International Commission Report on Kosovo, p. 107.

61   ICG, *Waiting for UNMIK*, Oct. 1999.

62   Interview with Susan Manual.

63   Joly Dixon, the first head of the EU Pillar in Kosovo, a position which also made him a deputy to the SRSG, speaking to Iain King in 2000.

64   Victor Gomes, providing figures from a public AidCo document, 2004.

65   BRITFOR Press Officer, Sept. 2000.

66   Interview with Lars Tummers, Aug. 2004.

67   Tim Wilson, volunteer with Oxfam, quoted from 2000

68   Interview with Blanca Antonini, 2005.

69   Ibid.

70   Susan Manuel.

71   Interview with contemporary international employee in the Office of the TMC, Aug. 2004.

72   *Koha Ditore*, Aug. 1999.

[73] For more on this, see the ICG report from Nov. 1999, *Violence in Kosovo: Who's Killing Whom?*

[74] Susan Manuel, 2004.

[75] Karin von Hippel, 2004.

[76] Senior member of UNMIK's Civil Administration Pillar, 2004.

[77] Lars Tummers, Aug. 2004.

[78] Note that many Albanians conspired or refused to pay taxes during the 1980s and 1990s. Tax collection rates under Milosevic are hard to come by, but it is clear that what was left of the old tax collection system had ceased to function in Albanian-dominated areas by 1999.

[79] Michael Palliret has written extensively on this subject; many of his works are available on the website of the European Stability Initiative.

[80] The stability of the DM made it popular even with many Serbs, who had nationalist reasons to prefer the dinar. When the main Trepca plant was taken over in Aug. 2000, many Serb workers opted to receive a payment from UNMIK in DM rather than dinars.

[81] Interview with UN employee, Aug. 2004.

[82] The EU Pillar managed to re-establish a basic energy market with Serbia, allowing both territories to sell electricity to each other when a mechanical failure disrupted domestic supply. For the first few years after the war, importing electricity from Serbia proved far more effective than repair and reconstruction of Kosovo's existing power plants as a means of meeting electricity demand.

[83] Witnessed by Iain King, 2000.

[84] Speech made by Roy Dickinson, 2001.

[85] Technical meeting of donors in Pristina, 25-6 February 2001, co-chaired by the European Commission and the World Bank.

[86] Dr Bernard Kouchner, 12 Jan. 2001.

CONSOLIDATION

[1] *Focus Kosovo*, Oct. 2001.

[2] Dana Stinson, Special Assistant to the UN Regional Administrator in Mitrovica.

[3] Tony Welch, UN Regional Administrator in Mitrovica, email interview July 2004.

[4] Ibid.

5   R. Jeffrey Smith, Washington Post Foreign Service, Sunday, 29 July 2001; p. A01, quoting an internal UN report.

6   Ibid.

7   Ibid.

8   'British troops' error led to bus bomb', (London) *Sunday Times*, Bob Graham Pristina, http://www.sunday-times.co.uk/news/pages/st`i/2001/07/29/stifgneur02006.html. Ejupi was eventually tracked down and locked away in 2005.

9   Amnesty International *Report*.

10   For more information on this, read the reports of the OSCE Legal Monitoring unit, available through www.osce.org.

11   Steve Bennett.

12   *Focus Kosovo*.

13   Former Police Spokesperson Derek Chappell, 2004.

14   *Focus Kosovo*, Oct. 2001, p. 17.

15   Kofi Annan's 2002 visit was preceded by an attack on a Serb Orthodox church 36 hours earlier; Chris Patten's visit was preceded by physical attacks on Serbs; Harri Holkeri's appointment in Aug. 2003 was also preceded by the murder of Serb teenagers in Gorazdevac.

16   *Focus Kosovo*, Chronicle, Oct. 2001.

17   ICG report on Presevo Valley, Aug. 2001.

18   The brother of Ramush Haradinaj, a future Prime Minister of Kosovo, Daut, reportedly fought with the NLA. Daut Haradinaj was placed on the US blacklist for his alleged activities; the list was read out publicly by US President Bush in July 2001.

19   ICG report on the Presevo valley crisis, Aug. 2001, researched and written by Whit Mason.

20   Michael Hartmann, UNMIK Prosecutor.

21   This regulation was enacted on 15 Dec. 2000.

22   USIP. report on Kosovo's judiciary.

23   Senior figure within the UNMIK Department of Judicial Affairs.

24   Michael Hartmann, USIP.

25   The need for careful scrutiny by the international prosecutor of police investigation and evidence before initiating a request for a judicial investigation was especially important given the complexity of the legal elements and factual determinations in war crimes cases. Many of these and other high-priority cases are interrelated, as the criminal power structures, including organised crime, are also involved in terrorism and inter-ethnic violence.

26   Verena Knaus of ESI.

27   This comment was made to the authors by several international employees in a position to form a reasonable view.

28   UNMIK crime figures, available in the quarterly reports of the Secretary-General to the Security Council.

29   *Assessment of the Situation of Ethnic Minorities in Kosovo, March through Aug. 2001*, UNHCR/OSCE, p. 23.

30   Haekkerup's speech to UN Security Council, Sept. 2001.

31   Witnessed by Iain King, 2000 and 2001.

32   UK Adviser from the MOD deployed in Kosovo.

33   EU regional representative, Valerie Bour.

34   This scenario was played out in Podujevo, among several Albanian-majority municipalities; they were recounted by the OSCE.

35   Interview with Tania Mechlenborg, 2004.

36   IWPR report, 'Rexhepi Offers Serbs Olive Branch', May 2002.

37   A very senior Kosovo Albanian politician, quoted via a senior UN official, 2004.

38   Interview with former head of the EU Pillar Andy Bearpark, Dec. 2004.

39   International Crisis Group, Report, Oct. 2000, p. 5.

40   Witnessed by Iain King, Oct. 2000.

41   This astute analysis was offered by Roy Dickinson, who often represented the EU at meetings of the Interim Administration Council.

42   Andy Bearpark, contemporary quote.

43   Accounts provided by UN staff who provided secretarial support to the body which drafted the Constitutional Framework under Johan van Lamoen's chairmanship.

44   'Kosovo: Landmark Election', *Europe Report No. 120*, 21 Nov. 2001.

45   Ibid.

46   Ibid.

47   Article drafted by Whit Mason in *Koha Ditore*, 7 Nov. 2001.

48   Anecdotes to this effect were recounted to the authors by several members of Haekkerup's office.

49   Interview with Andy Bearpark, Dec. 2004.

50   Dana Eyre, recounted at the time. contemporary quote.

51   Andy Bearpark, contemporary quote.

52   The OSCE conducted an extensive survey of voters' concerns. UNMIK probably drew on the survey much more than local politicians.

53   This episode was witnessed by Iain King.

54   ICG, 'Reaction in Kosovo to Kostunica's Victory', 10 Oct. 2000, p. 2.

55   ICG Report, Oct. 2000.

56   This power was subject to review by the Media Hearing Board
57   UNMIK regulation 2000/4.
58   UNMIK regulation 2000/37.
59   Comments from the Office of the Temporary Media Commissioner.
60   TMC Report, 2002, p. 101.
61   TMC Report, 2002, p. 103.
62   TMC's *Annual Report* for 2002.
63   World Bank/Kosovo Statistical Office, May 2003.
64   Scott Bowen, EU Regional Office, Peje.
65   Reports that some UN staff in the region were condoning or even inciting
      Serbs to protest against the enforcement of tax were given to Iain King from
      several people working in Mitrovica at the time.

CONFRONTATION AND STAGNATION

1   Henley, 'Kosovo 1999', *The Guardian*, 29 May 2003.
2   Ibid.
3   Ibid.
4   *Focus Kosovo*, Aug. 2002, p. 18.
5   Interview with Michael Steiner, Dec. 2004.
6   Ibid.
7   Witnessed by Whit Mason, Aug. 2004.
8   This comment was made by several members of the international commu-
      nity, including SRSG Steiner.
9   Henley, 'Kosovo 1999', *The Guardian*, 29 May 2003.
10   ICTY Case Information Sheet, Case IT-03-66.
11   IWPR report, 'KLA Men Indicted', 20 Feb. 2003.
12   UN SG's *Report to the UN Security Council*, Jan. 2003.
13   This comment was made independently by two high-level international of-
      ficials knowledgeable about the case.
14   'KLA Trial Backlash', Arben Qirezi, IWPR, 31 July 2002.
15   Anonymous source In the Department of Justice, 2004.
16   A court later determined that its evidence showed only that Ivanovic had
      thrown something — not necessarily a grenade — and gave him a two-
      month suspended sentence.
17   'UN facing backlash', Arben Qirezi, IWPR, 23 Aug. 2002.
18   The victims belonged to the Armed Forces of the Republic of Kosovo FARK,
      the armed wing of the LDK-led government in exile.

19   Shkelzen Maliqi, Nov. 2004.
20   Witnessed by Whit Mason.
21   British officer, speaking in 2002.
22   Interview with Reno Harnish, 2004.
23   One military expert reckoned that about half of the military personnel in Kosovo had support roles, and half could be described as 'frontline'.
24   Senior military secondee to UNMIK, interviewed in 2004.
25   UNDP, Small Arms Survey, 2003, p. 24; quoted in Catherine Clarke, 'Criminality and the Rule of Law in Contemporary Kosovo', MA thesis, Kings College, Aug. 2005.
26   United States Institute for Peace, Feb. 2003.
27   Veseli was found guilty of murdering Ekrem Rexha, aka Commander Drini. The international community had regarded Drini as its most trusted interlocutor from within the KLA; analysts concluded that it was this good relationship with UNMIK and KFOR that had cost him his life.
28   IWPR, 'Policing the Protectors', 30 June 2003.
29   Andrew Cumming, March 2005.
30   This paragraph draws heavily on Eleanor Beardsley's article, 'A Chronology of Confusion', Focus Kosovo, Oct. 2002.
31   This operation was experienced first hand by Iain King.
32   Eleanor Beardsley, 'A Chronology of Confusion'.
33   Ibid.
34   Ibid.
35   Haselock, 'Reading Kosovo's Elections', Focus Kosovo, Oct. 2002.
36   SRSG Michael Steiner's address to the UN Security Council, 30 July 2002.
37   In the Stolic case, care was taken to make sure the bounty was not divisible by three, implying that it symbolised how much the lives were worth.
38   This figure features in a number of contemporary documents produced by UNHCR and UNMIK's Returns Unit.
39   UNMIK, 'The Right to Sustainable Return', 17 May 2002.
40   UNMIK, Manual on Sustainble Returns, 2002.
41   UNMIK, 'The Right to Sustainable Return'.
42   Ibid.
43   This request was made in the Klina and Peje municipalities, and probably also in several other places.
44   Military secondee to UNMIK, recounted from 2003.
45   IWPR, 'Kosovo Serb Despair', 7 Oct. 2002.
46   IWPR, 'Kosovo Serbs Making Progress', 17 Oct. 2002.
47   From the Constitutional Framework.

48   Peter Schumann, Principal International Officer in the Ministry of Public
       Services, contemporary quote.
49   UNMIK Press Release 771, 2002.
50   The Kosovo Assembly elected the LDK leader Ibrahim Rugova President;
       Bajram Rexhepi, a surgeon and former mayor of Mitrovica with little fol-
       lowing of his own, Prime Minister; and Nexhat Daci, a professor of chemis-
       try in whom UNMIK initially placed great hopes, President of the Assembly
       with responsibility for managing the agenda of Kosovo's first democratically
       elected legislature.
51   SRSG's speech to the Assembly, from UNMIK Press Release 732, 9 May
       2002.
52   Specifically, the Assembly resolution rejected the recent agreement between
       Belgrade and Skopje which adjusted the border of Kosovo and Macedonia,
       moving a small piece of territory from Kosovo into Macedonia.
53   UNMIK media monitoring, 24 May 2002.
54   Ibid.
55   Ibid.
56   Ibid.
57   Ibid
58   Ibid.
59   Observations made at the UNMIK Energy Committee.
60   This charge was made by the European Stability Initiative in 2003, and gen-
       erated much publicity.
61   According to a UNDP survey of voters' concerns in Feb. 2003, the elector-
       ate's top priorities were crime, jobs, electricity and status (independence);
       the findings were largely ignored by local politicians.
62   Interview with Michael Steiner, Dec. 2004.
63   Interview with Minna Järvenpää, June 2005.
64   'Pillar Talk', June 2002.
65   This quote was made in a gathering of municipal representatives in Feb.
       2003, eight months after the 'Pillar Talk' email on letting go of power. About
       one third of municipal representatives saw their role in this way; a further
       third tried to empower locally elected representatives as they were sup-
       posed to; and the rest were somewhere between these two positions.
66   Interview with Steiner, Dec. 2004.
67   Belgrade and Pristina did eventually hold a purely symbolic joint meeting,
       but not till six months later.
68   Jolyon Naegele, 'Taking the First Step', Focus Kosovo, Dec. 2003.
69   Ibid.

70   Interview with Michael Steiner, Dec. 2004.

71   Not realising that the idea had originally emanated from Steiner, the new staffers in UNMIK's Political Affairs Department were affronted by Grossman imposing such an idea on the UN without prior consultation.

72   *Focus Kosovo*, 'Aiming for Decentralisation', Oct. 2002.

73   Interview with Järvenpää, June 2005.

74   Interview, *Koha Ditore*, 6 May 2002.

75   Interview with Steiner, Dec. 2004.

76   In March 2004 the government and presidency retained Haselock and a consulting firm he had founded to advise them on their own communications strategy. Whit Mason worked for this firm, Albany Associates.

77   Henley, 'Kosovo 1999', *The Guardian*, 29 May 2003.

78   Ibid.

79   Quote provided by a senior international official working closely with PM Rexhepi.

80   Speech by SRSG Steiner, Jan. 2003.

81   *24 Ore*, translated by UNMIK media monitoring, June 2002.

82   Arben Qirezi, IWPR, 'Kosovo: Media Watchdog Bites Back', 9 Aug. 2002.

83   Comments from Di Lellio to Whit Mason, Autumn 2003.

84   Published by *Koha Ditore* on 27 Sept. 2002

85   The disintegrated nature of Kosovo society was very much a product of the region's history, in particular the Ottoman Empire's approach to government. For more on this, see Chapter 1.

86   World Bank Studies on the Kosovo Economy.

87   UNMIK Report to Donor Conference, Nov. 2002.

88   These figures are from the World Bank. Figures from the Statistical Office of Kosovo claiming that roughly 50 per cent of Kosovans are unemployed are, in the opinion of the authors, less reliable, for several reasons, including their failure at one point to delete from their lists the names of employment seekers who subsequently found work.

89   ESI report, *The Ottoman Dilemma*, 2002.

90   Senior source in the UNMIK Department of Justice.

THE RECKONING

1   UNMIK police confirm that a total of 19 persons died in the violence, of whom 11 were Kosovo Albanians and 8 were Kosovo Serbs. Two were seriously injured and died later, bringing the total number of deaths directly

brought about by the March riots to 21. A total of 954 civilians were treated for injuries. In addition, 65 international police officers, 58 KPS officers and 61 KFOR personnel also suffered injuries. More than 150 vehicles, including more than 100 belonging to UNMIK and 12 to the Kosovo Police Service, were destroyed or severely damaged. KFOR suffered the destruction of one armoured personnel carrier and three cars. Approximately 730 houses, 36 Orthodox churches, monasteries and other religious and cultural sites were damaged or destroyed (Report of the Secretary-General on the United Nations Interim Administration Mission in Kosovo to the Security Council, 30 April 2004, S/2004/348). Some 4,100 Serbs and Roma were displaced by the violence. Many have still not returned to their homes.

2   http://www.osce.org.

3   Senior UN source present at a meeting of the Contact Group. in Pristina, March 2004.

4   Alban Kurti, *Irish Times*, 5 Jan. 2005.

5   Interview with Massimo Gambi, 2004.

6   Interview with Gilles Everts, 2004.

7   UNMIK Press Release, Aug. 2004.

8   Petersen's speech to the OSCE Permanent Council, Feb. 2005.

9   Veton Surroi, *Koha Ditore*, July 2004.

10 Peterson's speech to NATO, Sept. 2004.

11 This analogy was used by a senior member of UNMIK's Pillar One.

12 High-level international official.

13 High-level international official in the Department of Justice, 2004.

14 High-level international official.

15 Senior KFOR officer.

16 *Eide Report*, July 2004.

17 Ibid.

18 Interview with Minna Järvenpää, Aug. 2004.

19 Interview with senior international official, Aug. 2004.

20 Interview with international diplomat in Pristina, Aug. 2004.

21 Nikola Krstic and Jeta Xharra, 'Murders Reignite Serb Fears', IWPR 2 Sept. 2005

22 *The Independent*, July 2003.

23 Interview with senior Kosovo official, March 2005.

24 StratFor, 'The Growing Militant Threat in the Balkans', 24 Oct. 2005.

25 Interview with Vittrup, 2004.

26 Nikola Krstic and Jeta Xharra, 'Murders Reignite Serb Fears', IWPR, 2 Sept. 2005

27 Ibid.

28 Zana Limani and Ibrahim Kelmendi, 'Armed Group Roams Western Kosovo', IWPR, 21 Oct. 2005.

29 Serbs still qualified for the ten seats guaranteed to them by the Constitutional Framework.

30 Interview with UNMIK employee, Aug. 2004.

31 This exchange was witnessed by Iain King, Feb. 2003.

32 Sullivan, 'Special report: Is Kosovo up to Standard?', Balkan Crisis Report No. 549, IWPR, 1 April 2004.

33 Interview in Mitrovica, Aug. 2004.

34 Petersen's speech to the OSCE, Feb. 2005.

35 Petersen speech, May 2005.

36 UNDP survey, March 2005 — the percentage is 46 per cent.

37 Ibid. — 41 per cent.

38 Ibid. — 84 per cent.

39 73 per cent of Serbs blamed ethnic tensions on the attitude of Kosovo Albanian leaders, while 26 per cent blamed insufficient effort by Albanians to help them integrate.

40 UNDP survey, March 2005. At home, 33 per cent of Kosovo Serbs felt 'somewhat safe' or 'safe'; 67 per cent felt 'somewhat unsafe' or 'very unsafe'; on the street, the corresponding figures were 21 per cent and 79 per cent.

41 Ibid. — 92 per cent.

42 UNDP survey, March 2005. The poll of 1,262 persons was fairly representative though slightly skewed toward the young among Albanians, the old among Serbs and men across all communities.

43 Interview with UN employee of the Returns Unit, Aug. 2004.

44 *Secretary-General's Report to the UN Security Council*, Nov. 2004.

45 http://www.kosovo.com.

46 UNDP Survey, March 2005. 62 per cent of Kosovo Albanians favoured return 'to some degree'; 38 per cent did not agree 'at all' with the concept.

47 Interview with Hicks, 2004.

48 Ibid.

49 In Eide's Assessment of Kosovo's suitability for status talks, published in Oct. 2005.

50 'Albanian Divisions May Hamper Kosovo Talks', Jeta Xharra and Artan Mustafa, Balkan Investigative Reporting Network.

51 Interview with Terence Bellingham, Aug. 2004.

52 Ibid.

53   Ibid.
54   *Eide Report*, July 2004.
55   Anonymous eye-witness.
56   Haradinaj open letter, Feb. 2005.
57   Sullivan, 'Special report: Is Kosovo up to Standard?', Balkan Crisis Report No. 549, IWPR, 1 April 2004.
58   Jeta Xharra, 'Time to End Destructive Kosovo Clan Warfare', IWPR, April 2005.
59   Internal document, given to Whit Mason, March 2005.
60   Eide, 'A Comprehensive Review of the Situation in Kosovo', 7 Oct. 2005, available at www.reliefweb.int/library/documents/2005/unsc-ser-7oct.pdf
61   TMC Report on March 2004 events, available through the OSCE website.
62   'Joint Agreement Between the Office of the TMC and Radio Television Kosovo Relating to RTK Broadcasting on March Events 2004', 15 Dec. 2004.
63   Ibid.
64   *Kosovo Opinion Survey*, Dec. 2004.
65   Throughout former Yugoslavia, there had been a tradition of funding public broadcasters through a fee added to electricity bills; this system was re-instituted in Kosovo in 2002, but, largely because of KEK's poor bill collection rates, proved insufficient to fund RTK.
66   Various interviews, spring 2005.
67   *Economist* journalist, Kosovo, April 2005.
68   UNDP survey, March 2005.
69   Ibid.
70   Ibid.
71   Ibid. Only 35 per cent of Kosovo Albanians were dissatisfied to some degree.
72   Ibid.
73   Ibid.
74   Ibid.
75   Interviews conducted in Aug. 2004.
76   OSCE, *OMIK's Role in Youth and Education Issues*, 12 Aug. 2004.
77   OSCE employee.
78   'Playing the Fool in War's Shadow', by Jeta Xharra, BCR No 579, 14 Oct. 2005.
79   Petersen's address to the Security Council, 2004.
80   For more on this, see the Kosovo Development Plan, available at http://www.euinkosovo.org.

81   Source, IMF *Report*, March 2004.

82   International employee in the Kosovo Trust Agency, 2004.

83   Lambsdorff interviewed on BBC Radio Four, March 2004.

84   The plan was not a huge innovation — it was a re-working of an old idea, hammered out between German and American lawyers under Steiner, and rejected at the time by UN lawyers.

85   Under the new arrangement, the UN was protected from claims because compensation to previous creditors was capped: old owners, mainly Serbs, could not claim more than the amount each SOE raised at auction, even if the firm had been asset stripped since they last visited.

86   UNMIK Press Release 1361.

87   ESI, *The Ottoman Dilemma*, 2002.

88   Kosovo Ministry of Agriculture, Aug. 2004.

89   Kosovo Development Plan, available through http://www.euinkosovo.org.

90   Catherine Clarke, unpublished MA thesis, Kings College, London, Aug. 2005.

91   These figures are drawn from several sources, principally the World Bank's Economic Memorandum of May 2004; UNMIK's *Kosovo Outlook*, 2004, also from May 2004; the International Monetary Fund's Aide Memoire of March 2004; and work done by Michael Palairet for the European Stability Initiative. All of these figures involve a degree of professional estimation — they are illustrative rather than absolute.

PART II. WHY THE WORLD FAILED TO TRANSFORM KOSOVO
EXPLAINING FAILURE

1   See Chaim Kaufmann, 'Possible and Impossible Solutions to Ethnic Civil Wars,' *International Security,* Vol.20, no.4 (Spring 1996), pp. 136-53.

2   See Nancy Bermeo, 'What the Democratization Literature Says — or doesn't Say — about Postwar Democratization', *Global Governance* 9 (2, 2003), pp.159-77.

3   This view has been expressed conversationally by several long-time observers of internal conflicts who are familiar with Kosovo.

4   Discussion on the Kosovo Standards Implementation Plan, Nov. 2003. This comment was made by Francisco Bastagli, head of Pillar II. It exemplifies the point of view in question, but Bastagli was not a weak link in the chain

of command. He was, quite rightly, regarded as one of the most effective members of the mission.

5   While Kouchner appreciated the importance of the media in shaping public attitudes and under Steiner/Haselock UNMIK's Division of Public Information was energetic and prominent in the bureaucratic hierarchy, most parts of the mission never understood that changing attitudes was at the heart of what the mission was trying to do.

6   Roland Paris, *At War's End* (2004), pp. 189-190.

7   Ibid.

8   For more on this, read the Brahimi Report, available through http://www.un.org.

9   Many UNMIK offices, including those of senior decision-makers, were electronically bugged; the Albanian newspaper *Zeri* often published transcripts of important high-level meetings, which were not minuted by UNMIK staff. Some local staff were also feeding information to interested factions within Kosovo.

10   The Kosovo Trust Agency.

11   'America's Role in Nation-Building from Germany to Iraq', RAND, 2003.

12   This observation was made by the American political commentator Walter Lippmann.

DOING BETTER

1   This statistic is correct as of Feb. 2006.

2   Immanuel Kant, 1784.

INDEX

299